PARLIAMENT, THE CONSTITUTION, AND PROPERTY IN THE UNITED KINGDOM

This book considers whether Parliament recognises a constitutional right to property.

Parliament is supreme: in theory, there is nothing to stop it from passing laws to confiscate property. Nevertheless, MPs often argue that a proposed law would be unconstitutional. What does this mean in a system without a written constitution? What counts as a sound argument about constitutional rights? And what influence do constitutional arguments have on the legislative process?

The book takes a close look at these questions. It reviews legislation and debates from the Middle Ages through to more recent legislation, and covers a wide range of topics, such as land reform, nationalisation, taxation, regulatory laws and retrospection. It also looks at the most recent debates and considers the relevance of constitutional thinking to election manifestos of the main political parties.

Parliament, the Constitution, and Property in the United Kingdom

Tom Allen

• HART •
OXFORD • LONDON • NEW YORK • NEW DELHI • SYDNEY

HART PUBLISHING

Bloomsbury Publishing Plc

Kemp House, Chawley Park, Cumnor Hill, Oxford, OX2 9PH, UK

1385 Broadway, New York, NY 10018, USA

29 Earlsfort Terrace, Dublin 2, Ireland

HART PUBLISHING, the Hart/Stag logo, BLOOMSBURY and the Diana logo are trademarks of Bloomsbury Publishing Plc

First published in Great Britain 2024

A catalogue record for this book is available from the British Library.

A catalogue record for this book is available from the Library of Congress.

Library of Congress Control Number: 2024944192

ISBN: HB: 978-1-50996-575-5
ePDF: 978-1-50996-577-9
ePub: 978-1-50996-576-2

Typeset by Compuscript Ltd, Shannon

CONTENTS

TABLE OF CASES

TABLE OF STATUTES

Enacted prior to 1600

Enacted after 1600

Introduction

In debates on taxation in the American colonies, Lord Camden claimed that 'the many private bills, as well as public, passed every session' showed that Parliament 'cannot take away any man's private property without making him a compensation'.[1] In a later debate on quartering troops in the colonies, William Pitt the Elder, Lord Chatham, referred to the

> fundamental rules of the English constitution; and that it is an essential unalterable right in nature, ingrafted into the British constitution as fundamental law, and ever held sacred and irrevocable by the subjects within this realm – that what a man has honestly acquired, is absolutely his own; which he may freely give, but which cannot be taken from him without his consent.[2]

What did they mean by this, given that there was (and still is) no written constitution? By their time, the supremacy of Parliament was beyond doubt: the executive and the courts were bound by any Act that Parliament chose to pass. Yet, in their view, the rights of property holders were at stake and, aside from anything else, that was a good reason for Parliament to observe limits on its power.

Other parliamentarians have echoed the claims of Camden and Chatham. Over a century later, Parliament debated a clause in Home Rule Bill 1893 that would have barred an Irish legislature from enacting laws 'whereby private property may be taken without just compensation'.[3] John Rigby, the Solicitor General, argued that courts could derive the meaning of 'just compensation' from existing laws and practices.[4] Like Lords Camden and Chatham before him, he believed that there was evidence that Parliament had respected rights of private property; moreover, it had established precedents from which one could discover constitutional principles, even in the absence of a written constitution.

Over 80 years after the Home Rule debates, the House of Commons considered the rights of the shareholders in companies targeted for nationalisation by the Aircraft and Shipbuilding Industries Bill 1977. The Examiners found that the Bill was hybrid, because of the impact on their rights of property, and therefore the shareholders had the right to appear before Parliament to argue against its enactment. The Examiners stated that there are few constitutional rights 'of such

[1] *Cobbett's Parliamentary History of England*, XVI, 167 (1766).

[2] *Cobbett's Parliamentary History of England*, XVII, 1356 (1774).

[3] See generally T Allen, 'Constitutional Rights in the Irish Home Rule Bill of 1893' (2018) 39 *Journal of Legal History* 187.

[4] HC Deb 11 April 1893, vol 11, col 112.

importance as the right of a subject to plead his cause before Committees of either House'.[5] In the Commons, Sir Derek Walker-Smith argued that 'though the House is master of its own procedure, the exercise of that power is subject to the inherent constraint that it must not be used in violation of the fundamental rights of the individual citizen'; anything to the contrary would be 'a breach of the principles of our unwritten constitution'.[6] Parliament was supreme, but there were principles that it should follow when considering bills affecting private property.

A final example is seen in the reports of the House of Lords Constitution Committee, where it has raised questions over retrospective bills, including those that affect rights of property as established by judgments of the courts.[7] The Committee's remit is 'To examine the constitutional implications of all public bills coming before the House; and to keep under review the operation of the constitution.'[8] Its reports on different bills follow, in broad terms, the positions taken by Lord Camden, Lord Chatham, John Rigby, the Examiners and Sir Derek Walker-Smith: Parliament may be supreme, but it should be guided by constitutional principles, despite the absence of any external review of parliamentary action.

These views reflect earlier thinking that 'fundamental law' bound the King, Parliament, the courts, and ordinary subjects.[9] Writers including Grotius,[10] Locke[11] and Blackstone[12] said that there were limits on the sovereign's powers over private property. In her study of the history of the expropriation in Europe, Susan Reynolds found that there has never been a period in which property in land was considered inviolable, but equally there has never been a period in which it was thought that the sovereign could simply take property without compensation or good reason.[13] Of course, there were many statutes that did authorise the taking of property, but such laws were legitimately done with consent, either to the specific bill or through the consent given by the legislature as the representatives of the people. These principles were central to the conceptions of fundamental law. However, fundamental law was considered distinct from positive law. Before 1688, there was no consensus on the key question: if there was a conflict between

[5] House of Lords, Sessional Papers 1976–77 vol 5, 71.

[6] HC Deb 27 May 1976, vol 912, cols 696–97.

[7] House of Lords Constitution Committee, *Jobseekers (Back to Work Schemes) Bill* (HL 2012–13, 155).

[8] House of Lords Constitution Committee, *Reviewing the Constitution: Terms of Reference and Method of Working* (HL 2001–02, 11) para 1.

[9] See ES Corwin, 'The "Higher Law" Background of American Constitutional Law' (1929) 42 *Harvard Law Review* 365; JW Gough, *Fundamental Law in English Constitutional History* (Clarendon, 1955); TC Grey, 'Origins of the Unwritten Constitution: Fundamental Law in American Revolutionary Thought' (1977) 30 *Stanford Law Review* 843.

[10] H Grotius, *De Jure Belli ac Pacis* (translated by F Kelsey) (first published 1625, Clarendon, 1925) 807.

[11] J Locke, *Two Treatises of Government* (first published 1689, Fenn 1821) 308–309.

[12] 1 Bl Comm 135.

[13] S Reynolds, *Before Eminent Domain: Toward a History of Expropriation of Land for the Common Good* (University of North Carolina Press, 2010) 7. See also FA Mann, 'Outlines of a History of Expropriation' (1959) 75 *LQR* 188, 189 and *De Keyser's Royal Hotel Ltd v The King* [1919] 2 Ch 197, 221 (CA) Swinfen Eady MR (upheld in *Attorney-General v De Keyser's Royal Hotel Ltd* [1920] AC 508).

them, should positive law yield to fundamental law and, more importantly, who would decide that there was a conflict and determine the consequences? This was, of course, ultimately resolved in favour of parliamentary supremacy. Nevertheless, property was still seen as a fundamental right: Parliament might be supreme, but many MPs believed that it should not undermine rights of private property.

These examples might suggest that there is a consensus that the right to property is part of the United Kingdom's (UK) constitutional traditions. However, there have been contrary voices. In the debates on the taxation in the colonies, Lord Mansfield challenged Lord Camden, saying that: 'I deny the proposition that parliament takes no man's property without his consent: it frequently takes private property without making what the owner thinks a compensation.'[14] With the Home Rule Bill, George Wyndham said that the precedents actually showed that 'The Imperial Parliament was every day engaged in passing laws, extinguishing the rights of property in a manner some believed to be due and others believed to be undue'.[15] More recently, JAG Griffith's claim that 'the constitution is no more and no less than what happens' has produced a large volume of literature questioning whether parliamentarians observe constitutional standards on lawmaking.[16] Finally, it is worth noting that, although the Constitution Committee has raised concerns over the impact of different bills on rights of the individual, it has not specifically said that a right to property is one of the rights that should be protected under the unwritten constitution.[17]

Against this background, this book takes a closer look at the claims regarding constitutional rights to property, by asking questions such as: what do parliamentarians regard as the sources for an argument about rights? How do they interpret their sources? And what is the impact of constitutional argumentation on the legislative process? It follows in the line of recent scholarship that considers the substantive norms of the British constitution. Some of the scholarship concentrates on the judiciary and in particular the extent to which the courts articulate and apply constitutional standards in the interpretation of legislation.[18] The role of the executive, whether in relation to the drafting of laws or their implementation, is also considered.[19] However, other scholarship focuses on Parliament

[14] *Cobbett's Parliamentary History of England*, XVI, 172 (1766).

[15] HC Deb 15 June 1893, vol 13, col 1129.

[16] JAG Griffith, 'The Political Constitution' (1979) 42 *MLR* 1, 19; see A Tomkins, 'What's Left of the Political Constitution?' (2013) 14 *German Law Journal* 2275; G Gee, 'The Political Constitutionalism of JAG Griffith' (2008) 28 *Legal Studies* 20; G Gee and GCN Webber, 'What Is a Political Constitution?' (2010) 30 *OJLS* 273; R Bellamy, 'Political Constitutionalism' in H Kumarasingham and P Cane (eds), *The Cambridge Constitutional History of the United Kingdom: Exploring the Constitution* (Cambridge University Press 2023) vol 1.

[17] House of Lords Constitution Committee (n 8) para 34.

[18] See, eg, M Elliott and K Hughes, *Common Law Constitutional Rights* (Bloomsbury Publishing, 2020); Christina Lienen, *Shaped by the Nuanced Constitution: A Critique of Common Law Constitutional Rights* (Bloomsbury Publishing, 2023).

[19] See, eg, A Blick, *The Codes of the Constitution* (Hart Publishing, 2016) 217–30; Howard A Scarrow, 'Policy Pressures by British Local Government: The Case of Regulation in the "Public Interest"' (1971)

itself, as it investigates the role of constitutional norms in the legislative process.[20] This often concerns changes aimed at enhancing scrutiny of bills, such as the creation of the Joint Committee on Human Rights and the House of Lords Select Committee on the Constitution. The question for scholars is often whether these reforms have had the desired effect: can specific constitutional norms be identified, and do they receive appropriate consideration in the legislative process? This book asks similar questions, but it examines the specific claim that there is a constitutional right to property, how it developed and what it might include. This provides the opportunity to take a long view of constitutional standards, as Parliament keeps returning to the same issues regarding the relationship between state power and the individual: when does the public interest justify overriding rights of private property? Where justification is present, how should the interests of individuals be safeguarded: by compensating affected parties, and if so, by what standard? Would a weaker requirement of fair or proportionate treatment be sufficient? What are the procedural rights of the affected parties: can they appear before the decision-making body to voice their objections? And who should make these decisions: parliamentary committees, the courts or administrative bodies?

In terms of its scope, this book concentrates on parliamentarians and how they see the unwritten constitution. For the most part, it does not address the legal constitution. To be sure, the courts have some power to protect property, through the interpretation of statutes and the development of administrative law. In some cases, courts have cited the constitution as a source of general presumptions of interpretation in favour of the rights of the individual.[21] Clearly, to do so, they must have a conception of the nature and content of those rights. These judicial conceptions are not, however, the focus of this book. In addition, it does not closely examine international law, although the House of Lords Constitution Committee has included 'Membership of the Commonwealth, the European Union, and other international organisations' as one of the five 'basic tenets' of the UK constitution.[22] Indeed, as discussed in the concluding chapter, Parliament and Ministers now give more consideration to the right to property under the European Convention on

4 *Comparative Politics* 1; C Stebbings, 'The Equity of the Executive: Fairness in Tax Law in Nineteenth-Century England' in PG Turner (ed), *Equity and Administration*, 1st edn (Cambridge University Press, 2016); P Grez Hidalgo, 'Legislative Scrutiny on Constitutional Grounds in the United Kingdom Parliament' PhD thesis (Edinburgh, 2019) 189–99.

[20] See, in addition to the works cited in n 16, J Waldron, 'The Core of the Case Against Judicial Review' (2006) 115 *Yale Law Journal* 1346, 1384–85; C Pinelli, 'Constitutional Reasoning and Political Deliberation' (2013) 14 *German Law Journal* 1171; J Simson Caird, 'Identifying the Value of Parliamentary Constitutional Interpretation', PhD thesis (Queen Mary University of London, 2014); J Simson Caird and D Oliver, 'Parliament's Constitutional Standards' in A Horne and A Le Seuer (eds), *Parliament: Legislation and Accountability* (Hart Publishing, 2016); J Simson Caird, R Hazell and D Oliver, *The Constitutional Standards of the House of Lords Select Committee on the Constitution*, 3rd edn (The Constitution Unit, 2017); Grez Hidalgo (n 19).

[21] See the works cited in n 18.

[22] House of Lords Constitution Committee (n 8) para 51.

Human Rights (ECHR) than any similar right under the unwritten constitution.[23] These legal aspects are important but lie beyond parliamentarians' view of the unwritten, political constitution and hence they are not examined in detail. This also means that the role of the executive is given relatively little attention, although the capacity of governments to control and influence parliamentary business is beyond doubt. The book does not ignore the executive's role: in particular, when considering debates on bills, the book looks closely at the statements of Ministers and Law Officers. With private bills, departments often gave advice to parliamentary committees on issues of constitutionality.[24] Nevertheless, as important as the judicial and executive conceptions of constitutional rights may be, this book focuses on parliamentary conceptions of the constitution.

I. Political and Legal Constitutions

Most states have written justiciable constitutions that include a right to property. However, this book looks at the non-legal, political aspect of a right to property. To be sure, the Human Rights Act (HRA) 1998 allows for domestic application of the ECHR, including the right to the peaceful enjoyment of possessions under Article 1 of the First Protocol to the Convention. Parliament has not, however, considered any bills with proposals to enact a right to property for application in the UK. Instead, it has enacted a mass of rules, both statutory and procedural, regarding specific forms of expropriation, regulation and other interferences with rights of property. These are very much collections of rules rather than broad principles. For example, one of the most important statutes on compulsory purchase is the Land Clauses Consolidation Act 1845, which pulled together the statutory precedents from private Acts. However, as its title suggests, it consolidated the law: it contains a multitude of details but leaves out the points that would be most important in the drafting of a general constitutional or human right to property. It does not say, for instance, that an owner is entitled to compensation. It also does not say that the expropriation must serve the public interest, although, when read in conjunction with the Standing Orders, it is clear that Parliament expected the promoter to show that their scheme did so. British legislation on property is characterised by detail, where constitutional principles may lie in the background but are rarely articulated. Hence this book concentrates on the detail and asks whether general principles emerge from it.

[23] Article 1 of the First Protocol contains the right to the peaceful enjoyment of possessions: Protocol to the Convention for the Protection of Human Rights and Fundamental Freedoms (Paris, 20 March 1952).

[24] See Scarrow (n 19); the role of the Law Officers and obligation of Ministers and officials to seek their advice on constitutional (as opposed to legal) matters is described in Cabinet Office, *Cabinet Manual* (Cabinet Office, 2011) para 6.6–6.7.

This raises the question: do parliamentarians act on principle? Parliamentary restraint may be possible in theory but that does not necessarily mean that it is evident in practice. Jeremy Waldron observes that many scholars of the American legislative process doubt that legislators are guided by principle to any extent. As he puts it, 'our jurisprudence is pervaded by imagery that presents ordinary legislative activity as deal-making, horse-trading, log-rolling, interest-pandering, and pork-barreling – as anything, indeed, except principled political decision-making'.[25] A less cynical view holds that a principled approach is possible and, at least in the UK, it is sometimes evident.[26] Recent scholarship considers how well Parliament does formulate and follow principles.[27] The scholarship tends to focus on the period from the European Communities Act 1972 and especially through to HRA 1998 and the Blair government reforms, and specifically on the existence and enhancement of a culture of justification within Parliament. They consider, for example, the impact of parliamentary committees such as the House of Lords Constitution Committee and the Joint Committee on Human Rights. The work of departments and civil service is also relevant, as shown by the publication of the Cabinet Office guidance for Ministers and MPs regarding the importance of constitutional issues in the preparation of bills.[28] These are not just modern developments: as many of the examples discussed in this book demonstrate, the Law Officers have been called upon to introduce or defend bills that raise complex constitutional issues. In addition, the Houses regularly revised their Standing Orders to protect rights of individuals. Moreover, parliamentarians have been aware of the importance of precedent, with the House of Commons creating the Court of Referees in 1865 specifically to enable the collection of precedent on questions of standing. Going back to Waldron, legislatures are not incapable of acting on principle; however, there is no guarantee that they would do so.

This therefore raises two points for this book. The first is whether constitutional principles do guide parliamentary decisions relating to property. This book shows that there is at least some evidence of this, in relation to certain aspects of legislation affecting rights of property. As chapter one will argue, the threshold point of evidence is the existence of a culture of justification relating to property. To some extent, the existence of a culture of justification should not be controversial. It is safe to assume that most people share a commitment to fundamental rights, although they may disagree on their precise content and the institutional arrangements for their determination and vindication.[29] However, as long as there is broad agreement that rights are important, it is likely that MPs would reflect this

[25] J Waldron, *The Dignity of Legislation* (Cambridge University Press, 1999) 1–2. See also J Waldron, 'The Dignity of Legislation' (1995) 54 *Maryland Law Review* 633, 644.

[26] Waldron believes that this is possible, although his focus was on the American scene.

[27] See, eg, Tomkins (n 16); Blick (n 19); Simson Caird and Oliver (n 20); Simson Caird, Hazell and Oliver (n 20); Grez Hidalgo (n 19).

[28] See Cabinet Office (n 24); see also D Grieve, 'The Role of Human Rights in a Law Officer's Work: Challenges Facing the HRA and the ECHR' (2012) 17 *Judicial Review* 101.

[29] Waldron (n 20) 1364–66.

agreement in their deliberations. Where there are questions regarding the impact of a bill on core rights, Ministers would seek to justify their actions and MPs, especially in the opposition, would seek to test their reasoning. Hence, there is a culture of justification, but only in a loose sense.

The real question for this book is whether this culture of justification, as it relates to rights of property, has developed into something more precise and relevant to the specific situation. By way of comparison, where courts have jurisdiction to interpret constitutional or human rights to property, the doctrine is usually quite complex. Courts articulate principles on, for example, the scope of constitutional standard, the right to compensation, the nature and proof of a public interest in support of a bill and the requirements for notice, audience and other procedural rights. The question is the extent to which Parliament has moved beyond the general requirement that all legislation should be justified to a more particularised form of justification for an interference with property. Has Parliament developed specific points of reference for the constitutional scrutiny of bills affecting rights of property? The chapters show that there is good evidence for these points of reference in several areas: the rights of notice and audience in the processes for deciding on takings, as discussed in chapter two, and compensation for loss on expropriation and nationalisation, with valuation by an independent body, as discussed in chapters three and four. This is also the case with retrospection that interferes with property: as chapter six shows, Parliament has consistently expressed concern that retrospective laws undermine the rule of law. It has not adopted a categorial rule against all retrospective laws, but it has developed a set of criteria for judging whether retrospection is justified. Beyond this, however, the evidence for specific points of reference is equivocal or insufficient to establish a constitutional standard, as it does not move past very general statements that laws should treat the holders of rights of property with fairness. To be sure, this is the underlying value that Ministers and MPs refer to most often in argument and debate: it helps to understand the source and development of the standards and their likely direction of evolution, but this book takes the view that something more specific is required to enhance the scrutiny of bills. In other words, on its own, it does not exist as a right to property: where fairness is raised in contexts other than expropriation, nationalisation or retrospection, it generally adds little to debate, because it simply lacks the detail and structure that would allow for the kind of careful argumentation that would enhance scrutiny. The general value of fairness should be expressed in more specific points of reference.

The second question follows the first. If there is evidence that parliamentarians believe that a constitutional right to property does exist, does it also indicate how their belief affects or enhances the scrutiny of bills? Given that we are working with the political constitution, this is difficult to answer. At the highest level of generality, the constitution has not failed, as Parliament remains the key institution in resolving conflicts between different interests in matters relating to property. In the twentieth century, the parliamentary battles over the People's Budget and Labour's post-World War II nationalisation programme were probably the most serious conflicts concerning rights of property that it faced. However, they were ultimately resolved by parliamentary processes, including the enactment of the Parliament Acts 1911 and 1949. Parliament did not hand over key decisions to the courts and the leading political parties did not abandon Parliament or democratic politics as the forum for resolving disputes. In that sense, the political constitution has not failed. However, going further, the question is also whether constitutional scrutiny of legislation affecting property has enhanced the legislative process. Some constitutional arguments are impressively focused – this is most evident with retrospective laws that interfere with rights of property – but there are debates where invocations of the constitution add very little to scrutiny. MPs often make claims regarding constitutionality without identifying the source for their views or how they apply to the measures at hand. Bald assertions regarding constitutionality provide no focus for scrutiny and are unlikely to enhance the legislative process. Indeed, the book shows that parliamentary scrutiny has declined in recent years. This is partly due to the rise of legal human rights, as many MPs and Ministers seem to find that Convention rights provide a better frame than the unwritten constitution for expressing concerns regarding rights of the individual. If nothing else, human rights law is more precise than the unwritten constitution: in general, the body of jurisprudence provides material for a more closely reasoned argument than the unwritten constitution. Indeed, to a limited extent, Parliament has sought to provide a similar body of precedent for some constitutional issues, as the establishment of the Court of Referees demonstrates. However, in relation to substantive matters, the Convention seems to be gaining ground on the unwritten principles, at least in relation to rights of property. Indeed, the Constitution Committee suggested, in its first report, that rights of property are unlikely to command its attention to the same degree as other constitutional concerns.[30] It is also the case that the constitutionality of bills is more likely to arise where bills proposed radical change, as in the case of the People's Budget of 1909 and the nationalisation programmes of the Attlee and Callaghan governments. In recent years, property issues have not been the political battleground of earlier periods. This, of course, could change: the unwritten constitution of property could come back into focus if, for example, a Conservative government sought to repeal the HRA 1998 and break the connection with Strasbourg, or if a Labour government sought to embark on a new programme of nationalisation.

II. Chapter Outlines

Following this Introduction, chapter one begins by describing the general aims and methodology of the book. Its starting point is Jack Simson Caird and Dawn

[30] House of Lords Constitution Committee (n 8) para 34.

Oliver's description of 'parliamentary constitutional standards'.[31] They put forward four criteria for standards that help to identify the characteristics that a right to property would have. First, parliamentary constitutional standards are formulated and applied by parliamentary actors in parliamentary fora. Accordingly, the book focuses on statutes, parliamentary rules, debates and other material in seeking evidence of parliamentary constitutional standards. Secondly, they are concerned with constitutional matters. Parliament may recognise other types of standards: for example, in 2011, the House of Commons Treasury Committee adopted the *Principles of Tax Policy*.[32] Accordingly, in each chapter, the book seeks to distinguish constitutional from other parliamentary standards, and constitutional standards that are concerned with property as a fundamental right from those that are not. For the third criterion, Simson Caird and Oliver say that standards are not politically partisan: the majority of MPs across the parties would agree on the basic content of standards – for example, that compensation should be paid on the expropriation of land – even if they disagree on the detail. Finally, the constitutional standards are distinct from legal standards: the courts have no jurisdiction over the legislative process and do not lay down standards for application by Parliament. Parliamentary constitutional standards, as described by Simson Caird and Oliver, provide a framework for debate: parties may take different sides in a debate whilst agreeing that the debate is important and should address certain issues. As such, they can contribute to a culture of justification. This is a theme that the book returns to in each chapter: is there evidence of a culture of justification relating specifically to property as a fundamental right? As part of this, there should be a reasonably precise structure for review, with points of reference that allow MPs to identify constitutional issues and the factors that should be considered when reaching conclusions on specific issues.

Chapter two considers the aspects of legislative procedures that have had an impact on the development of constitutional norms, with close attention to those procedures that focus attention on substantive issues regarding the rights of property owners. This begins with a consideration of the right to petition for legislation (usually, a private or local Act) overriding the property rights of others, or to request the right of audience before Parliament to challenge such petitions. It also covers constitutional conventions, as well as Standing Orders, rulings of the Speaker, the Examiners and the Court of Referees, to the extent that these procedures help to indicate where Parliament has been particularly careful in deciding whether to intrude on rights of private property. It concludes with the distinction between public, hybrid and private bills, with a discussion on the conflict over the Aircraft and Shipbuilding Industries Bill 1977 and the most recent decisions concerning large infrastructure projects such as the High Speed Rail links.

[31] Simson Caird and Oliver (n 20).

[32] House of Commons Treasury Committee, *Principles of Tax Policy* (HC 2010–11, 753).

In chapter three, the book considers the compulsory purchase of land, which historically has provided the greatest volume of material relating to property and the unwritten constitution. It traces the development of compulsory purchase statutes from the first examples in the sixteenth century through to the modern era. As such, it covers the acquisition of property from the owner, but not its regulation or destruction, which is covered in chapter five. There is evidence of takings of land well before the sixteenth century, but they were either under a prerogative power or in response to a breach of a legal obligation, or it is unclear from the record whether the taking was compulsory or consensual. Compulsory purchase is distinct: it is statutory and need not be consensual. Moreover, there is no default by the owner. The justification is simply that the public interest would be better served if someone else owned the land. Usually (but not invariably), the expropriator has a development scheme for which they must acquire the land. The chapter finds evidence of constitutional principles in early statutes, and then through the wave of private Acts of the eighteenth and nineteenth century, to the near-complete delegation of decision making to administrative bodies in the twentieth century. Through this, it follows two key issues: the nature of the public interest required to justify the grant of compulsory purchase powers, and the requirement for compensation. This considers matters such as takings for private parties, whether in the form of commercial utilities buying land for their projects or tenants seeking to buy the freehold of the property. It also considers questions of compensation, and in particular the principle that compensation should reflect the value to the owner, as independently assessed; and, from the late Victorian period, the extent to which compensation may be adjusted to reflect moral claims against the land and its value. It shows that there is a clear culture of justification, based on standards that show remarkable durability over their long history.

The book considers nationalisation in the following chapter. Nationalisation is a relatively modern activity, dating from the first part of the nineteenth century. State enterprises were not a new phenomenon at that time: the establishment of the Post Office under Charles II and the Navy Board under Henry VIII are two well-known examples. In addition, many early chartered companies, such as the East India Company, had public and private characteristics. However, nationalisation under modern law began in the nineteenth century, when local authorities took an increasingly important role in the provision of water, electricity, transportation, communications and medical services. The first modern nationalisations – where an industry is taken into national ownership – were the acquisition of the lighthouses in 1834 and then the telegraph network in 1870. Nationalisation can be highly controversial. The debates over the Iron and Steel Bill in 1949 and then over the Aircraft and Shipbuilding Bill in 1977 show that the opposition is sometimes prepared to exploit all possible procedural avenues to block legislation. Hence, it is perhaps surprising that governments, irrespective of political party, have agreed that shareholders and owners should receive 'fair compensation' on nationalisation. This chapter therefore examines the parliamentary understanding of 'fairness', both as it applies between the state and the owner and between different owners. It also shows that, despite the consensus on 'fair compensation', there is considerable variation in the actual terms, with the result that they have led to some of the most protracted debates over property rights. In some cases, 'fair compensation' has been very generous to owners; in others, it has been much less so. The key question, however, is whether one can say that there is any constitutional standard at all. In one debate after another, MPs and Ministers have clashed over the meaning of fairness, but almost never explicitly refer to the constitution as a source of relevant standards. As a result, it is not clear that governments or MPs regard 'fair compensation' as a constitutional standard or simply a political necessity to secure passage of a bill. It also points out that, perhaps because of this, recent parliamentary discussions on compensation have focused almost entirely on the ECHR, with no discussion of parliamentary precedent. This is also evident in political statements, such as the Labour Party's manifesto and related policy documents for the 2019 general election.

Chapter six looks at laws that reduce the value or utility of property, without a formal expropriation. This includes everything from regulatory restrictions on the use of property to orders for the destruction of assets or the extinction of rights of property. No state completely bars compulsory purchase, but equally no state bars all regulations that restrict the exercise of rights of property or otherwise diminish their value. Neither do they require compensation for losses caused by regulation. However, in many states, there is a constitutional right to compensation in at least some cases. In the UK, no such right has been recognised. Parliament has required compensation for some regulatory losses, but as a response to political and economic considerations rather than constitutional rights. There is, however, evidence of something less precise. The legislative record shows that regulatory laws that delegate powers to commissioners, Justices of the Peace, boroughs and other public officials and bodies often state that any burdens that they impose must be reasonable and distributed fairly. The chapter also considers whether there are constitutional standards relating to the substantive aspects of taxes and rates. There is a parallel with the statements on regulatory losses, as governments often say that taxes and rates are 'fair'; usually, this means that they should be set according to the ability to pay, or to the benefit received from the expenditure of the funds, or some combination of them. In practice, however, it is not clear that these statements are precise enough to disclose a constitutional standard.

The final chapter, chapter seven, considers a topic that overlaps with the protection of property: retrospective legislation that has the effect of depriving subjects of rights of private property. This can cover many situations, but the most issues relevant to this book concern laws that reverse a civil judgment of the courts. As a general comment, it is difficult to imagine that any lawyer would defend retrospective legislation, except where there is no harm to individuals. However, this chapter shows that Parliament frequently enacts retrospective laws that have the effect of taking or modifying rights of property. Indeed, it refers to Willes J's observation that 'it would fill a long chapter in history to enumerate all the instances of retrospective legislation'.[33] He said this in 1870, and subsequent experience confirms that Parliament continues to employ retrospective laws with similar regularity. Parliament has accepted that retrospection is only constitutionally legitimate where appropriate justification is given and subject to certain conditions. The chapter therefore considers, within this focus, how parliamentary standards have emerged and changed over time, and their significance in the progress of bills through Parliament.

The concluding chapter summarises the main findings of the previous chapters. Evidence drawn from the different areas of legislative activity supports the existence of parliamentary constitutional standards. Moreover, in broad outline, they follow the main points of legal rights to property found in constitutional and human rights law: a deprivation of property should serve a legitimate purpose, which should be defined with some precision for delegated powers; compensation should be provided for an expropriation but not necessarily for other deprivations of rights; and arguably there should be fair treatment where compensation is not required. However, as an element of a political constitution, the unwritten right to property lacks the precision of most legal rights to property. MPs who wish to construct a detailed argument can refer to statutory precedents but cannot draw on anything corresponding exactly to the reasoning of a judgment (except in the quasi-legal processes on procedures, such as the decisions of the Court of Referees). Debates and other material do provide material to supplement the statutory precedents, but even so, the attention to argumentation and reasoning in legal judgments is usually not present in parliamentary material. The conclusions then turn to a point that arises across the chapters: are parliamentarians turning to legal standards in preference to the older parliamentary standards?

[33] *Philips v Eyre* (1870) LR 6 QB 1, 25.

1

Parliamentary Constitutional Standards

This chapter considers the question that lies at the heart of this book: when MPs and Ministers talk about a constitutional right to property, what do they mean? What are the materials for their argument: where do they find the sources for constitutional rights and how do they interpret them? This chapter considers these questions over three sections. The first borrows from the work of Jack Simson Caird and Dawn Oliver and in particular their definition of 'parliamentary constitutional standards'.[1] This provides the context for the next section, which considers the source of standards. It explains that MPs treat legislation and conventions as the primary source of standards, but also considers secondary sources such as debates, reports of parliamentary committees, and any other material in which parliamentary actors articulate standards. The final section considers the question of interpretation. Describing standards and identifying sources provides only part of the answer to the primary question of this book. Sources must be interpreted, but do MPs share common views on the methods of parliamentary interpretation? This section acknowledges that there is relatively little to go on. The legislative process does not include anything quite like the detailed reasoning of a legal judgment. Indeed, there are many cases in which MPs appear to see no need to set out their reasoning. Simple assertions regarding constitutionality are enough. Nevertheless, the section shows that MPs do at least share a common view of what is not a valid argument on constitutional standards. From this, the methodology for the rest of the book can be derived.

I. 'Parliamentary Constitutional Standards'

Jack Simson Caird and Dawn Oliver identify four characteristics of parliamentary constitutional standards: they are articulated by parliamentary actors in parliamentary fora; they are concerned with constitutional matters, including the fundamental rights of the individual; they are not politically partisan, although they may arise in highly partisan debates; and finally they are not enforceable in the courts. Simson Caird and Oliver's characteristics are particularly helpful

[1] J Simson Caird and D Oliver, 'Parliament's Constitutional Standards' in A Horne and A Le Seuer (eds), Parliament: Legislation and Accountability (Hart Publishing, 2016).

because they share this book's focus on substantive and constitutional norms of legislation, as the following discussion of each characteristic demonstrates.

A. Parliamentary

The standards are *parliamentary* because they are articulated by parliamentary actors.[2] It is in parliamentary fora – the Lords, Commons, the committees, the Court of Referees, the meetings of the Examiners – that the expressions of standards are found. Other state actors – especially judges but also Ministers – also articulate constitutional standards, but it is Parliament's own activity that is central to our inquiry. Hence, the focus is not on the case law that develops the legal constitution. The courts have been active in defining the rights of property owners: for example, cases such as *R v Hampden*,[3] *Entick v Carrington*,[4] *Bowles v Bank of England*[5] and *Burmah Oil v Lord Advocate*[6] set down principles on the relationship between the state and the individual, and there are general principles of statutory interpretation that safeguard rights of property.[7] However, as these have been set down by the courts rather than Parliament, they fall outside the scope of our analysis. Similarly, departments or administrative bodies may issue statements on their views of the constitutionality of the exercise of powers over private property.[8] Again, these would not be considered sources of parliamentary standards. To be sure, one would not expect the legal or executive constitutional standards to depart significantly from parliamentary standards, especially in a system where Members of Parliament comprise the Cabinet and senior judges sit in one of the Houses. Nevertheless, parliamentary standards are articulated by parliamentary actors.

The distinction between judicial, executive and parliamentary standards is evident in the practice that parliamentary actors only look to parliamentary activity as the source of their standards. They do not look to judicial or executive statements when articulating constitutional standards, even if they deal with similar topics. Peter Rees MP expressed this view in debates on the Finance Bill 1978, where he considered whether constitutional standards applicable to retrospective legislation should be derived from general conceptions of the rule of law:

> I do not like to bandy the phrase 'the rule of law', because perhaps it has a slightly trite, almost pedagogic ring about it. It is perhaps too closely associated with the legal

[2] ibid 64.

[3] *R v Hampden* (1637) 3 State Tr 826.

[4] *Entick v Carrington* (1765) 19 Howell's State Trials 1029; 95 ER 807.

[5] *Bowles v Bank of England* [1913] 1 Ch 57.

[6] *Burmah Oil v Lord Advocate* [1965] AC 75.

[7] See F Bennion, Diggory Bailey and Luke Norbury, *Bennion, Bailey and Norbury on Statutory Interpretation*, 8th edn (LexisNexis UK, 2022) s 27.2.

[8] See HA Scarrow, 'Policy Pressures by British Local Government: The Case of Regulation in the "Public Interest"' (1971) 4 *Comparative Politics* 1; C Stebbings, 'The Equity of the Executive: Fairness in Tax Law in Nineteenth-Century England' in PG Turner (ed), *Equity and Administration*, 1st edn (Cambridge University Press, 2016).

> profession, and I do not think that we should look at this tonight as lawyers, if indeed we are. I think that this is a matter of constitutional significance which we have to judge as parliamentarians.[9]

Rees was not suggesting that the rule of law is not part of the constitution, but that the parliamentarians should not look to the law and legal precedent as the source of parliamentary standards.[10] Rather, parliamentary standards are articulated by parliamentary actors. In terms of sources, Rees said that 'If our constitution can be spelled out, it depends on precedent and convention.'[11] As numerous examples in this book demonstrate, most MPs would accept this view.

Peter Rees did not say why precedent and convention were the sources of constitutional standards. Indeed, statutory precedent would have been given less weight before supremacy of Parliament was firmly established as the core principle of the United Kingdom (UK) constitution, following the Glorious Revolution. Before then, it was widely agreed that fundamental law bound the Crown, Parliament, the courts, public officials and subjects.[12] Fundamental law was not positive law; rather, it was based on natural law and reason. A positive law might express principles of fundamental law; ideally, it would be at least consistent with it. However, it was also possible that positive law could conflict with fundamental law. Whether an Act contrary to fundamental law was valid was not resolved until parliamentary supremacy took hold after 1688, but ideas of fundamental law continued to influence constitutional thinking. However, the doctrine of supremacy focused attention on Acts as the source of principle. In effect, every Act carries the implicit statement that Parliament regards it as a constitutional expression of its power. This is the point made by Rees in his focus on parliamentary material as the source of principle for parliamentarians, and by Simson Caird and Oliver in their description of *parliamentary* standards.

Parliamentary debates are also studied extensively in this book and are particularly useful when examining methods of interpretation. The use of debates is, of course, subject to the usual caveats. Debates reflect the views of individuals rather than Parliament as a corporate body. Furthermore, they cannot always be accepted at face value. As Danny Nicol says, in relation to the debates on joining the European Economic Community, 'Doubtless some politicians deliberately did not say what they knew, so a certain caution is advisable.'[13] However, Nicol argues that debates are still useful: MPs know that their speeches form part of a public record and hence are likely to be careful in what they say.[14] As discussed below, the

[9] HC Deb 12 July 1978, vol 953, col 1679; he made a similar comment in the Standing Committee debate, at SC Deb (A) 6 June 1978, col 709.

[10] Indeed, his formulation of principles regarding retrospection were based on the importance of stability and predictability in the law, 'that a person should not be prejudiced without due notice of what he is likely to incur': SC Deb (A) 6 June 1978, col 720.

[11] HC Deb 12 July 1978, vol 953, col 1682.

[12] See JW Gough, *Fundamental Law in English Constitutional History* (Clarendon, 1955).

[13] D Nicol, *EC Membership and the Judicialization of British Politics* (Oxford University Press, 2001) ix.

[14] ibid.

quality of analysis and argumentation varies: often, MPs simply make assertions about the constitution without any backing. However, it is still the case that many parliamentarians see debate on constitutional points as sufficiently important that they are willing to devote time and energy in making sound arguments. Moreover, they refer to prior debates as sources of constitutional standards. Indeed, in the debates on the Finance Bill, Rees put forward four principles drawn from the precedents regarding retrospective anti-avoidance measures, which since became known as the 'Rees Rules'.[15] They have been cited by MPs in later debates as a valuable expression of the constitutional standards governing retrospection. Whilst the debates do not themselves constitute statutory precedent, they do indicate how the precedent has been used by MPs and how the standards developed.

A possible alternative to Rees's views on constitutional sources is evident in reports of the House of Lords Constitution Committee. It was set up in 2001 with the following remit: 'To examine the constitutional implications of all public bills coming before the House; and to keep under review the operation of the constitution.'[16] It has, in some reports on specific bills, used statements from the courts to explain constitutional points. To be sure, it does not cite cases as a source of parliamentary standards in the way that a court would cite legal precedents as a source of law. Instead, it uses them as elegant statements of general principles that are likely to be uncontroversial.[17] Indeed, some reports use passages from the works of leading writers such as Alfred Venn Dicey[18] and Tom Bingham (in his non-judicial capacity).[19] Nevertheless, the Committee's use of non-parliamentary sources may suggest that it does not distinguish between parliamentary and judicial standards as sharply as Peter Rees did. However, the Constitution Committee has, in some cases, asked Ministers for statutory precedents in support of the constitutionality of controversial measures.[20] This suggests that their approach is not as far from that of Peter Rees as it might appear: statements of general, foundational principles might be found in a variety of sources, but the statutory precedents help to understand their application to specific measures. Indeed, even in quasi-judicial

[15] For a full discussion, see chapter six, section IV.C.

[16] House of Lords Constitution Committee, *Reviewing the Constitution: Terms of Reference and Method of Working* (HL 2001–02, 11) para 1.

[17] For example, in its report on Part 1 of the Legal Aid, Sentencing and Punishment of Offenders Bill, the Committee cited *R v Secretary of State for the Home Department, ex parte Leech* [1994] QB 198, *R v Lord Chancellor, ex parte Witham* [1998] QB 575 (both cited at para 5) and *Ambrose v Harris* [2011] UKSC 43 (at para 18): see House of Lords Constitution Committee, *Part 1 of the Legal Aid, Sentencing and Punishment of Offenders Bill (Twenty-First Report)* (HL 2010–12, 222). In its report on the Tribunals, Courts and Enforcement Bill, it cited *R v Somerset County Council, ex parte Fewings* [1995] 1 All ER 513: House of Lords Constitution Committee, *Tribunals, Courts and Enforcement Bill (First Report)* (HL 2006–07, 13) para 12.

[18] Eg House of Lords Constitution Committee, *Serious Crime Bill (Second Report)* (HL 2006–07, 41) 2006–07, para 3, quoting AV Dicey, *Introduction to the Study of the Law of the Constitution*, 10th edn (MacMillan, 1959) 207–208.

[19] Eg House of Lords Constitution Committee (n 17) para 7, quoting T Bingham, *The Rule of Law* (Penguin, 2010) 85 and 88.

[20] See below, text to nn 63 and 64, on the Jobseekers (Back to Work Schemes) Bill 2013.

proceedings, parliamentary committees look to parliamentary precedents rather than legal precedents in determining rights of standing, even though the issues are similar and hence could be useful when resolving them. To give a specific example, when the Court of Referees considers whether individuals have standing to challenge a private bill before a special committee, the question is fundamentally the same as it would be for an administrative body considering the question of standing. Indeed, as administrative bodies now perform many of the functions formerly exercised by parliamentary private bill committees, one might have thought that they had built up a body of precedent that would be useful to the Court of Referees. Nevertheless, it looks to parliamentary rather than judicial precedent the source of constitutional standards.

B. Constitutional

Simson Caird and Oliver's second criterion states that standards are '"constitutional" because they are based on principles or norms relating to the working of constitutional relationships and procedures'.[21] In defining a 'constitution', most MPs would probably accept the Constitution Committee's working definition, as set out in its first report, as being:

> the set of laws, rules and practices that create the basic institutions of the state, and its component and related parts, and stipulate the powers of those institutions and the relationship between the different institutions and between those institutions and the individual.[22]

In the report, it also sets out five 'basic tenets' of the UK constitution.[23] These include the rule of law and protection of fundamental rights of the individual. The Constitution Committee did not go further than this, but as the examples in the Introduction show, many MPs have said that a right to property is one of the core rights of the individual. To be more precise, there are a number of candidates for specific constitutional rights relating to the protection of property. The first concern Parliament's own procedures, as it has long recognised rights to notice and audience for bills that specially and directly affect an owner of property. In terms of legislation, Parliament has consistently said that fair compensation should be paid to anyone subject to a compulsory expropriation of their property. As a matter of procedure, it has also said that an independent body, rather than the acquiring party, should have the final say on the valuation of property for compensation. Another standard states that laws should not have retrospective effect unless the circumstances are exceptional. There are other candidates, although their claim to existence is weaker.

[21] Simson Caird and Oliver (n 1) 64.
[22] House of Lords Constitution Committee (n 16) para 20.
[23] ibid para 21.

There are also standards that are constitutional, but not directly concerned with the fundamental rights of the individual. The fiscal constitution is particularly important for property, but it is not the focus of this work because it is more concerned with the relationship between the Houses of Parliament and the Crown rather than the state and the individual. Conversely, other parliamentary standards are not constitutional, although they are relevant to legislation affecting property. For example, in 2011, the Treasury Committee published the *Principles of Tax Policy*, in which it set standards in taxation.[24] This was an initiative of the Coalition government, but it was accepted by all members of the Committee as a non-partisan set of principles by which tax laws could be measured. The Committee identified two basic principles: that the tax system should be fair and that it should promote growth. In addition, there were three key procedural principles: tax rules should be reasonably certain, stable and practicable. Fairness is a value that often arises in constitutional discussions, and governments and MPs have long regarded it as an essential element of legislation imposing taxes, rates or other compulsory contributions. However, as shown in chapter five, their discussions focus on the efficacy of taxation rather than the protection of individuals from state power. For example, in the 1970s, some Conservative MPs argued that tax avoidance was an inevitable consequence of high marginal rates at the upper tax bands.[25] Their concern was more with principles of taxation than constitutional standards. They did not argue, for example, that higher rates violated the rule of law because they were arbitrary or set by the executive without statutory authority. Instead, they claimed that compliance amongst higher earners was weakening because the sense of fairness was breaking down. One may question whether the argument was valid but in any case it was not a constitutional argument.

C. Not Politically Partisan

For the third criterion, Simson Caird and Oliver say that parliamentary constitutional standards are not politically partisan. MPs and Ministers may differ on their content or their application in a specific context, but they agree that the standards exist.[26] For example, when Parliament debated the War Damage Act 1965, the Government did not argue that there were no constitutional standards regarding retrospective legislation. The debate was whether the legislation satisfied those standards.[27] Similarly, chapter four shows that, in debates on nationalisation bills, the overwhelming majority of MPs of all parties have agreed that fair compensation should be paid to the owners. They have often disagreed on formulae for

[24] House of Commons Treasury Committee, *Principles of Tax Policy* (HC 2010–11, 753).

[25] HC Deb 12 July 1978, vol 953 col 1657 (Tim Renton): 'There is no doubt that the root cause [of tax avoidance] is high and oppressive taxation. It is this that leads people and companies constantly to seek ways of reducing their tax burdens.'

[26] Simson Caird and Oliver (n 1) 74–75.

[27] See chapter six, section IV.C.

arriving at 'fair' compensation but not that there is a core standard of fair compensation. Standards exist above or independently of partisan politics, although there is room for debate on the application of those standards to the specific situation.

D. Not Enforceable in the Courts

Finally, Simson Caird and Oliver say that parliamentary constitutional standards are not legally binding, in the sense that the courts have no power to compel parliamentary actors to follow them. Neither may they refuse to apply legislation that was passed in contravention of parliamentary standards.[28] Parliament could, of course, consider statutory mechanisms by which the courts might exercise some control over its own lawmaking: the European Communities Act 1972 and the Human Rights Act (HRA) 1998 are probably the best-known examples. At one point, oaths were used as an instrument of control: the Catholic Relief Act 1793 and the Catholic Relief Act 1829 lifted restrictions on voting or standing for election by Roman Catholics, provided they took an oath to 'defend to the utmost of my power the settlement and arrangement of property in this country, as established by the laws now in being'.[29] The requirement was removed by the Parliamentary Oaths Act 1866, but as there is no evidence that anyone who took the oath ever violated it, its efficacy was never tested.

Simson Caird and Oliver's description is particularly valuable because it allows us to focus the inquiry. It does not lie on conventions (with some exceptions), or judicial standards or the constitution in the courts. Moreover, it distinguishes constitutional standards from non-constitutional standards. These points lead to the next set of issues: it may be possible to describe parliamentary constitutional standards, but that does not prove their existence or impact. Neither does it explain how standards emerge or how arguments regarding their content and application are framed. We now turn to these questions.

II. Constitutional Interpretation in Parliament

As discussed in the Introduction, there is evidence for the existence of standards. The frequency with which MPs explicitly raise matters as constitutional issues is one example; Parliament's creation of the Constitution Committee is another. The willingness of the executive to adopt constitutional principles for drafting bills

[28] This has been an issue in a number of cases concerning private Acts, where there is evidence of apparent breaches of Standing Orders that are intended to protect the interests of third parties. In *Edinburgh and Dalkeith Railway Co v Wauchope* (1842) 1 Bell 278, 8 Cl & Fin 710, 8 ER 279 the Court acknowledged that the absence of notice could be relevant to the interpretation of ambiguous provisions. See also *British Railways Board v Pickin* [1974] AC 765.

[29] T Allen, 'Constitutional Rights in the Irish Home Rule Bill of 1893' (2018) 39 *Journal of Legal History* 187, 194.

also confirms the importance of constitutional norms. However, this evidence is general rather than specific. It does not explain how MPs establish that a particular standard exists or whether it applies to specific measures of a bill. There is nothing as detailed as the judicial consideration of interpretive methods relating to judicial precedents or legal instruments. Arguably, there is less need for the articulation of rules of interpretation in the parliamentary context. As Jack Simson Caird observes, 'within a political context, interpreters can afford to be more creative, and less legalistic in their approach to deciding the meaning of a particular constitutional norm'.[30] Nevertheless, it is worth asking whether there is a concern with interpretive methods in Parliament.

A preliminary observation is appropriate here. That is, the distinct constitutional nature of the standards that this book considers suggests that the interpretive methods would be distinct from those relating to other parliamentary standards.[31] That is, what counts as a constitutional argument might not count as an argument on the economic implications of a bill, and vice versa. For example, an argument on *Principles of Tax Policy* would probably draw upon an economic analysis or compliance theory rather than statutory precedent.[32] In addition, as noted above, parliamentary interpretation is distinct from legal interpretation: parliamentarians do not look to judicial precedents or arguments to articulate parliamentary norms. To be sure, there are aspects of constitutional principles where the distinctions are not as clear as they once were. For example, most scholars would follow the Constitution Committee's statement that membership of the Commonwealth and other international organisations is one of the basic tenets of the part of the UK Constitution.[33] Hence, the parliamentary interpretation of treaty provisions may consider the legal interpretation of the same provisions. There is a specific overlap in this regard, as the European Convention on Human Rights (ECHR) contains a right to property, in Article 1 of the First Protocol.[34] However, the constitutional standards of property have not been merged with the human rights principles, although they cover similar ground.

A. The Use of Precedent

Usually, the strongest evidence of a constitutional standard is found in a long-standing, consistent pattern relating to a relatively narrow issue.[35] The clearest

[30] J Simson Caird, 'Identifying the Value of Parliamentary Constitutional Interpretation' PhD thesis (Queen Mary University of London, 2014) 49; see also 128.

[31] ibid 44: 'parliamentary constitutional interpretation is a distinct form of reasoning within the UK Parliament's legislative process'.

[32] House of Commons Treasury Committee (n 24).

[33] House of Lords Constitution Committee (n 16) para 21.

[34] Protocol to the Convention for the Protection of Human Rights and Fundamental Freedoms (Paris, 20 March 1952).

[35] This section concentrates on parliamentarians' use and interpretation of statutory precedent. There are situations in which parliamentary bodies may act in a legal role, and hence rely on judicial

examples are found in private Acts on enclosures, the modification of settled estates and compulsory purchase for infrastructure works. Over many years, Parliament passed thousands of Acts on these topics, following common patterns relating to their substantive content. As discussed in chapter three, MPs usually regarded these practices as setting standards for the protection of individual rights that, at the very least, should not be disregarded without good justification. A number of specific points emerged: Parliament would require the promoter to show that enactment of the bill would be in the public interest; if there was a loss to the owner (as in compulsory purchase), it should be compensated, with an independent valuation of the loss and rights of appeal. Parliament would also ensure that directly affected individuals would be given notice and rights of audience before the committee considering the bill. Another example of a consistent practice is evident with retrospective legislation aimed at tax avoidance schemes. Clearly, retrospectivity raises questions over the rule of law, but Parliament has adopted a practice of limiting retrospection to the date on which the Government gave a specific prior warning of the intention to legislate retrospectively. Arguably, over the last century or so, this practice has been repeated so frequently that it should be treated as a parliamentary constitutional standard. These practices are good candidates for constitutional standards because they have been followed consistently; where there is a suggestion that legislation may depart from them, governments are careful to provide reasons for doing so or to argue that there is in fact no departure from the practice.

It is also worth noting that the absence of a practice has suggested that there is no constitutional standard to follow. Chapter five discusses the Town and Country Planning Act 1947, under which the right to develop land was taken from the owners, without compensation. After 1947, owners could only change the use of land if they applied for planning permission and paid a development charge to the Central Land Board. The Act clearly took something of value from owners, but the Government said that no compensation was due for taking the right to develop from owners, on the basis that there was no practice of compensating for regulatory losses. A similar example arises with nationalisation, where there has been no consistent practice on the mode of payment. In many cases, compensation is in the form of long-term securities issued by the state corporation, rather than a cash payment. There is, clearly, no standard that full compensation should be paid in cash on acquisition.

The case for a parliamentary standard becomes weaker when the practice is less frequent. Nevertheless, there are cases where MPs have treated a single Act

methods of interpretation. The House of Lords, sitting as a judicial committee of the Lords, operates as a court and hence relies on judicial precedent. In *Viscountess Rhondda's Claim* [1922] 2 AC 339, the Committee for Privileges took a similar approach, and treated the interpretation of the Sex Disqualification (Removal) Act 1919 as a legal question to be resolved by the application of legal principles and precedents. The Court of Referees relies on its own precedents for its decisions; the chairs of special committees on hybrid bills also consider the Court's precedents as well as their own precedents.

as establishing a principle of constitutional significance. Indeed, the HRA 1998 is a recent example of importance to property, as it incorporates the right to property of the ECHR, but legislation does not need to carry such obvious constitutional significance to establish a precedent. For example, the Tramways Act 1870 included compensation terms for the compulsory purchase of assets that ignored the value of a business as a going concern.[36] This broke with the practice that had applied prior to it. Subsequently, 'tramway terms' became known as one of the possible ways of assessing loss on the acquisition of an undertaking. Similarly, the Housing of the Working Classes Act 1890 established that compensation for land may be reduced where its value is partly attributable to illegal or immoral activity.[37] If, for example, the landlord earned a higher income from the property (and thereby increased the capital value) by exceeding the lawful occupancy, compensation would only reflect the value with lawful occupancy. Both of these statutes broke the prior practice regarding compensation and loss. As such, they indicated Parliament's views on the scope of legitimate interference with private property and became important precedents.

At face value, it would seem that a long-standing practice regarding the content of legislation should always provide strong evidence of a standard, especially if it is also clear that Parliament expects that any departure from the practice should be justified. However, some MPs have doubted whether a legislative practice does establish a constitutional standard. Paul Scott raises the eighteenth century debate in Parliament over its power to impose taxes in America.[38] As noted in the Introduction, Lord Camden argued that 'the many private bills, as well as public, passed every session' showed that Parliament 'cannot take away any man's private property without making him a compensation'.[39] Lord Mansfield challenged Camden, saying that: 'I deny the proposition that parliament takes no man's property without his consent: it frequently takes private property without making what the owner thinks a compensation.'[40] Scott's point is important: even if we accept the existence of constitutional standards, we should look carefully at the evidence of a practice before concluding that one has been established. With the Camden-Mansfield debate, one might argue that Lord Mansfield was objecting to a principle that Lord Camden did not in fact put forward. That is, Lord Camden argues for compensation, objectively determined, but Lord Mansfield counters by saying that there is no principle of subjective compensation. It is not unusual for MPs to employ straw man arguments, but this raises a second issue. Even if standards could be established by a practice, the evidence is often likely to be so weak or equivocal that their existence is open to doubt.

[36] See chapter four, section I.

[37] See chapter three, section III.A.

[38] P Scott, 'Entick v Carrington and the Legal Protection of Property' in A Tomkins and P Scott (eds), *Entick and Carrington: 250 Years of the Rule of Law* (Hart Publishing, 2015) 137–39.

[39] *Cobbett's Parliamentary History of England*, XVI, 167 (1766).

[40] *Cobbett's Parliamentary History of England*, XVI, 172 (1766).

Doubts over the relevance of a practice have been expressed in Parliament as well, with the debates on the Home Rule Bill of 1893 perhaps the best example.[41] The Prime Minister, William Gladstone, sought to assuage fears that an Irish legislature would confiscate and redistribute land, by including a bill of rights with a right to property in the Bill. Accordingly, the final version of clause 4(5) barred the Irish legislature from enacting laws

> Whereby any person may be deprived of life, liberty or property without due process of law in accordance with the settled principles and precedents, or may be denied the equal protection of the laws, or whereby private property may be taken without just compensation.

After lengthy debate, the House of Commons passed the bill, although it was later rejected by the House of Lords. From our perspective, the most interesting aspect of the Commons debate concerned the effect of clause 4(5). The Attorney-General, Charles Russell, said that 'settled principles and precedent' would give the courts enough to apply the clause to concrete situations. He gave the example of habeas corpus: the Irish legislature would have the power to suspend it, but only where, 'according to established precedent, there was an emergency or a state of circumstances justifying the action'.[42] Similarly, the Solicitor-General, John Rigby, argued that the meaning of 'just compensation' would be governed by 'what the Irish and English laws at the present time think to be just' and 'the fundamental laws of justice in granting compensation'.[43] By contrast, the opposing MPs saw little value in precedent. On this point, Dunbar Barton stated that 'In no country had historical precedents been used in deciding legal questions'.[44] His concern, of course, was with judicial interpretation rather than the interpretation of precedent in Parliament, but he and other MPs doubted that precedent established patterns that could be seen as evidence in any context. In any case, he doubted that precedent actually established anything, at least in relation to the highly controversial laws regarding the laws of 'coercion' that had been applied to Ireland. Echoing Lord Mansfield, he said that 'if they [precedents] could be used there would be nothing to prevent the Irish Legislature following the coercive policy of the present Government in past years'.[45] Similarly, in relation to the laws on tenancy reforms and compulsory purchase of land in Ireland, George Wyndham argued that the Land Law (Ireland) Act 1881 and the Land Law (Ireland) Act 1887 demonstrated that 'The Imperial Parliament was every day engaged in passing laws, extinguishing the rights of property in a manner some believed to be due and others believed

[41] See Allen (n 29).

[42] HC Deb 15 June 1893, vol 13, col 1116; see also the Solicitor-General, HC Deb 15 June 1893, vol 13, cols 1111–12.

[43] HC Deb 11 April 1893, vol 11, col 112.

[44] HC Deb 16 June 1893, vol 13 cols 1209–10.

[45] ibid.

to be undue'.[46] If precedents were relevant to the existence of standards, the courts would find it impossible to develop legal rules from them in concrete situations.

The Unionists' position on clause 4(5) also reflected a more general point, as they were determined to reject any argument that suggested that a written constitution could be drafted that would protect the Protestant minority from a Catholic-majority legislature. For them, only a continued union within the UK would provide effective constitutional protection for the minority. It was the composition of Parliament itself that protected the Protestants and their property: any practices in existence had always been contingent on the balance of power within Parliament rather than a commitment from MPs to follow the practice. Indeed, the Unionists seemed to accept some truth in Waldron's and Griffith's description of legislatures: they were a place of negotiation and deal-making rather than high principle.[47]

This view certainly exists, but it is not accepted by many MPs, Ministers and government departments. Their practices demonstrate that standards are important to them and that they can be established by statutory precedent. Nevertheless, the analysis of precedent can be perfunctory. Often, Ministers and MPs refer to the claim that a standard is relevant and that it is established by precedent, but without identifying the precedents. There are some rare exceptions, with the debates on the War Damage Act 1965 an interesting example. When the Attorney-General introduced the War Damage Bill in the Commons, he explained that it would retrospectively overturn the judgment of the House of Lords in *Burmah Oil v Lord Advocate*.[48] He recognised the constitutional issues of retrospectivity, but cited the Indemnity Act 1920, the War Charges Validation Act 1925, the Charitable Trusts (Validation) Act 1954, the Wireless Telegraphy (Validity of Charges) Act 1954 and the Finance Act 1960 as precedents for the Bill. He went through each, arguing that they showed that more contentious aspects of the Bill were not novel and that the justifications given for the Bill were consistent with the justifications for earlier legislation.

The Attorney-General's defence of the Bill suggests that precedent was important. Edward Gardner, an opposition MP, pointed out that compensation was available under the 1920 Act but not under the Bill. He also argued that the Act was not a relevant precedent, because it 'was not put into law with any particular target in view',[49] whereas 'This Bill came into being because of a particular company and the claim made by that company, and in order to defeat that claim.'[50] The Attorney-General addressed both points. He argued that the 1920 Act established

[46] HC Deb 15 June 1893, vol 13, col 1129. The Land Law (Ireland) Act 1881 and the Land Law (Ireland) Act 1887 allowed for the compulsory modification of rents and other terms of a lease.

[47] JAG Griffith, 'The Political Constitution' (1979) 42 *MLR* 1; J Waldron, *The Dignity of Legislation* (Cambridge University Press, 1999).

[48] *Burmah Oil v Lord Advocate* [1965] AC 75.

[49] HC Deb 12 May 1965, vol 712, col 596.

[50] ibid col 597.

that legislation could set a fair level of compensation, and in this case, it was fair to provide none;[51] in any event, the 1920 Act did not provide any compensation for damage that occurred overseas.[52] Insofar as targeting specific proceedings was concerned, he pointed out that the Government was expecting other claims to come forward, as a number of companies were waiting for the outcome of the Burmah Oil litigation. Finally, in relation to stopping proceedings that had already resulted in a judgment, he argued that the 1920 Act had non-suited the claimants in *Newcastle Breweries Ltd v Attorney-General*, which was 'almost exactly parallel' to the situation in the *Burmah Oil* case.[53]

It is clear that the Attorney-General and Gardner did consider the statutory precedents carefully. However, except for Gardner, none of the opposing MPs referred to specific precedents.[54] Given that many of them asserted that the constitutional issues were important, their lack of interest in precedent is striking. For them, constitutionality could be deduced from broad principles, rather than induction from precedent. This is a general observation: often, MPs seem to invoke the constitution without reference to specific precedent or indeed to any sources at all. Indeed, in some cases, references to 'precedent' and 'the constitution' seem to mean stability in the most general sense. During the land reform debates of the late nineteenth century and first part of the twentieth century, it was clear that many members of the House of Lords regarded the distribution of land as a constitutional matter, so that any law aimed at changing the established order was seen as unconstitutional.[55] Hence, there is a gap in the parliamentary method: there is common ground on the sources of standards but not their interpretation. In effect, there should be a theory of interpretation. There might, of course, be disagreement, just as judges and lawyers often differ on the appropriate method for interpreting a legal instrument.

B. Parliamentary Committees and Constitutional Interpretation

In principle, the close consideration of statutes as precedent should arise in parliamentary committees. However, they do not disclose a clear methodology for the

[51] Claims could be made to a compensation tribunal, but only on principles as set out in the Act.

[52] HC Deb 12 May 1965, vol 712, cols 532, 533–34.

[53] ibid col 606.

[54] N MacDermot, Financial Secretary to the Treasury, on the same day, also discussed the Indemnity Act 1920, but for the Government: see HC Deb 12 May 1965, vol 712, col 531.

[55] See the discussion of the Salisbury 'doctrine' in G Dymond and H Deadman, 'The Salisbury Doctrine' (2006) House of Lords Library Note Number LLN 2006/006. Dymond and Deadman quote GHL Le May's comment: 'The national will was supreme, and the Conservative Party represented it. The House of Lords was the instrument that ensured the national will should be respected.' GHL Le May, *The Victorian Constitution: Conventions, Usages and Contingencies* (Duckworth, 1979) 144, in Dymond and Deadman, ibid 9.

use of precedent. For example, the Royal Commission on Churches (Scotland) considered whether to recommend that Parliament overturn a House of Lords judgment with retrospective effect.[56] It acknowledged the constitutional difficulties, saying that reversal should only be a last resort.[57] However, the Commission stated that an 'equitable adjustment' of assets would be appropriate, as it would enable two factions of a church that had split to serve their congregations and missions.[58] One might have thought that the Commission, and later Parliament, would have considered whether there were statutory precedents for an 'equitable adjustment', but none were given. By contrast, the Leasehold Committee's 1950 report went into some depth on the precedents regarding residential leasehold enfranchisement. The majority advised against granting tenants a right to compulsory purchase of the freehold. This was based on its interpretation of the statutory precedents, from which it concluded that enfranchisement would be a significant departure from existing laws.[59] For that reason, it could not be justified without strong evidence of a clear public benefit. The Committee did not find this evidence and hence it recommended that no change be made. The minority carefully considered the precedents, arguing that the majority had not described them correctly and that enfranchisement would not be a radical step.[60] The majority's view held, but Parliament would follow the minority's view in the next decade. However, both seemed to agree that the precedents were important and both considered them carefully. They differed on their interpretation of the precedents, but not on their significance.

The Constitution Committee's role in articulating constitutional standards has been considered by a number of scholars.[61] To date, none of the Committee's reports acknowledge that there is a constitutional right to property. Its silence does not mean, however, that there is no such constitutional right, as it has not attempted to issue a comprehensive list of fundamental rights. Silence may only reflect the relatively low profile given to constitutional issues regarding property in recent years. Indeed, in the Committee's first report, it acknowledged that its terms of reference require it to examine all public bills but said that only some bills would be the subject of a substantive report to the House. It gave the example of the Countryside and Rights of Way Bill: 'although it was concerned with rights of access to land, might not be thought to have raised

[56] Royal Commission on Churches (Scotland), *Report of the Royal Commission on Churches (Scotland)*, vol 1 (Cd 2494, 1905); *General Assembly of Free Church of Scotland v Overtoun* [1904] AC 515; see chapter six, section IV.C.

[57] Royal Commission on Churches (Scotland), ibid, 17.

[58] ibid 20–22.

[59] Leasehold Committee, *Final Report* (Cd 7982, 1950) 27–39.

[60] ibid 133–38, 142–44.

[61] See J Simson Caird, R Hazell and D Oliver, *The Constitutional Standards of the House of Lords Select Committee on the Constitution*, 3rd edn (The Constitution Unit, 2017); P Grez Hidalgo, 'Legislative Scrutiny on Constitutional Grounds in the United Kingdom Parliament' PhD thesis (Edinburgh, 2019) 122–38.

significant constitutional issues'.[62] In the light of this, it is not surprising that the Committee has had little to say about statutory precedents relating to a constitutional right to property. Its most extensive consideration of the impact of legislation on property concerned the Jobseekers (Back to Work Schemes) Bill of 2013. Even here, the focus was on retrospectivity and the extinction of judgments rather than property alone. The Government introduced the Bill into the House of Commons on 14 March 2013, in response to *R (Reilly and Wilson) v The Secretary of State for Work and Pensions*, where the Court of Appeal held that recipients of jobseeker benefits had been unlawfully denied benefits and then subjected to sanctions that were also unlawful.[63] The Bill declared, with retrospective effect, that the recipients had not been entitled to the benefits and the sanctions could be imposed. The Constitution Committee's report on the Bill included a recommendation that the House should 'consider whether retrospectively confirming penalties on individuals who, according to judicial decision, have not transgressed any lawful rule is constitutionally appropriate in terms of the rule of law'.[64] The Committee did call upon the Government to provide constitutional precedents for retrospection but none were provided. There were further debates on the Bill, but no discussion of the constitutionality of the retrospective provisions.[65] Ultimately, it seems that constitutional standards and precedents were not seen as particularly significant beyond the Committee – a point to which we return in chapter six.

The Constitution Committee's reports on other fundamental rights have varied in their use of statutory precedent. There are reports where it has expressed concerns over the lack of precedent for measures in a bill: the Jobseekers Bill is one example. Similarly, in its report on the Prevention of Terrorism Bill, it specifically noted that 'There is no direct precedent for the powers granted to the Secretary of State by this Bill'.[66] Its report on the Child Maintenance and Other Payments Bill did refer to statutory precedents to support its position.[67] However, it did not refer to any of the numerous statutory precedents on retrospection in its

[62] House of Lords Constitution Committee (n 16) para 34. There had been, in fact, some discussion in the debates about the status of property as a fundamental right in the debates on the bill: see HC Deb 20 March 2000, vol 346, cols 720, 763 (Christopher Gill), cols 720, 721 (Michael Meacher, Secretary of State for the Environment), col 734 (Archie Norman), col 754 (Peter Atkinson), col 790 (Andrew Hunter) and HL Deb 26 June 2000, vol 614, col 688 (Earl Ferrers), col 712 (Earl of Arran) and cols 723–24 (Lord Luke).

[63] *R (Reilly and Wilson) v The Secretary of State for Work and Pensions* [2013] EWCA Civ 66, which was upheld on appeal (*R (Reilly and Another) v The Secretary of State for Work and Pensions* [2013] UKSC 68), although not until after the Act came into effect.

[64] House of Lords Constitution Committee, *Jobseekers (Back to Work Schemes) Bill* (HL 2012–13, 155) para 15.

[65] See chapter six, section IV.C.

[66] House of Lords Constitution Committee, *Prevention of Terrorism Bill (Second Report)* (HL 2004–05, 66) para 10.

[67] House of Lords Constitution Committee, *Child Maintenance and Other Payments Bill (Third Report)* (HL 2007–08, 27) para 5.

report on the Nationality, Immigration and Asylum Bill, and this is more typical of its approach.[68] In many reports, it offers little more than a statement of a broad constitutional principle, followed by the specific measures of concern and a recommendation that the House subject the measures to closer scrutiny on constitutional grounds. Often, it cites no authorities in support of its statement. Either the statutory precedents are so well-known that there is no need to list them, or the principle is so clearly a part of a sound constitutional order that it exists irrespective of specific statutory precedent.

C. Parliamentary Reasoning

It may be the case that most MPs believe that standards exist and that precedent is important in uncovering them, but they only rarely discuss methods of interpretation. By contrast, when judges interpret legal instruments, they may be guided or directed to follow specific methods of interpretation. The choice of method may be uncertain: for example, it may not be obvious whether a judge should adopt a plain meaning or purposive approach to interpretation. Nevertheless, judicial interpretation itself is thought to be subject to methodological principles, even if contested. With parliamentary constitutional interpretation, there is no clear methodology. It is not clear, for example, whether the Constitution Committee's basic tenets should be the starting point for interpretation. Jack Simson Caird's observation is apt: 'Constitutional interpretation in the UK is often not a question of discovering the intention of the original authors, because many of the principles are unwritten or uncodified.'[69]

Given that it is difficult to identify principles or methods of parliamentary constitutional interpretation, it may be easier to focus on the opposite: are there principles or methods that parliamentarians regard as invalid. If so, it might affirm that there are positive principles, even if they are difficult to discern. In this respect, the literature on constitutional interpretation in the American courts may be valuable. David E Pozen and Adam M Samaha list forms of constitutional interpretation that would not be considered valid in the American courts.[70] These are ones based on policy, ideology or religion, partisan politics, emotion, popular opinion, 'logrolling' and trade-offs, as well as more general principles 'such as norms against logical contradiction, explicit indifference to enacted text, or personal bias against a party to a dispute'.[71] In the UK, the supremacy of Parliament makes the identification of specific methods of constitutional interpretation more complex. It can always choose to enact a new constitutional rule, whether by

[68] House of Lords Constitution Committee, *Nationality, Immigration and Asylum Bill Further Report (Seventh Report)* (HL 2001–02, 129).

[69] Simson Caird (n 30) 128.

[70] DE Pozen and AM Samaha, 'Anti-Modalities' (2021) 119 *Michigan Law Review* 729.

[71] ibid 767.

explicit legislation, such as the Parliament Acts 1911 and 1949. Or, it may modify or extend a specific standard by enacting a statute contrary to the precedents, as with the compensation principles of the Housing of the Working Classes Act 1890 and the curtailment of the right to petition under the Town and Country Planning 1947 and Transport and Works Act 1992.[72] Or, MPs may argue that there are no relevant precedents: in the debates on the Indemnity Act 1920 and actions taken in World War I, the Attorney-General (Sir Gordon Hewart) acknowledged that 'that there has never been such an Indemnity Bill as this. Be it so. I would add that there has never been such a war as this'.[73]

To start with, Pozen and Samaha state that American courts do not accept policy objectives as an aid in determining the meaning of constitutional clauses. In the British context, there is the example of the *Principles of Tax Policy*. In applying the *Principles*, an MP might apply an economic analysis: for example, some MPs might argue that high tax rates harm economic growth and hence should not be used.[74] This, however, would not be a constitutional argument: it would not be accepted as establishing a constitutional right not to be subjected to high taxation or (as some MPs have suggested) excusing tax avoidance.

Pozen and Samaha's second example – ideology and religion – is reflected in the parliamentary view of constitutional interpretation. Neither are accepted as providing alternative sources of constitutional standards, or of providing principles for interpretation. This is not to say that they have not shaped the law of property. The nineteenth century lifting of disabilities by the Catholic Emancipation Act 1829 and the Jews Relief Act 1858 are examples.[75] Some aspects of land law – such as chancel repair liability – still reflect the interests of the Church of England. However, neither religion nor ideology provide criteria for selecting constitutional sources or the ways in which they are interpreted. Even the arguments of the spiritual Lords on property legislation affecting the Church's interests have been secular in nature. For example, the Archbishop of Canterbury argued that the compensation for the nationalisation of coal reserves, as provided by the Coal Bill 1938, would be inadequate, but did not invoke faith as the basis for an argument on constitutionality.[76]

[72] For the Housing of the Working Classes Act 1890, see chapter three, section III.A.

[73] HC Deb 3 May 1920, vol 128, col 1840.

[74] See, eg, HC Deb 12 July 1978, vol 953 col 1657 (Tim Renton).

[75] For the parliamentary context for each, see: RW Davis, 'The House of Lords, the Whigs and Catholic Emancipation, 1806–1829' (1999) 18 *Parliamentary History* 23; URQ Henriques, 'The Jewish Emancipation Controversy in Nineteenth-Century Britain' [1968] *Past & Present* 126.

[76] HL Deb 3 May 1938, vol 108, cols 774–777 (the Ecclesiastical Commissioners received the largest royalty income from reserves in the country). Indeed, even in the debates that seem more likely to raise religious arguments, MPs may acknowledge the importance of their faith in developing their moral views on a bill, but they still frame arguments in secular terms: see, eg, the debates on the Medical Termination of Pregnancy Bill 1966, HC Deb 22 July 1966, vol 729, col 1067ff and HL Deb 19 July 1967, vol 285, col 258 ff (although see Norman St. John-Stevas HC Deb 22 July 1966, vol 732, cols 1153, 1157 and the Lord Privy Seal (Earl of Longford) HL Deb 19 July 1967 vol 285, cols 311–12).

Pozen and Samaha's third form of invalid reasoning involves forms of argument that inject partisan politics into constitutional interpretation. There is a counterpart in parliamentary constitutional interpretation: as noted above, Simson Caird and Oliver describe constitutional standards as politically neutral. In practice, it is unlikely that MPs would argue that the interests of their party define constitutional standards. For example, they are unlikely to claim that an Act does not create a valid precedent merely because their party was not in government when it was enacted. Nevertheless, some arguments have been coloured by partisan politics: for example, where MPs cite speeches in support of a constitutional argument, they tend to cite senior members of their own party. For example, Conservative MPs regularly refer to the Rees Rules and the later 'Dorrell Statement' in relation to retrospection and anti-avoidance tax measures, whereas Labour MPs are more likely to refer to the 'Primarolo Statement'.[77] To be sure, there are differences between the statements, but it is also apparent that MPs prefer to cite their own party members as constitutional authorities. The effect is a little contradictory: they cite their own MPs to give the impression that their party pays more attention to constitutional values, and yet by doing so they undermine the neutrality that should characterise constitutional interpretation. Nevertheless, although there is an element of partisan politics, the focus is still on statutory precedent as the source of standards.

Parliament has taken a view similar to the American courts in relation to Pozen and Samaha's next category of invalid argument, regarding emotion. In Parliament, MPs often discount arguments based on emotion or 'sentiment'. For example, in the debates on the retrospective aspects of the War Damage Bill 1965, and again in debates on extending firearms restrictions on handguns, a number of MPs stated that emotion and sentiment should not be a basis for decision.[78]

Pozen and Samaha's point that judges reject arguments that resort to popular opinion is interesting in the parliamentary context, given that legislation should reflect popular opinion in a democracy. Indeed, some constitutional principles give weight to expressions of popular opinion. The Salisbury convention requiring the House of Lords not to reject bills that were promised in the Government's election manifesto is one example; the weight given to a referendum is another.[79] However, even where public opinion does carry weight, it does not dictate the

[77] See chapter six, section IV.C.

[78] On the War Damage Bill, see, eg, HC Deb 3 February 1965, vol 705, col 1129 (Ivor Richard), col 1139 (Sir J Foster), col 1144 (Sydney Silverman) and col 1165 (Harold Lever). On the firearms proposals, see HL Deb 16 December 1996, vol 576, col 1365 (Viscount Thurso) and HC Deb 18 November 1996, vol 285, col 763 (Sir Patrick Cormack) and col 765 (Austin Miller). Not all MPs agreed that emotion should not provide reasons: see HC Deb 18 November 1996, vol 285, col 760 (David Mellor) and HC Deb 18 November 1996, vol 285, col 780 (Alice Mahon): 'I am completely unapologetic about saying that my overwhelming reason for supporting a total ban on handguns is emotional. I am not ashamed of that. Emotion is a valuable human asset that differentiates us from lower species. Logic also dictates that it is rational to support a total ban.'

[79] Dymond and Deadman (n 55); N Johnston, 'Referendums' (2016) House of Commons Library Briefing Paper Number 7692.

choice of precedent or the manner of their interpretation. That is, popular opinion may be reflected in an Act, but that Act remains a precedent even if it is subsequently repealed. Conservative governments have reversed nationalisations, but that does not mean that the nationalisation Acts are not precedents and would not be relevant to future nationalisations.

Finally, Pozen and Samaha identify trade-offs as an invalid form of argument. As a political matter, trade-offs are common in legislatures and are often essential to get bills through Parliament. However, where constitutional issues arise, MPs do not say that an Act is not a precedent because it was part of a legislative bargain. Trade-offs may occur regularly, but constitutional argument is distinct. Indeed, in the nineteenth century, many MPs resisted reforms of private bill procedures that restricted the opportunity for trade-offs, as they thought that bargaining was essential to protecting the interests of their constituents.[80] Even so, bill committees were still expected to consider the constitutional requirements of notice, proof of public advantage, and that the bill should guarantee compensation as assessed by an independent body.

Overall, the evidence of principles of interpretation lacks the clarity or detail that is seen in judicial interpretation of legal instruments. Precedent is valuable, but it seems that MPs often see no need to identify the precedents that they use or how they use them. The existence of invalid forms of constitutional argument suggests that there must be valid forms, but identifying those forms has not been possible, given the lack of close analysis in debates and reports. Moreover, the task is rendered more difficult because invalid forms of constitutional argument may be valid as other forms of argument. In addition, different forms of valid argument may be jumbled together in a single debate (and often in a single speech). Nevertheless, the evidence confirms that Rees was correct, in that Acts are a primary focus of interpretation (and parliamentary practice for conventions). Reasoning and interpretive method is more difficult to uncover. It seems to comprise little more than the general principle that 'like cases should be treated alike', but without a theory on the identification of likenesses.

III. Conclusion

The remaining chapters of this book focus on two key questions. First, is it possible to identify specific standards in relation to measures that modify or take rights of property? That is, is there evidence of a culture of justification relating to laws that interfere with rights of property, with specific points of reference for heightened parliamentary scrutiny? If so, can we describe them, and comment on their impact? Primary sources follow those of parliamentarians: statutory law,

[80] See chapter two, section II.

parliamentary procedural rules such as conventions, Standing Orders, and decisions of the Speaker, Examiners, Court of Referees and committee chairs. Debates and committee reports are also important, to help understand how parliamentarians understood the constitutional issues and the impact of legislation. They are also useful in identifying whether an MP saw an issue as constitutional: for example, did a concern with the fairness of a law arise from constitutional matters or was it more about the efficacy of tax measures?

The second question asks how parliamentarians establish these points of reference. To what extent do MPs look to statutory precedent and other parliamentary material to support their constitutional arguments? As subsequent chapters show, there are many debates in which some MPs have claimed that a bill is constitutional or unconstitutional, but provide nothing in support of their argument. On the other hand, there are also debates in which a careful examination of precedent is laid out for the House. This is therefore also a recurring theme of the book: can we identify a parliamentary view of constitutional interpretation?

2

Rights in the Parliamentary Process

This chapter considers the procedural rights in the legislative process of bills directly affecting property. For the most part, the procedures are the same as they are for any other bill, regardless of the subject matter. There are, however, a few points that either concern interests in property or arise more frequently with property than other types of bills. The focus on procedure is a departure from the focus on substantive issues considered elsewhere in this book. However, the culture of justification, as it relates to the constitution and property, emerged from procedures that Parliament developed for the consideration of bills, and especially from its consideration of private bills. Parliament now spends very little time on private bills, but this was not always the case: in the eighteenth and nineteenth centuries, Parliament passed thousands of private Acts, covering a very wide range of activity. The volume declined in the twentieth century, as legislation constituted various administrative bodies with the power to issue orders allowing the modification or interferences with rights of property. Consequently, 'compared with their nineteenth-century heyday, private bills have become something of a parliamentary backwater'.[1] Even in the nineteenth century, Frederick Clifford remarked that 'private bills have ever been the humble companions of public measures, largely ignored at one period in the statute book, hardly noticed by contemporaries, almost wholly neglected in history'.[2] Nevertheless, we consider them because the numerous proceedings on private and hybrid bills provide evidence of constitutional rights to property that are relevant to modern legislation. In addition, in recent years, governments have used the hybrid proceedings for significant infrastructure projects, such as the Channel Tunnel Rail Link Act 1996, Crossrail Act 2008 and the HS2 rail legislation.[3] Hence, constitutional rights still play a role in at least some legislative processes.[4]

This chapter proceeds by considering, first, the right to petition for and promote a private Act and then the corresponding right to petition for the opportunity to challenge a bill before Parliament. In the final section, it considers the recent use

[1] N Besly and others, *How Parliament Works*, 8th edn (Routledge, 2019) 237.

[2] F Clifford, *A History of Private Bill Legislation* (Butterworths, 1885) vol 1, 1.

[3] High Speed Rail (London–West Midlands) Act 2017; High Speed Rail (West Midlands–Crewe) Act 2021.

[4] On procedure as a general constraint on parliamentarians and governments, see P Norton, 'Playing by the Rules: The Constraining Hand of Parliamentary Procedure' (2001) 7 *Journal of Legislative Studies* 13.

of hybrid procedures for large transportation infrastructure schemes and whether it has had an impact on the constitutional rights.

I. The Right to Promote a Bill

An unusual aspect of the procedural system is petitioning, and in particular that anyone can petition for a bill that would override the property rights of others. The Joint Committee noted that 'It is a right of every subject to be able to promote a private bill before Parliament, and the Committee would not wish to see that right abrogated in any way.'[5] Evidence that individuals or groups petitioned the Crown for relief of one kind or another goes back to the reign of Edward I.[6] Where it appeared that a petition required a response that neither the courts nor the Chancellor could provide, it would be referred to Parliament for consideration.[7] If it was accepted, a bill would be issued for royal assent. Petitions could cover a wide range of issues:[8] a petitioner might pursue their own interests, for matters relating to personal status such as naturalisation, restitution by blood, annulment or divorce. Or, they might seek a modification or simply a clarification of their interests in land. A local group or town might petition to protect their market from forestalling or other harmful trade practices. Petitions also came forward for various local projects, such as the clearing of obstacles to river navigation, the draining of marsh lands, the raising of flood defences, the repair and improvement of highways and harbours, or for urban projects such as the paving of streets and the development of new water supplies. Often, the petition would include a request for authority to set tolls or impose local rates or charges to cover the costs of the project. In some cases, petitions requested a redistribution of rights, as in the case of enclosures. By the sixteenth century, petitioners were seeking powers to use or acquire land for local works such as waterways, sewers, port facilities and the like, if necessary by compulsion. Later, during the industrial age, petitions allowing the assembly of land for turnpikes, canals, railways, local tramways, electric and gas lighting and other infrastructure came forward in increasing numbers. In addition, in the nineteenth century, municipal bodies regularly promoted bills in support of their own activities in improving local infrastructure, slum clearances, and the provision of services. In all of these cases, the petitions often included a

[5] Joint Committee on Private Bill Procedure, *Private Bill Procedure* (1987–88, HL 97, HC 625) para 19; see also its final recommendation, at para 205.

[6] P Brand, 'Petitions and Parliament in the Reign of Edward I' (2004) 23 *Parliamentary History* 14.

[7] This remains a core principle: see Joint Committee on Private Bill Procedure (n 5) at para 205: '… there will continue to be private legislation as long as the citizen enjoys the right to petition Parliament for relief not obtainable elsewhere, and Parliament owes a duty to the people to give such legislation time and attention'.

[8] General references are: Clifford (n 2); F Clifford, *A History of Private Bill Legislation* (Butterworths, 1885) vol 2; RJB Morris, *Private Bill Legislation in the Nineteenth Century: Parliamentary Promotion from 1797 to 1914* (Cambridge Scholars Publishing, 2022).

request for powers to override the private interests of others. Given the interference with private property, Parliament has sought to ensure that the private bill procedures allow for due scrutiny.

The right to promote a bill only applies to private bills. Private persons have no right to promote a public bill. The distinction between public and private bills is therefore crucial. Traces of it appeared in the thirteenth and fourteenth centuries, although the differences were not fully clear until the late eighteenth century.[9] RW Perceval reports cases where the King refused assent to a private bill because it would affect the commonalty of the Realm; conversely, there were cases where petitioners were told to withdraw and resubmit a public bill as a private bill because it only affected the petitioner or a small group.[10] This reflected from the fundamental distinction that a private Act would only affect the rights of the parties named in it, but a public Act would affect everyone.[11] The breadth of application is still the key question in classification. Two rulings from the Speakers on the London Rating Bill lay down the governing principles: in 1895, Arthur Peel stated that 'the magnitude of its scope, the magnitude of the area, and the multiplicity of the interests involved'[12] were the key factors in classification. In 1939, the Speaker, JH Whitley, adopted Peel's principles and added that a bill should be treated as a public bill if 'it raises questions of public policy of great importance, and affects interests of vast magnitude, interests which are much more than local'.[13]

The distinction is crucial in formal terms, but in practical terms, it was relatively unimportant before the procedural reforms of the eighteenth and nineteenth centuries. Promoters were likely to use the private bill procedures if they had already obtained the consent of all or most of the affected parties, as this would speed the process through Parliament.[14] If, however, obtaining consents was impracticable, they could ask a sympathetic Member of Parliament to introduce the bill as a public bill. Each method had advantages and disadvantages. Obtaining consents for a private bill could be a lengthy and costly process; however, the

[9] Clifford (n 2) 266–76, 344–45; RW Perceval, 'The Origin and Essence of Hybrid Bills' (1949) 2 *Parliamentary Affairs* 139, 140. For the modern distinctions between private and public bills, and the division of private bills between personal and local bills, see D Natzler and M Hutton, *Erskine May's Treatise on the Law, Privileges, Proceedings and Usage of Parliament*, 25th edn (LexisNexis UK, 2019) paras 24.2, 26.2, 42.1; J Innes, *Inferior Politics: Social Problems and Social Policies in Eighteenth-Century Britain* (Oxford University Press, 2009) 79–80; S Lambert, *Bills and Acts: Legislative Procedure in Eighteenth-Century England* (Cambridge University Press, 1971) 84.

[10] Perceval (n 9) 140.

[11] This explains the differences in the statutory interpretation of public and private Acts, see MK Heatley, 'The Continued Use of Private Acts of Parliament in United Kingdom' (*UK Constitutional Law Association*, 4 October 2021), available at ukconstitutionallaw.org/2021/10/04/mark-k-heatley-the-continued-use-of-private-acts-of-parliament-in-united-kingdom; F Bennion, D Bailey and L Norbury, *Bennion, Bailey and Norbury on Statutory Interpretation*, 8th edn (LexisNexis UK, 2022) para 2.14.

[12] HC Deb 8 February 1939, vol 343, col 710 (Peel's ruling was described by the Speaker in 1939).

[13] HC Deb 8 February 1939, vol 343, col 953. The most difficult cases arise in relation to local government bodies. For example, bills promoted by London County Council have usually been treated as public bills, given their breadth of application; by contrast, bills promoted by other local authorities were normally treated as private bills: see Morris (n 8) 170–71; Natzler and Hutton (n 9) para 42.4.

[14] Innes (n 9) 103–105.

progress of a public bill could be less predictable, as the promoter was less able to control proceedings. An added consideration was cost, as Parliament charged fees for private bills, in addition to the costs faced by the petitioner in preparing and arguing the case for the bill.[15] Morris states that, well into the eighteenth century, 'House of Commons officers were reputed to judge between public and private Bills very simply, by whether they could extract fees from someone'.[16] Moreover, witnesses could be called to give evidence relating to any bill and MPs were free to participate in proceedings for either type of bill.[17] Hence, the real question for the promoter often came down to practical questions of cost and delay rather than formal distinctions and constitutional rights.

The increase in private bill business in the industrial age led both Houses to review their procedures. The House of Commons first adopted detailed Standing Orders on private bills in 1774; the House of Lords soon followed. Both Houses subsequently revised their procedures on multiple occasions, so as to secure greater efficiency.[18] The impact of these developments was clear. Julian Hoppit states that

> In the ten parliamentary sessions before then [1688] only 10 percent of attempts to obtain an act succeeded. Thereafter regular, predictable, much better-ordered sessions saw the success rate change profoundly, so that for most of the eighteenth century it was around 75 percent. This contributed to an explosion in the numbers of enactments.[19]

The increase was across multiple areas, with bills on turnpikes,[20] canals,[21] enclosures[22] and settled estates[23] being the most prominent before the railway boom of the 1800s.

By the mid-nineteenth century, it was apparent that the further reforms would be needed if Parliament were to cope with the volume of private bills coming

[15] The costs of preparing the bill could be substantial: see S Jack and A Jack, 'Nineteenth-Century Lawyers and Railway Capitalism: Historians and the Use of Legal Cases' (2003) 24 *Journal of Legal History* 59.

[16] Morris (n 8) 55, fn 66, citing JE Neale, The Elizabethan House of Commons (Jonathan Cape, 1949) 336.

[17] Perceval (n 9) 142; Innes (n 9) 45–46.

[18] See Morris (n 8).

[19] J Hoppit, 'The Nation, the State, and the First Industrial Revolution' (2011) 50 *Journal of British Studies* 315; see also J Hoppit, 'Patterns of Parliamentary Legislation, 1660–1800' (1996) 39 *Historical Journal* 109; Morris (n 8) 93.

[20] See W Albert, *The Turnpike Road System in England, 1663–1840* (Cambridge University Press, 1972) app B and C.

[21] For an early example, see B Rudden, *The New River: A Legal History* (Oxford University Press, 1985) 13–14, 265–67; see also L Lead, '"They Flow for Country and People": Landowners and Early Canal Development in England' (2014) 38 *Railway & Canal Historical Society* 73.

[22] See generally M Turner, *English Parliamentary Enclosure: Its Historical Geography and Economic History* (Dawson, 1980) 26, 67–68; GE Mingay, *Parliamentary Enclosure in England: An Introduction to Its Causes, Incidence and Impact 1750–1850* (Longman, 1997) 14–31; FA Sharman, 'An Introduction to the Enclosure Acts' (1989) 10 *Journal of Legal History* 45, 48. Sharman notes that legislation often confirmed agreements that had already been reached; see also Lambert (n 9) 133; M Turner, *Enclosures in Britain 1750–1830* (Macmillan Press, 1984) 33–35.

[23] See generally Lambert (n 9) 110–28. K Dimitruk, '"I Intend Therefore to Prorogue": The Effects of Political Conflict and the Glorious Revolution in Parliament, 1660–1772' (2017) 22 *European Review of*

before it. The next step was to delegate parliamentary authority to administrative bodies.[24] Initially, Parliament only authorised administrative bodies to determine the facts prior to committee hearings.[25] Later, they were authorised to issue orders against property that would take effect on positive confirmation by Parliament; then to issue orders that took effect if there were no objections in Parliament. The New Towns Act 1946 and the Town and Country Planning Act 1947 bypassed the Parliament entirely: orders were subject to Ministerial confirmation and review, but as confirmations were not laid before Parliament, there was no opportunity for MPs to consider or reject specific orders.[26] As important as this legislation was, there were still many important cases for which petitions for private Acts could be brought forward. The legislative scheme did not cover, for example, railway works, tramways, ports and harbours, for which the private bill system was still used. This came into focus with a private bill deposited by the Felixstowe Dock and Railway Company in 1984. The Bill was intended to confer authority to expand the Felixstowe docks. Ann Clywd, the Labour member of the select committee considering the bill, withdrew from the committee before proceedings were completed. This dropped the committee below its quorum, but Clywd argued that private bill proceedings allowed the promoters to avoid the more rigorous and open procedures under a public inquiry:

> Parliament must re-examine its procedures so that wealthy companies do not obtain planning permission by the back door through private Bill routes. They are able to obtain permission for their proposals without them receiving proper scrutiny. They bypass ministerial decisions on important matters of national policy.[27]

Other MPs asked whether it was possible or even desirable for MPs to act in a disinterested, quasi-judicial manner when there were political considerations at stake. In this case, the Felixstowe project would have had an impact on docks and employment elsewhere in the country, on which MPs might divide on party lines.[28] The direct rights of specially and directly affected parties were intact, but the procedure as a whole suggested that Parliament was not protecting all the interests that it should protect.

Economic History 261; J Habakkuk, 'Presidential Address: The Rise and Fall of English Landed Families, 1600–1800: II' (1980) 30 *Transactions of the Royal Historical Society* 199.

[24] M Grant, 'Environmental Court Project Final Report: Report to the Department of Environment, Transport and the Regions' (Department of Environment, Transport and the Regions, 2000) 294–99; S Anderson, 'Parliament' in W Cornish and others (eds), *The Oxford History of the Laws of England: Volume XI: 1820–1914 English Legal System* (Oxford University Press, 2010) 325–41.

[25] To some extent, there was nothing novel about the suggestion, as it had long been the practice for legislation that authorised the compulsory purchase of land to refer questions of valuation to a jury for an independent assessment following quasi-judicial procedures: see chapter three. In theory, extending this to other issues would greatly reduce the amount of time that would be spent in the committee stage. However, valuation as fact-finding occurred after the parliamentary process, rather than before.

[26] Grant (n 24) 292.

[27] Felixstowe Dock And Railway Deb 12 February 1986, col 1022. Ultimately, Parliament decided to lower the quorum so that the committee could continue.

[28] ibid cols 1037–38 (Colin Fatchett).

A Joint Committee on Private Bill Procedure considered the issues and recommended that it would be better to consider these projects through public inquiries and ministerial orders, for which the legal framework would be set up under a public Act.[29] The Committee agreed that this would allow for wider and more effective participation by the public than the private bill proceedings. For example, in the debate on the Lords on the Joint Committee's Report, Lord Montagu noted that the Court of Referees had denied English Heritage standing in relation to King's Cross Railway Bill, even though its statutory constitution required it to advise the Secretary of State on heritage.[30] The Transport and Works Act 1992 largely followed the recommendations of the Joint Committee, as it introduced a system by which, on the conclusion of a public inquiry, a Ministerial order would grant authority for the construction of new transport infrastructure without the necessity or option of petitioning for a private Act.[31]

Neither the changes in 1946 and 1947 nor 1992 produced significant debate about the right to promote a bill. As pointed out at the beginning of this section, the Joint Committee highlighted the importance of the right to promote private bills.[32] However, it also pointed out that Parliament had already delegated extensively under the planning legislation, which operated without direct parliamentary intervention. There appeared to be no constitutional reason for the differences: the choice of procedure 'has been more a matter of historical evolution than rational design'.[33] In effect, the constitutionality of taking the approval process out of Parliament had already been resolved by the New Towns Act 1946 and the Town and Country Planning Act 1947, both of which allowed someone to submit plans in respect of land they did not own and hence to request an order for compulsory purchase, as under the private bill procedures. Similarly, the Transport and Works Act allowed parties to obtain the powers that were formerly available through private bill proceedings. In practical terms, the Acts provided promoters with the same opportunity to override the rights of others as the private Acts, but without direct parliamentary scrutiny. Accordingly, there was no erosion of the constitutional right.

II. The Right to Challenge a Bill

The procedural reforms of the industrial age and after focused on improving the certainty and efficiency of the legislative process.[34] Nevertheless, Parliament had

[29] Joint Committee on Private Bill Procedure (n 5).

[30] Joint Committee on Private Bill Procedure Deb 17 May 1989, col 1194. The decision of the Court of Referees is at [1983–1991] LSR 38–39.

[31] Section 9 of the Act includes a mechanism by which the Secretary of State may refer 'schemes of national significance' to Parliament for consideration; this followed the recommendations of the Joint Committee on Private Bill Procedure (n 5).

[32] Above, text to n 5.

[33] Joint Committee on Private Bill Procedure (n 5) para 20.

[34] The reforms did not always meet with success, as noted by Hoppit, 'Patterns' (n 19) 131: 'At times almost farcical situations could develop, with parliament unable or unwilling to legislate in an

long recognised that procedural fairness requires that anyone whose rights would be specially and directly affected by legislation should be entitled to notice of the bill and to challenge it. Clifford described this right as one of 'immemorial usage', with documentary evidence going back to the sixteenth century.[35] Standing Orders on private bills consistently required the promoter to provide evidence of notice to all specially affected parties. Similarly, a public bill that specially and directly affects individuals will be treated as hybrid, so as to permit rights of audience. The task of classification falls to the Examiners, who have stated that there are few constitutional rights 'of such importance as the right of a subject to plead his cause before Committees of either House'.[36]

The specific requirements for notice varied from one type of bill to another. For bills that were likely to have a broader impact, such as canal and turnpike bills, notice might include publication in local newspapers.[37] With bills concerned with more personal matters, such as interests in settled estates, there was no need for wider publicity.[38] However, in all cases, some form of notice was essential for the protection of the interests of affected parties.[39] Parliament took the notice requirements seriously: during proceedings, the promoter could be subject to numerous demands for additional information, such as proof that all affected parties had been properly notified or that the project would have the wider benefits that were claimed for it.[40] As a result, the costs of obtaining an Act could be very high. Sybil and Adrian Jack state that the costs of the Act for the London and Birmingham Railway were £72,868; for the Great Western Railway, the promoters spent £88,710, of which 40 per cent went on their legal expenses.[41] It is clear that the process of notification and recording consents or objections added considerably to the expense, but it is also clear that Parliament saw it as important.

The core principle – that a petitioner has the right to appear before Parliament if they are specially and directly affected by a bill – has never been controversial.

adequately positive or general fashion. It had, for example, to pass ten separate acts – not to mention the ten failed attempts – to allow the building and maintenance of Westminster bridge.'

[35] Clifford (n 8) 850–51, 866 ('immemorial usage' is at 866); see also O Williams, *The Historical Development of Private Bill Procedure and Standing Orders in the House of Commons*, vol 1 (His Majesty's Stationery Office, 1948) 27–35.

[36] House of Lords, Sessional Papers 1976–77 vol 5, 71; see also L Blake, '"Hybrid Bills" and Human Rights: The Parliament Square Litigation 2002–2007' (2008) 19 *King's Law Journal* 183, 189–90.

[37] CT Ellis, *Practical Remarks, and Precedents of Proceedings in Parliament* (B McMillan, 1802) 161–242 provides a comprehensive set of precedent forms for practitioners, including forms for notices for different types of bills.

[38] Lambert (n 9) 121: 'Since these [estate bills] were quite private matters it was possible to identify all the parties concerned, and the rules of the House of Lords made certain that all were consulted and had an opportunity to voice opposition.'

[39] See ibid 134–40 on the efforts made to ensure notice and consents: committees demanded evidence that all interested parties had indicated whether they were for, against or neutral.

[40] It was also the case that, although the cost of complying with the notice requirements could be very high, notice often provided the poor with little or no practical opportunity to challenge bills and the impact on the peasantry was often harsh: see Sharman (n 22) 66–67; Mingay (n 22) 124–47 and the sources listed in R Tennyson, 'From Unanimity to Proportionality: Assent Standards and the Parliamentary Enclosure Movement' (2013) 31 *Law and History Review* 199, 202, fn4.

[41] Jack and Jack (n 15) 63; Morris (n 8) 91–120.

However, it is not always clear that a specific individual has standing to challenge a specific bill. Initially, the question of standing was determined by the committee hearing the bill. By the middle of the nineteenth century, it was widely acknowledged that this was not ideal. In 1866, James Mellor Smethurst said that it was often impossible to make more than a 'mere guess' whether a committee would allow standing, because there was 'no uniformity' in their decisions.[42] If the bill would interfere with vested rights, the holder would have standing. This, however, lead to confusion over, for example, holders of contingent interests, riparian rights, easements, rights of pasture, company shareholders and municipalities and other statutory bodies. Committees could exercise discretion in the absence of an interference with vested rights, but again there was confusion. So, for example, there was considerable uncertainty over the position of traders and businesses who would be affected by transportation schemes, especially where they might be charged tolls or levies for access.[43] Similarly, existing railways often sought to challenge bills from potential or existing competitors; committees took different views on allowing standing in very similar cases.[44]

Historically, questions of standing became more important when Parliament began to restrict membership of the private bill committees. Initially, the committees regularly included all MPs of the region where the scheme would operate.[45] It was accepted that these committees could be partisan. Indeed, MPs often voted on bills without having heard any of the evidence presented to the committee.[46] This was not, however, seen as a defect by many MPs: rather, they saw it as part of their constitutional responsibility to represent constituents' interests. Hence, it was appropriate for them to rely on their own information and investigation into a proposed scheme, and to represent the interests of constituents who did not have standing. However, Parliament found it increasingly difficult to get through its business as the volume of private bills rose and considered whether impartial committees would be quicker in disposing of business. Accordingly, in 1837, the House of Lords required committee members to have no interest in the bills before them. They were expected to have no prior knowledge of the issues or the locality and county and to make their decisions solely on the basis of the information put before them during the proceedings.[47] Furthermore, under the 1837 Standing Orders, a committee would comprise five members only. This, it was thought, would reduce the delays and the obstructive tactics of MPs who had taken sides in a local dispute over a proposed scheme. Although similar measures were proposed in the Commons, it did not finally stop including local MPs in private bill committees until 1855.[48]

[42] J Mellor Smethurst, *A Treatise on the Locus Standi of Petitioners Against Private Bills in Parliament* (Stevens and Haynes, 1867) vi.
[43] ibid 29–31.
[44] ibid 33–47.
[45] Clifford (n 8) 869.
[46] ibid 831; Morris (n 8) 81–85.
[47] Clifford (n 8) 828.
[48] ibid 843.

In theory, the movement to impartial committees left MPs less able to defend unrepresented interests. Opponents argued that it would lead to 'the oppression of the lower classes'.[49] Realistically, the defence of partiality was more a defence of political power and the opportunity for patronage and corruption. The changes probably had little impact on those that the old system supposedly protected. For example, in principle, promoters were required to give notice in time for interested parties to make representations in Parliament. In practice, they often delayed notice until it was too late for smaller landowners and others to put forward an effective challenge. Indeed, as Frank A Sharman observes in respect of enclosures, the petitioner might claim that it had held public meetings but it was not always clear that they had done so, and weaker parties would not have had the resources to fight their case in Parliament. Furthermore, with enclosures,

> the poor, without landed rights, got little or nothing and the small commoners and strip owners received small allotments of land which, proportionately, bore more of the costs, were expensive to fence and were not of a commercial size. They usually sold out to the larger landowners.[50]

In principle, MPs with local knowledge could protect the more vulnerable interests. Nevertheless, the reforms went through. The constitutional arguments regarding MPs as the protectors of unrepresented interests faded in the face of the demand for more efficient procedures.

As noted above, James Mellor Smethurst observed that impartial committees proved to be no better in providing certainty in relation to standing decisions.[51] In 1865, the House of Commons constituted the Court of Referees to determine whether petitioners should have standing before a private bill committee.[52] This, it was hoped, would produce greater consistency and a body of precedent that would guide petitioners in future. The Court's decisions were published and reviewed in treatises as well as parliamentary reports and publications.[53] Its relevance has declined in recent years: it met in 2016 and before that in 2002.[54] Through this period, the Court did not make any significant changes to the rules. There have been some changes in the Standing Orders: the most important was in 1881, when local authorities were given an absolute right to oppose lighting or water supply bills if their town or district would be injured.[55]

[49] ibid 832–34, 839.
[50] Sharman (n 22) 66–67.
[51] Smethurst (n 42).
[52] For private bills before the House of Lords, counter-petitions are considered by the committee to which the bill was referred: see Natzler and Hutton (n 9) para 46.23.
[53] See T Landers, *Procedure and Practice Relating to Private Bills in Parliament: Shewing the Progress of a Bill from Its Inception to Royal Assent, Together with Numerous Forms and Precedents* (Stevens and Sons, 1919). Frederick Clifford and Pembroke S Stephens began the Locus Standi Reports series in 1870; there were five volumes in the first 20 years after the Court of Referees came into existence. The most recent volume is [1991–2006] LSR, which has reports on only five cases, with the most recent from the 2001–2002 parliamentary session.
[54] Natzler and Hutton (n 9) para 44.4, fn 5.
[55] Clifford (n 8) 869.

Despite this, there have been cases where a government bill has an exceptional impact on the rights of specific persons, and yet the Examiners classified it as a public bill. The leading example is the Churches (Scotland) Act 1905, which authorised the appointment of a commission to redistribute the assets of the Free Church and the United Free Church. As explained in chapter six, the Act effectively reversed the judgment in *General Assembly of Free Church of Scotland v Overtoun*, where the House of Lords declared that the trustees of the Free Church held assets that had been used by members of the United Free Church.[56] The Bill was a government bill, so the only real issue was whether it should be treated as hybrid and hence subject to the private bill Standing Orders, as it specifically targeted the trustees' property. It was referred to the Examiners, who decided that it could be treated as a purely public bill.[57] Why the bill was not treated as a hybrid bill was not clear: identified parties would suffer the uncompensated loss of their property and yet they would not be entitled to plead their case before either House.[58] It was not even the case that the number of specially and directly affected parties would have been unmanageable, as only the two churches were directly affected. However, there was a very strong public interest in support of the Bill, as housing, employment and education provided by the church bodies were at risk and prompt action was needed.

There have also been cases where the Examiners classified a bill as hybrid and yet the Government requested the Commons to dispense with the private bill procedures. This is clearly bound to be controversial, as it denies standing to parties.[59] The best-known case concerns the Aircraft and Shipbuilding Industries Bill 1976. After Second Reading, Robin Maxwell-Hyslop, a Conservative MP, asked the Speaker for a ruling that the Bill was hybrid. As the hybrid procedures would have prolonged a process that had already been lengthy, the Labour Government put up strong resistance. His argument focused on the exclusion of the Marathon company from its Bill's application. Marathon was taken over by an American company in 1972, under an agreement with the Conservative Government (supported by the Labour opposition) that it would not be nationalised. The Bill was therefore drafted to exclude Marathon, but it did so indirectly, by omitting it from the list of companies to be nationalised and by limiting its application to manufacturers of 'ships' over a certain size.[60] It was thought that, as Marathon only manufactured drilling rigs, it would be outside the scope of the Bill. Moreover, as the Act would

[56] *General Assembly of Free Church of Scotland v Overtoun* [1904] AC 515.

[57] Natzler and Hutton (n 9) para 42.8.

[58] House of Lords, Sessional Papers 1976–77 vol 5, 71.

[59] The test of hybridity is whether a public bill 'affects a particular private interest in a manner different from the private interest of other persons or bodies of the same category or class': HC Deb 10 December 1962, vol 669, col 45 (Mr Speaker Hylton-Fraser). The question of standing is distinct; it is considered by the select committee on the bill and turns on whether a petitioner is specially and directly affected (see Examiners of Petitions for Private Bills, *Holocaust Memorial Bill: Report from the Examiners and Statement of Reasons* (HC 2022–23, 1403) para 6).

[60] Aircraft and Shipbuilding Industries HC Bill (1975–76), para 221, sch 2, cls 3 and 6.

still apply to shipbuilders as a class, it would not be hybrid. However, Maxwell-Hyslop argued that a rig that was being manufactured by Marathon was a 'ship' and hence Marathon should have been within the scope of the Bill. As a result, its exclusion meant that the Bill was hybrid. The Speaker accepted that this was the case and classified the Bill as 'prima facie hybrid'. Under the usual procedure, the Speaker would have referred the Bill to the Examiners for a final determination. In this case, however, the Government tabled a motion for dispensing with the private bill procedures. Against this, the Opposition tabled a motion that the bill should proceed directly to a select committee without reference to the Examiners.

The debates on the motions were protracted and acrimonious. The vote on the Opposition motion was held first. The House split 303–303, with the Speaker following precedent by submitting a casting vote against the motion. The Government's motion followed immediately, but it succeeded by a margin of 304–303, as a Labour MP who was in a pairing arrangement voted anyway. The Prime Minister subsequently acknowledged this to be wrong and it was agreed that the Opposition should be permitted to submit their motion again, as a means of providing a fair vote on the issue. This time, Labour prevailed by a wider margin of 311–297 against the Conservative motion.

The effect of the vote in the House of Commons is not clear. It does confirm the key constitutional principle that the House is the master of its procedure. Several MPs, including Robin Maxwell-Hyslop, argued that the rights of the individual secured by the hybrid procedure could not be extinguished by procedural resolutions, but only by an Act.[61] Plainly, this was not the view of the Labour majority and it was not pressed by other Conservative MPs. Self-restraint was still necessary, however. For example, the Conservative MP Sir Derek Walker-Smith said that

> though the House is master of its own procedure, the exercise of that power is subject to the inherent constraint that it must not be used in violation of the fundamental rights of the individual citizen, and that for Ministers to invite the House to act in that way is a breach of the principles of our unwritten constitution.[62]

The second point concerned the relationship between the purpose and scope of hybridity. The Liberal Party stated that all bills for the nationalisation of manufacturing industries should be treated as hybrid from the start, 'so that petitioners can be heard and the legislation can be considered properly'.[63] Whether Marathon was exempt or not was beside the point: the impact of the Bill was both serious enough, and selective enough, that all property owners subject to expropriation should be heard. In effect, the Liberals argued that the constitutional safeguards are necessary and should be broadened to ensure that they serve their purpose.

[61] HC Deb 7 June 1976, vol 912, cols 949–50; see also HC Deb 29 June 1976, vol 914, cols 299–301 (Charles Fletcher-Cooke).

[62] HC Deb 27 May 1976, vol 912, cols 696–97.

[63] HC Deb 29 June 1976, vol 914, col 1006 (Richard Wainwright).

Neither Labour nor the Conservatives supported the Liberal proposal. Arguably, they were content with the principles of classification, despite their disagreement over the basis for departing from the usual procedures.

There was a further issue on the scope of the Standing Orders and precedents. Michael Foot, the Leader of the House, maintained that they only dealt with hybridity that had been found before Second Reading. As the Bill had passed Second Reading, the House had already given its support to it in principle. Hence, to allow a challenge after Second Reading would not further parliamentary democracy but frustrate it.[64] As a related argument, the Government stated that it had acted in good faith in proceeding on the basis that the Bill was a public bill.[65] Indeed, there were hints that some Conservative MPs were aware that Marathon was manufacturing the rig before Second Reading was completed, but did not bring it to the attention of the Speaker in order to maximise the delay.[66] The Conservatives did not address the point directly, except that they were clearly not willing to see the timing as a valid reason for dispensing with the ordinary procedures. On these points, the Speaker agreed with the opposition, by classifying the Bill as prima facie hybrid.

Several other points were left unresolved. The Government argued that its motion would not undermine important individual rights in any practical sense. If its motion were successful, it would only affect Marathon, which was content to be left out of the scope of the Bill in any case.[67] The Conservatives argued that this would be unfair to the companies that did fall under the Bill. Michael Heseltine said that 'The issue is that the Government are denying that company and its workers their rights to put their case for parity of treatment with an American company [Marathon] to a Select Committee of this House. We find that precedent repugnant'.[68] This raises a fundamental question of constitutional purposes of private and hybrid procedures. The Conservative argument was not simply about the right of affected parties to challenge the legislative interference with their rights of property solely of the impact on their own interests, but to raise the general question of fairness. That is, they argued that a property owner should be able to challenge a bill on the basis that other similarly-placed persons would be treated more favourably, whether in terms of compensation or an exemption from the legislation. This is an important issue, but the nature of the debate and voting in this case meant that it was aired but not resolved.

[64] HC Deb 27 May 1976, vol 912, cols 681–82 (Eric S Heffer) and cols 750–51, 753–54 (Michael Foot).

[65] Labour did not argue that individuals should only have rights in cases of bad faith of MPs, but that this was one of a number of factors that might be weighed in determining whether a departure from the usual procedures would be justified: see, eg, Eric G Varley, Secretary of State for Industry, HC Deb 27 May 1976, vol 912, cols 632–35.

[66] HC Deb 27 May 1976, vol 912, cols 685–86 (Eric S Heffer).

[67] See, eg, HC Deb 27 May 1976, vol 912, col 736 (John P Mackintosh); HC Deb 29 June 1976, vol 914, cols 269–70 (Bryan Gould).

[68] HC Deb 29 June 1976, vol 914, col 224.

The House of Lords eventually considered the Bill and passed 59 amendments to it. These were seen by the Government as wrecking amendments.[69] The Bill did not survive the end of the parliamentary session but was re-introduced in the following session. It was the Government's intention to use the Parliament Acts 1911 and 1949 to force it through. However, the House of Lords referred it to the Examiners, who found it to be hybrid. At this point, the Government deleted the provisions applying to the ship repairing industry and the Bill then passed through both Houses.[70]

III. Hybrid Bills and Rights of Audience

As noted above, the Felixstowe project raised questions about the use of private bill procedures for projects that have a wide impact. By petitioning, the promoter was able to avoid a public inquiry and the more extensive examination that it would have involved. This question also arises where governments prefer the hybrid procedures for its own projects, as has occurred with a number of large infrastructure schemes.

Strictly speaking, the right to appear before Parliament to challenge a bill is not affected, as the hybrid procedures preserve these rights. The advantage, to the Government, is that the hybrid proceedings are likely to be quicker than a public inquiry. This seems to have been the lesson drawn from the inquiry into the Sizewell B nuclear project.[71] The inquiry opened in January 1983 and closed on March 1985, after hearing 340 days of evidence. The Deputy Chief Whip in the House of Lords, Viscount Davidson, described it as 'the longest and most exhaustive planning inquiry in our history'.[72] Since then, governments have relied on the hybrid procedures for large-scale projects.[73] However, this has been controversial because it avoids the requirement to call a public inquiry. For example, in 1986, the Conservative Government introduced the Channel Tunnel project as a hybrid bill rather than submit it to a public inquiry. This was 'widely perceived by the public as a shirking of responsibilities by the government to listen and pay heed to local objections'.[74] In particular, the select committee did not hear evidence

[69] HC Deb 8 November 1976, vol 919, cols 96–97 (Eric Varley, Secretary of State for Industry).

[70] See NDJ Baldwin, 'The House of Lords and the Labour Government 1974–79' (1995) 1 *Journal of Legislative Studies* 218.

[71] See M Purdue, R Kemp and T O'Riordan, 'The Context and Conduct of the Sizewell B Inquiry' (1984) 12 *Energy Policy* 276; T O'Riordan, R Kemp and M Purdue, *Sizewell B: An Anatomy of the Inquiry* (Macmillan Press, 1988); G Greenhalgh, 'The Sizewell Inquiry – Is There a Better Way?' (1984) 12 *Energy Policy* 283.

[72] HL Deb 2 March 1987, vol 485, col 455.

[73] See R Kelly, 'Hybrid Bills (Background Paper)' (2018) House of Commons Library Briefing Paper Number 06736 17 for a list of all hybrid bills from 1983 to 2018.

[74] E Darian-Smith, *Bridging Divides: The Channel Tunnel and English Legal Identity in the New Europe* (University of California Press, 1999) 122; I Holliday, 'The Politics of the Channel Tunnel' (1992) 45 *Parliamentary Affairs* 188, 194–95.

regarding the need for the tunnel or the desirability of calling a public inquiry.[75] Later Labour governments continued this same strategy, by using hybrid bills for the Channel Tunnel Rail Link Act 1996 and the Crossrail Act 2008. More recently, Conservative governments did the same for the High Speed Rail legislation. Its decision was challenged in *R (HS2 Action Alliance Ltd) v Secretary of State for Transport*,[76] on the basis that the hybrid procedures fell short of the requirements of European Union law.[77] Clearly, no such challenge would have been possible under constitutional principles alone. However, from our point of view, the most interesting aspect concerned the importance of political considerations in the legislative process. The claimants argued, in part, that the legislative process fell short of the requirements of the Environmental Impact Assessment Directive 2011 because it would allow political factors to influence the environmental decisions.[78] In particular, they said that Parliament would not allow a free vote, and an MP might not take environmental factors into account. The arguments were therefore similar to those made about impartiality in the early nineteenth century, when many MPs felt that the process of approving railway projects should permit them to consider political factors in reaching a decision. As in the nineteenth century, the MPs of the late twentieth and early twenty-first centuries did not see this as negative: committees could manage the volume of business and allow for the kinds of negotiation and trade-offs that, at least for some MPs, are essential for achieving a fair and balanced resolution of competing interests involved in large scale projects. In any case, the Supreme Court held that the legislative process did satisfy the Directive. Accordingly, the High Speed Rail (London to West Midlands) Bill proceeded through Parliament as a hybrid bill and was enacted in 2017. Subsequently, the Government introduced the High Speed Rail (West Midlands to Crewe) Bill in 2017; it was enacted in February 2021.[79] Plainly, successive governments have preferred the hybrid procedures for complex infrastructure projects. Parliament has shown no appetite for closing down the possibility of employing these procedures in future.

It is worth noting that the hybrid bill select committees have the discretion to allow a wide range of petitioners to appear before them. In practice, they are reluctant to do so. Indeed, with private bills, committees have been more determined

[75] Darian-Smith, ibid 122.

[76] *R (HS2 Action Alliance Ltd) v Secretary of State for Transport* [2014] UKSC 3.

[77] See ML Wilde, 'All the Queen's Horses: Statutory Authority and HS2' (2017) 37 *Legal Studies* 765, 774–76.

[78] Directive 2011/92/EU of the European Parliament and of the Council on the assessment of the effects of certain public and private projects on the environment [2012] OJ L26/1; see *R (HS2 Action Alliance Ltd)* (n 76) paras 98–117. Wilde notes that the Committee encouraged the promoter to negotiate with petitioners for the withdrawal of their petitions: ibid 775.

[79] The High Speed Rail (Crewe to Manchester) Bill was introduced in January 2022 but the project has been cancelled; see M Benson, 'What Next for HS2?', House of Commons Library Insight, 24 November 2023.

to restrict standing than the promoters, although one might have thought that it would be the promoters who would be more interested in doing so.[80] In 1988, the Joint Committee on Private Bill Procedure had evidence from the Clerk of the House of Commons that 'promoters have been a little reluctant to raise objections to the *locus standi* of petitioners because the impression might be given that they are taking technical points against petitioners'.[81] The Joint Committee felt that this was wrong. It affirmed that 'it is a fundamental principle of private legislation procedure that *only* parties specially affected should be entitled to be heard' (emphasis added),[82] and it encouraged promoters to police the rules. This has carried over to hybrid bills. The House of Commons Select Committee on the Phase One Bill reported that it had not been strict enough in its approach to standing. It noted that, with the Crossrail Bill, the promoters did not challenge any petitions for standing. Initially, the promoter of the Phase One Bill and the Select Committee took a similarly relaxed view. However, in its final report, the Committee said that 'With the benefit of nearly two years' experience, we believe that there should be a stricter approach to locus standi'.[83] The process was 'too inclusive', and 'There should be less petitioning, with more focus on serious detriment'.[84] The House of Lords Select Committee on the Phase One Bill took the same view as the Commons Select Committee, as it said that the right to be heard was limited to petitioners who could establish

> the prospect of direct and material detriment to his or her property interests, either by compulsory acquisition or by interference with his or her property rights which amounts to a common law nuisance, or some other interference which would be actionable if not authorised by Parliament.[85]

In all other cases, standing was only allowed as a matter of discretion. For example, it did not exercise its discretion in favour of residents who raised concerns about the impact on their general neighbourhood or users of affected footpaths or public rights of way.[86] It did, however, exercise its discretion in favour of action groups that could offer 'accumulated knowledge and expertise' on the issues, especially in relation to 'topics of general, route wide significance',[87] or where it was clear that the petitioner would be putting forward views of those who did have a right

[80] The Court of Referees does not have jurisdiction over hybrid bills, but note Erskine May: Natzler and Hutton (n 9) para 44.4: 'It should be remembered, however, that decisions of the court are binding upon select committees on hybrid bills when they come to decide questions of the rights of petitioners to have their petition considered.'

[81] Joint Committee on Private Bill Procedure, *Report* (HL 1987–88, 97, HC 625) para 101.

[82] ibid.

[83] Select Committee on the Phase One Bill, *Second Special Report of Session 2015–16* (HC 2015–16, 129) paras 393–94.

[84] ibid para 385.

[85] Select Committee on the High Speed Rail (London – West Midlands) Bill, *Special Report of Session 2016–17* (HL 2016–17, 83) para 102.

[86] ibid paras 104–11.

[87] ibid para 103.

to standing but did not have the resources to present their case.[88] It was clear, however, that this was an exercise of discretion, rather than an extension of the constitutional right to audience.

The Commons Select Committee recommended a review of the hybrid bill procedures. Accordingly, in May 2016, the Chairman of Ways and Means and the Chairman of Committees opened a review. Its scope was to:

> consider and make recommendations about possible changes to the procedure and practice of both Houses in relation to hybrid bills so as to make the hybrid bill process simpler and less time-consuming for all those involved, without unfairly curtailing the right of those who are directly and specially affected by such bills to make their case effectively, or the right of the Government to ensure the passage of its legislation through Parliament.[89]

From this, it is quite clear that the Committee was not suggesting that there would be any extension of the right to standing, and the final report did not make any such recommendations. This did not completely block local representations, as local authorities were permitted to appear before it. In addition, new standing orders allowed Members of Parliament who wished to represent constituency interests to do so.[90] In both cases, however, it is clear that the individual's right to appear was not changed. The right to standing would not be curtailed, but otherwise the emphasis would be on restricting access rather than extending it, in order to improve efficiency.

IV. Conclusion

Constitutional rights to promote and object to bills affecting property rights have a long history in the British system. At one time, determination of rights occupied a considerable amount of time and energy in Parliament. In practical terms, they became much less important in parliamentary proceedings with the delegation of power to administrative bodies. Nevertheless, the rights remain in place, and they have provided the standard for the delegation of power to administrative bodies. It is worth noting, however, that there has been little appetite within Parliament to widen the rights of participation. The threshold remains a formal test of impact and, in particular, whether the petitioner's rights of property would be subject to a direct interference if the bill were enacted. This does not arise only in respect

[88] ibid paras 103–104.

[89] Chairman of Ways and Means, House of Commons and Senior Deputy Speaker, House of Lords, *Hybrid Bill Review Report* (2022) para 2, available at www.parliament.uk/globalassets/about-parliament/how-parliament-works/how-are-laws-made/hbr-final-covered-doc.pdf.

[90] Procedure Committee, *Revisions of Private Business Standing Orders* (HL 2017–19, 34) para 10, agreed in the House of Commons, HC Deb 7 November 2017, vol 630, col 1311 and the House of Lords, HL Deb 18 December 2017, vol 787, col 1138.

of rights of audience: with compulsory purchase, a loss is compensated only if there is a taking of an interest in property. It is not a universal rule, however. As chapter four on nationalisation shows, there is a consistent practice of safeguarding the interests of employees. With private and hybrid bills, rights of standing have been extended to local authorities and MPs whose constituents are affected. Nevertheless, the scope of the constitutional rights of individuals have not been revisited.

3

Expropriation of Land

This chapter considers the constitutional aspects of the expropriation of land. Expropriation does not appear in the statutory record until the sixteenth century and did not take the usual form of compulsory purchase until the eighteenth century. The first part of the chapter explains how the early legislation drew on precedents for purveyances and the writs for the valuation of land. These precedents established several substantive principles that are still part of modern law: the promoter of a bill must show that their project would produce a public advantage. This is still the case. It has also been the case that owners receive full compensation for their loss, as determined by an independent assessment. These points are firmly embedded in the practice and are reflected in the thousands of private and public Acts enacted over the centuries. MPs would almost certainly see any departure from them as a violation of the rights of the property holder and would expect the promoter to provide a very compelling justification before giving their support to a bill. As such, these principles satisfy the requirements for a parliamentary constitutional standard, as set out by Jack Simson Caird and Dawn Oliver and discussed in chapter one. Parliament has allowed variations in valuation so that it is not necessarily based on market value in every case. This chapter traces the evolution of these practices and standards from the earliest statutes, through to the increase in private bill activity of the eighteenth and nineteenth centuries and then the rise in public authority takings from the nineteenth century onwards. It shows how the standards developed and were adapted to the rise of the modern state, especially in relation to compensation. It shows that there is some flexibility in the constitutional standard: for example, compensation may be reduced where part of the value is attributable to wrongful conduct by the owner, or to investment in the property by the community or others.

I. Early History

The principle that land is subject to expropriation has not been particularly controversial. In Susan Reynolds' review of the history of the expropriation of land across western Europe, she found that

> in all the periods and in all the societies that I have considered, the right of the community to take land for the common good, with compensation to the owner, seems to have

> been taken for granted. There is no period in which I have found evidence that it was seen as an innovation.[1]

Initially, it was a power held by the Crown and, in some cases, the higher nobility. However, these powers were not unrestricted but defined by law; moreover, it was reasonably clear that Parliament could impose restrictions on their exercise.[2] One illustration is provided by the development of statutory controls over the prerogative power of purveyance.[3] The power gave the king, other members of his family, royal officials and the higher nobility the right to pre-empt the sale of goods and provision of carriage for their personal use. Goods were not simply confiscated, as the buyer was expected to pay a fair price for them. Nevertheless, purveyances became a regular subject of complaint, especially in the thirteenth and fourteenth centuries, when the Crown began to rely on them to supply English armies at war. Indeed, it was used as a means of generating surplus funds: WR Jones gives the example of the attempts by Edward I and later by Edward III to turn a profit by purveying England's entire wool crop for sale overseas.[4] As the royal demands for supply became more onerous, the wider community sought to restrain the prerogative by putting it on the same footing as a tax. This would have meant that the consent of Parliament would be required whenever a purveyance was sought on a national scale. The King resisted such attempts, refusing to concede that a purveyance was anything more than a sale and purchase of goods. Nevertheless, in 1362, the Statute of Purveyance required the seller to consent to the sale and the buyer to make immediate payment for the goods or carriage.[5] This appears to have settled the constitutional status of purveyances: they were treated as agreed sales and hence they did not require the consent of Parliament; nevertheless, the King and his agents were expected to pay for the goods and to

[1] S Reynolds, *Before Eminent Domain: Toward a History of Expropriation of Land for the Common Good* (University of North Carolina Press, 2010) 7. See also FA Mann, 'Outlines of a History of Expropriation' (1959) 75 *LQR* 188, 189: 'all the available evidence goes to show that at all stages of history the individual owner was liable to have his property taken from him'. In *De Keyser's Royal Hotel Ltd v The King* [1919] 2 Ch 197, 221 (CA), Swinfen Eady MR observed that, regarding the Crown's power to take land without compensation for defence, 'The result of the searches which have been made is that it does not appear that the Crown has ever taken the subject's land for the defence of the country without paying for it; and even in Stuart times I cannot trace any claim by the Crown to such a prerogative.' This did not rule out the possibility that payment may have been ex gratia payments or by prior agreement. The Court of Appeal's judgment was upheld on appeal to the House of Lords: *Attorney-General v De Keyser's Royal Hotel Ltd* [1920] AC 508.

[2] See Reynolds, ibid 11: most early legislation assumed that the right to expropriate existed; legislation 'regulated the right rather than established it, in effect stating what, given the evidence of practice, was already accepted in law: that is, that land could be taken only for the common good and with compensation'.

[3] See WR Jones, 'Keeping the Peace: English Society, Local Government, and the Commissions of 1341–44' (1974) 18 *American Journal of Legal History* 307; WR Jones, 'Purveyance for War and the Community of the Realm in Late Medieval England' (1975) 7 *Albion: A Quarterly Journal Concerned with British Studies* 300.

[4] Jones, 'Purveyance for War', ibid 304.

[5] 36 Edw III stat 1 chs 1–6 (1362).

act honestly and responsibly and only for appropriate purposes when acquiring them.[6] As discussed below, this provided the model for compulsory purchase in the industrial age and after. Moreover, it clearly indicated that Parliament could restrict the prerogative powers.

Early statutes were not solely concerned with the prerogative powers. As discussed in chapter two, subjects could petition for legislation affecting rights in property. For example, Parliament often considered petitions relating to local works and industries. Legislation addressed various aspects of the fishing industry, such as the removal of weirs causing obstructions, the forestalling of fish markets and the control of prices at markets.[7] It also addressed deficiencies in the customary laws for maintaining roads, ports, drainage, rivers and the like, by enabling local officials to require contributions of labour and working animals or to set tolls or compulsory levies.[8] These Acts provided a precedent for laws granting powers of compulsory purchase. They were, however, still quite distant from the later legislation, as the first clear examples of compulsory purchase did not appear until the sixteenth century. Moreover, many of the Acts purported to do no more than provide a means of compelling the performance of obligations that already existed by custom: this would not be the case with compulsory purchase.

Another important aspect of early practice relates to compensation. Reynolds could find no examples of the expropriation of land without compensation, although she acknowledges that 'the difference between a voluntary and compulsory sale of land by an individual to the ruler or rulers of a community on its behalf is sometimes invisible or hard to detect'.[9] Nevertheless, several principles emerged that were later adapted for compulsory purchase. Reynolds observes that, where compensation was provided, the amount was often assessed by a jury, which suggests that the Crown could not simply set a figure that it thought appropriate.[10]

Some scholars see the origins of constitutional principles on compensation in the writ *ad quod damnum*.[11] This writ would lead to an inquest under which a jury would determine the loss arising from a wrongful act. It was also used to assess the value of property held by the Crown, as in the case of property obtained by escheat or forfeiture. Similarly, the writ provided a procedure for determining the loss that would arise if the Crown acceded to a request to modify its rights or interests. Hence, it was regularly used where a landowner requested permission to stop or

[6] Jones, 'Purveyance for War' (n 3); EB Fryde, 'Edward III's Wool Monopoly of 1337: A Fourteenth Century Royal Trading Venture' (1952) 37 *History* 8.

[7] See, eg, 6 Rich II stat 1 c 11 (1382); 5 & 6 Edw VI c 14 (1551–52); 21 Ric II c 19 (1397–98); 2 Hen VI c 12 (1423).

[8] See, eg, 6 Hen VI c 5 (1427); 1 Hen VIII c 9 (1509–10); 9 Hen V stat 2 c 11 (1421–22); 22 Hen VIII c 5 (1530–31); 24 Hen VIII c 11 (1532–33); 25 Hen VIII c 8 (1533–34).

[9] Reynolds (n 1) 10.

[10] ibid 34–46.

[11] S Wanling, 'What Is Just Compensation?' (2019) 105 *Virginia Law Review* 1485, 1492–1503; S Gadd, 'The Emergence and Development of Statutory Process for the Compulsory Purchase of Land for Transport Infrastructure in England and Wales, c.1530–1800' (2019) 40 *Journal of Legal History* 1.

change the route of a public highway over its land. In such cases, the Crown was more likely to agree if the owner offered to compensate it for any damage. As part of this procedure, the writ might also include a direction to put a value on losses suffered by third parties. If, for example, the Crown received a request to stop and divert a public highway, the inquest would often assess the loss to both the Crown and to other parties.

The use of this writ is consistent with several important aspects of modern constitutional practice. First, the determination of loss and value was separate from the determination of the entitlement to compensation. This meant that loss was valued without an assessment of the conduct of the parties or the profit that one of them might have expected from any action that was taken. This has carried through to the modern practice: in general, valuation is objective, and it focuses on the owner's loss rather than the taker's gain.[12] This was also reflected in the 1362 Act on purveyances, where it is noteworthy that the price for goods was set at the market rate, rather than the value to the buyer on a more subjective assessment. Secondly, valuation was in the hands of a jury rather than the agents of the Crown or the parties. This is also seen in the modern practice. Juries are no longer used, but valuation is still seen as something that should be independent from the parties.

II. Compulsory Purchase Statutes

The first statutes authorising the compulsory acquisition of title appear in the statutory record in the sixteenth century.[13] Prior to that, there are no unequivocal cases of what we would now consider compulsory purchase: a transfer of ownership, for the public interest, on payment of compensation. Parliament had frequently directed the confiscation or forfeiture of land as a penal measure, usually for disloyalty to the Crown, but modern compulsory purchase does not depend on finding that the owner is guilty of a default of any type. In addition, Parliament

[12] The corollary, that there is no compensation for a taking in the absence of loss, was not established until the enactment of the Petroleum (Production) Act 1934. Section 1 provides that 'The property in petroleum existing in its natural condition in strata in Great Britain is hereby property in vested in His Majesty' and gave the Crown the 'exclusive right of searching and boring for and getting such petroleum'. No compensation was provided. The Secretary of State for Air, the Marquess of Londonderry, who introduced the Bill on Second Reading in the Lords, said that there was no need for compensation because 'the existence of oil in workable quantities is quite unknown … no land in this country has acquired any added value as potential oil-bearing property': HL Deb 19 April 1934, vol 91, col 675. The issue would resurface a few years later, when coal reserves were nationalised under the Coal Act 1938, but with generous compensation. Unlike petroleum, the location was known and the impact of nationalisation on the value of specific land was not trivial.

[13] WD McNulty, 'The Power of "Compulsory Purchase" under the Law of England' (1912) 21 *Yale Law Journal* 639; WB Stoebuck, 'A General Theory of Eminent Domain' (1971) 47 *Washington Law Review* 553; Gadd (n 11); Reynolds (n 1) 34–46. See below, text to n 44ff, on the adoption of the consensual sale as the form of the transfer.

often enacted laws to protect or regulate local markets and industries or to enforce obligations that were said to exist but not observed. For example, a statute might authorise the removal of unlawful obstructions on rivers or roads, or enact measures in support of customary obligations to contribute to the repair of sewers and flood defences, but neither case involved a new interference with existing rights of property.[14] Hence, there was no reason to compensate those that were affected. However, as legislation was based on substantive obligations that already existed, the potential for new developments was restricted. If a locality wished to construct a new bridge or develop a new water supply, the enforcement of existing law would not always be sufficient. If the project would intrude on rights of property, the promoters would need the consent of everyone holding those rights. In general, Parliament's role, so far as projects in the public interest was concerned, was to ensure that landowners fulfilled their customary and common law obligations but not to redistribute property or impose new obligations on owners. Barring some sort of default, landowners were not at risk of losing their property by legislative action.[15]

This began to change in the early sixteenth century, as Parliament began to authorise intrusions on rights of property without identifying a dereliction of duty on the part of the owner. As justification, petitioners cited the benefit to the 'common weal',[16] and compensation would be provided to the injured party where there was no breach of an obligation. The Conduits at Gloucester Act[17] and the Conduits in London Act[18] are sometimes cited as the earliest examples of parliamentary grants of the power to expropriate land. The Acts recite the hardships suffered by the townspeople due to the lack of a good water supply, and that the access to land for the construction of watercourses from new springs and sources would be desirable. The legislation granted access, without any suggestion that the landowners committed a wrong by refusing their consent; indeed, entry would have been actionable without the statutory authority. Hence, the legislation provided that the owners would be compensated for their loss. As such, the Acts

[14] See, eg, 25 Edw III stat 3 c 4 (1350–51); 45 Edw III c 2 (1370–71); 12 Ric III c 13 (1388); 21 Ric II c 18 (1397–98); 1 Hen IV c 12 (1399); 9 Hen V stat 2 c 11 (1421); 9 Hen VI c 9 (1430–31) and the examples cited above nn 7–8.

[15] In some cases, it could be argued that legislation extended customary obligations: see, eg, 9 Hen V stat 2 c 11 (1421), for the repair of certain roads and bridges: it allowed any subject to cut and take trees growing on roads for repair of the road 'as often as they please, for ever, without the Impediment or Impeachment of any one; any Title or Interest whatever … notwithstanding', which seems to go beyond the clearance of obstructions.

[16] On the origins of the 'common weal' as a justification for legislation, see J Watts, '"Common Weal" and "Commonwealth": England's Monarchical Republic in the Making' in A Gamberini, J-P Genet and A Zorzi (eds), *The Languages of Political Society: Western Europe, 14th-17th Centuries* (Viella, 2011); WM Ormrod, '"Common Profit" and "The Profit of the King and Kingdom": Parliament and the Development of Political Language in England, 1250–1450' (2015) 46 *Viator* 219. An example is the reference to the 'coen weale' to justify an Act allowing landowners to allow access to land for the construction of a new road: 14 and 15 Hen VIII, c 6, s 2 (1523).

[17] 33 Hen VIII c 35 (1541–42).

[18] 35 Hen VIII c 10 (1543–44).

were significant because they indicate that the community, with parliamentary authorisation, could interfere with private rights in land for the 'common weal', subject to compensation for the landowner.[19]

The two Acts confirmed Parliament's power to authorise takings, although neither one explicitly granted powers of compulsory purchase. Instead, they gave authority to enter land and construct permanent works for securing the supply of water but without a transfer of title. This was still an important step, and it remains the case that Parliament requires compensation for a permanent occupation of land.[20] They may have had a precedent in the Statute of Sewers 1427, which William B Stoebuck cites as the first example of expropriation, as it authorised sewer commissioners to take land 'where shall need of new to make'.[21] However, it did not require compensation, as in a compulsory purchase, and there was considerable doubt that it enabled the commissioners to construct new works.[22] Stephen Gadd makes a strong case for the Acte for the Mending of the Ryver of Exeter as the first clear example of expropriation.[23] The Act recites the difficulties faced regarding navigation of the River, and provides authority for the 'Maire Bayliffs and Comonaltie' of Exeter to 'plucke down digge moyne breke banke and caste upp'; all obstructions and nuisances to navigation. This aspect of the Act was not innovative. However, although the language is not entirely clear, the Act also conferred a power to acquire land as necessary for the project, in the following terms:

> in other placese and ground convenient and necessarie for the same whose soever they be, lyinge betwene your said Cittiie and the highe Sea; and further to doe and make all other things requisite and necessarie [to enable the River to be navigable] … gevinge and payinge therfore unto the Lorde or Lordes owners and owner of the soyle where suche digginge and mynynge shalbe, in recompence and satisfaction of and for the lande and grounde so to be digged and myned, after the rate of twentie yeres purchase, or else asmuche for the same as shalbe adjudged ordeyned and determined by the King's Justices of the Assise.

The language may be a little ambiguous, but Gadd has shown that the Act was understood and applied by the parties as authorising the acquisition of the land.[24] The key point from this Act, and the Gloucester and London Acts, is that the needs

[19] Gadd (n 11); JH Baker, *The Oxford History of the Laws of England* (Oxford University Press, 2004) vol 6, 17–18, 30–34.

[20] See McNulty (n 13) 643–44; Stoebuck (n 13) 563–66; Reynolds (n 1) 34–46; Gadd (n 11) 3–4. For modern rules on compensation and entry and construction of permanent works, and the issues regarding compensation, see J Rowan-Robinson and NE Hutchison, 'Utility Wayleaves: Time for Reform' 2001 *Journal of Planning and Environmental Law* 1247; NE Hutchison and J Rowan-Robinson, 'Utility Wayleaves: A Compensation Lottery?' (2002) 20 *Journal of Property Investment & Finance* 159.

[21] 6 Hen VI c 5 (1427); Stoebuck (n 13) 565–66. The Act was the first of a series: see FA Sharman, 'River Improvement Law in the Early Seventeenth Century' (1982) 3 *Journal of Legal History* 222, 223–27. Gadd (n 11) 3 argues that the Statute only authorised distraint to compel payment.

[22] See Sharman, ibid 223–27; LL Jaffe and EG Henderson, 'Judicial Review and the Rule of Law: Historical Origins' (1956) 72 *LQR* 347, 349.

[23] 31 Hen VIII c 4 (1539); Gadd (n 11) 14, fn 75.

[24] Gadd (n 11).

of the community were sufficient justification to override rights of private property. Moreover, unlike the Statute of Sewers and other earlier laws, the legislation was not restricted to the restoration of existing works or rights of way and there was no suggestion that withholding consent was a breach of a legal or moral obligation.

For compensation, the Ryver Exe Act required payment for the land at the rate of 20 years' purchase. This reflected the usual method of pricing land in private transactions,[25] although the multiplier could fluctuate over time and by region.[26] It was more precise than the standard set in the Gloucester and London legislation, which provided that the Mayor (and Dean, for the Gloucester Act) was required to 'satisfie content and pay' an amount 'as shall be adjudged and taxed by the Determination and Judgment of Three or Four indifferent Men'. If the 'Three or Four' men could not agree on the amount, the owner would be entitled to bring an action in trespass against the Mayor (and Dean). Unlike the Ryver Exe Act, the Gloucester and London Acts left it open to the 'indifferent Men' to choose the method and standard of valuation. This may have been because the land itself was not being acquired, or simply because precedents were still being established and there was no accepted practice. However, even a century later, the Great Fire legislation used language that still seems quite vague to modern lawyers.[27] Legislation was enacted for the creation of Fire Courts with the jurisdiction to determine interests in a site, and then to set regulations on reconstruction. It also authorised the expropriation of land for the widening of streets, but only called for 'reasonable satisfaction' to be given 'For all such Ground as shall be taken and imployed'. Failing agreement with the owners, a jury would be sworn 'to inquire and assesse such Damage and Recompence as they shall judge fitt to be awarded'.[28] There were instructions to juries to estimate the 'true and just value' of land that was not built upon in three years, with a view to expropriation, but no indication of years purchase or any other basis of valuation.[29] It seems that, in terms of the

[25] W Deringer, 'Pricing the Future in the Seventeenth Century: Calculating Technologies in Competition' (2017) 58 *Technology and Culture* 506, 511. Simple and compound interest discounting were also used by the seventeenth century, but more often in relation to financial instruments such as annuities: see HJ Habakkuk, 'The Long-Term Rate of Interest and the Price of Land in the Seventeenth Century' (1952) 5 *Economic History Review* 26; C Clay, 'The Price of Freehold Land in the Later Seventeenth and Eighteenth Centuries' (1974) 27 *Economic History Review* 173; RC Allen, 'The Price of Freehold Land and the Interest Rate in the Seventeenth and Eighteenth Centuries' (1988) 41 *Economic History Review* 33.

[26] See Habakkuk, ibid 44–45: records from the 13th and 14th centuries show that it was closer to 10 years; Clay, ibid 174; Allen, ibid 34 show that average multipliers were lower than 20 years in the 17th century and higher in the 18th century.

[27] An Act for erecting a Judicature for Determination of Differences touching Houses burned or demolished by reason of the late Fire which happened in London (1666) 18 & 19 Car II c 7 and An Act for rebuilding the City of London (1666) 19 Car II c 8. These were followed by An Additionall Act for the rebuilding of the City of London (1670) 22 Car II c 11, which extended the powers of the earlier Acts to other streets and buildings, subject to similar rules on compensation. See T Fiddian Reddaway, *The Rebuilding of London After the Great Fire* (Jonathan Cape, 1940).

[28] An Act for rebuilding the City of London (1666) 19 Car II c 8, s 23.

[29] ibid s 13.

precision of valuation, the River Exe case was the exception. In general, the details of valuation were not seen as sufficiently important to the owner or the acquiring body for Parliament to set it down in statute. Instead, it was left to independent assessors and ultimately to the courts.

After the Exeter, Gloucester and London Acts, compulsory acquisitions began to appear more frequently in the statutory record. Indeed, the scale of the reconstruction of London after the Great Fire of 1666 indicates that interfering with private property for the wider public benefit had become an accepted function of Parliament.[30] The Glorious Revolution established the supremacy of Parliament over the Crown, and in particular it ensured that the Crown could not take land and property without either the consent of the landowner or of Parliament. In principle, Parliament would protect the rights of owners, but debates on prominent eighteenth and nineteenth century public bills demonstrated that there were concerns over its willingness to legislate against property. Julian Hoppit raises the case of the Heritable Jurisdictions (Scotland) Act 1746, which abolished heritable jurisdictions in Scotland.[31] The Act ensured that office holders would be paid, but there were still concerns over the constitutional implications, not least the Acts of Union 1707 which declared that the jurisdictions were a form of property.[32] If any form of property should have been inviolable, it would have that property identified in a constitutional statute. Nevertheless, many MPs raised concerns in Parliament. Cobbett summarised them as follows:

> we cannot pass such a Bill, without making a plain encroachment upon the Articles of Union; that if we pass this Bill, or any Bill of a like import, we shall render the property of every man in the kingdom precarious; that by such a regulation as is thereby proposed, we shall bring our happy constitution into the utmost danger.[33]

The Act nevertheless passed. The Declaratory Act 1766 produced the debate between Lords Camden and Mansfield, as discussed in the Introduction; other public Acts also raised concern.[34] However, perhaps surprisingly, the public Acts settled relatively little in terms of constitutional standards. They were not directly concerned with the expropriation of land, but in any case, none of them were subsequently treated as constitutional precedents, in relation to either the public interest or the provision of compensation. Their terms were driven by political bargaining, with each determined by their specific context. For example, the question of slavery periodically arose after the Slave Trade Act 1807 and the Slavery Abolition Act 1833, but always in relation to events outside Britain or international treaties. Again, these Acts were not concerned with the compulsory purchase of land, but

[30] See the authorities cited above, n 27.
[31] See J Hoppit, 'Compulsion, Compensation and Property Rights in Britain, 1688-1833' [2011] *Past & Present* 93, 108–15.
[32] Acts of Union 1707, Art XX.
[33] *Cobbett's Parliamentary History of England*, XIV, 30 (1747).
[34] See Hoppit (n 31); D Bogart and G Richardson, 'Property Rights and Parliament in Industrializing Britain' (2011) 54 *Journal of Law and Economics* 241.

they illustrate the importance of political bargaining in relation to property. The compensation provisions of the 1833 Act were intended to ensure a majority gain in favour of the abolition of slavery. Indeed, no compensation was provided on the abolition of the slave trade. Parliament provided compensation to the holders of heritable jurisdictions under the Heritable Jurisdictions (Scotland) Act 1746 but not to the burghers who lost their offices as a result of the Municipal Reform Act 1835. Again, practical politics was more important than constitutional principle. Consequently, these public Acts, as important as they were, have not since been raised as precedents on constitutional standards relating to private property. They show that property is not inviolable, but little more than that.

It was through the consideration of private bills that Parliament developed its principles for the protection of property. By the eighteenth century, Parliament was spending a significant amount of its time on bills authorising compulsory purchase and other unconsented interferences with property. Julian Hoppit observes that the Parliament's willingness to override rights of private property, in both public and private Acts, raised 'uncertainties over property rights were sufficient for some to question whether property had a sound theoretical basis at all'.[35] Parliament did not ignore rights of property; given its composition at the time, it was highly unlikely that it would have done so. Nevertheless, there was sufficient common interest across political factions that legislative power did not become a tool for one group of landowners to deprive another of its property. Paul Langford argues, 'A feature common to very diverse kinds of legislation was a sense that statutory expropriation was an awesome responsibility for a Parliament obsessed with property rights', even though Parliament 'found its métier as an institution devoted to the remodelling and revision of property rights'.[36] Moreover, the repeat business of private bills led to the regularisation of procedures and content. The specific points of reference in relation to a constitutional right to property were being set down. The constitution was still political rather than legal, in that there was room for negotiation and bargaining over the terms of bills. This was most evident with the public bills, but as a practical matter, it occurred with private bills until well into the nineteenth century, when each House required the membership of private bill committees to be disinterested in the matters before them.[37] The political aspect did not mean, however, that there were no standards: they did exist, and they did provide MPs with points of reference for scrutiny of issues relating to the rights of individuals.

The first point of reference concerned constitutional procedural rights. Anxieties regarding private bills and compulsory purchase were addressed, if not fully resolved, by regularising the parliamentary procedures. As discussed in

[35] Hoppit (n 31) 93; see also P Langford, *Public Life and the Propertied Englishman 1689–1798* (Oxford University Press, 1994) 43–51.

[36] Langford, ibid 147 and 145.

[37] See chapter two, section II.

chapter two, Standing Orders were introduced and revised on several occasions, with refinements to the rules on notice, consent, evidence and the valuation process, and the value of impartial private bill committees was recognised and established in the early nineteenth century. In 1865, the Court of Referees was set up so that precedent could be collected to guide future decisions. These developments shaped modern law: Parliament has delegated its powers regarding compulsory purchase to planning and other administrative bodies, but the core principles that guide administrative proceedings were largely worked out through the consideration of the thousands of private bills that made their way through special committees in the preceding centuries. The desire to make the procedures more efficient often was the primary motivation, but at the same time the attention to procedure gave confidence that Parliament would not act arbitrarily. In particular, the procedures were reasonably transparent and therefore reduced the risk of fraud and corruption. The proceedings were reasonably balanced, in that the parliamentary committees were expected to check that promoters gave notice to interested parties and that they had the opportunity to be heard. They were also reasonably fair, as Parliament would ensure that compensation was paid to those who lost property or that they received other counterbalancing advantages.[38] Finally, in terms of substance, the accumulation of precedent provided a measure of predictability, especially with the passage of model Acts. The General Enclosure Act 1801 was the first statute with general clauses for incorporation in private bills. It was followed by the Land Clauses Consolidation Act 1845.[39] There were also consistent practices with other 'repeat bills', such as the Improvement Acts. These Acts, along with the Standing Orders and accumulated precedent, contributed to the culture of justification by making it easier for committees to notice and require justification of any departure from the practice. As discussed in chapter two, by the end of the twentieth century, Parliament had created administrative bodies and processes that did the work of private bill business, but always with a view to preserving the rights that it had recognised in its own procedures.

The second point concerned the compensation standard. Most private bills were promoted by commercial ventures, for which juries often set values that were favourable to owners subject to expropriation. Given that the promoters expected to make a profit from the scheme, and that they would do so by acquiring land without the owner's consent, generosity would not have seemed unfair.[40] The

[38] See, eg, GE Mingay, *Parliamentary Enclosure in England: An Introduction to Its Causes, Incidence and Impact 1750–1850* (Longman, 1997) 57–58.

[39] FA Sharman, 'An Introduction to the Enclosure Acts' (1989) 10 *Journal of Legal History* 45; FA Sharman, 'The History of the Lands Clauses Consolidation Act 1845 – I' (1986) 1986 *Statute Law Review* 13; FA Sharman, 'The History of the Lands Clauses Consolidation Act 1845 – II' (1986) 1986 *Statute Law Review* 78.

[40] Ministry of Reconstruction, *Second Report of the Committee Dealing with the Law and Practice relating to the Acquisition and Valuation of Land for Public Purposes* (Cd 9229, 1918) para 8 (hereafter 'Scott Report') para 8; S Jack and A Jack, 'Nineteenth-Century Lawyers and Railway Capitalism: Historians and the Use of Legal Cases' (2003) 24 *Journal of Legal History* 59, 72–73.

practice was to value land not only in its current use, but all potential uses. In 1919, the Scott Committee, in its report on compensation for land, remarked that

> under the cloak of this criterion merely hypothetical and often highly speculative elements of value which had no real existence have crept into awards as if they were actual; while elements of remote future value have too often been inadequately discounted, and valued as if there were a readily available market.[41]

In addition, it was the practice to add a 'solatium' to the compensation, usually at ten per cent of the value, to reflect the owner's loss of the opportunity to sell at a time and price of their own choosing.[42] As discussed in the next section, many of the reforms of the twentieth century were aimed at pulling back from the generosity of the nineteenth century.

Another point concerned the form of the transaction. The wave of private Acts used the consensual sale of land as structure for the transfer: it became known as a 'compulsory purchase', in the modern language. It did not follow the early Gloucester and London statutes, in that they granted immunity from trespass. Instead, the later Acts were closer to the form of a purveyance, where the acquisition followed the model of an ordinary consensual sale.[43] Arthur Lenhoff argues that only the adoption of the form of a sale would satisfy the desire to respect consent.[44] FA Mann traced the origins of the English idea of compulsory purchase to William Blackstone, who said that 'So great moreover is the regard of the law for private property, that it will not authorize the least violation of it; no, not even for the general good of the whole community.'[45] However, 'the legislature alone can, and indeed frequently does, interpose, and compel the individual to acquiesce'. As consent was now compelled, the transaction followed that of an ordinary contract: 'The public is now considered as an individual, treating with an individual for an exchange. All that the legislature does, is to oblige the owner to alienate his possession for a reasonable price.'[46] Adopting the form of a sale also allowed the owner certain procedural advantages: it could, for example, sue for the price of the land if the promoter did not pay when required.[47]

This raises a further question, concerning the distillation of principle from practice. Maitland famously commented that Parliament in the eighteenth century

> seems afraid to rise to the dignity of a general proposition; it will not say, 'All commons may be enclosed according to these general rules', 'All aliens may become naturalized if

[41] Scott Report, ibid para 8.

[42] ibid.

[43] Although, with a purveyance, the owner of goods could simply refuse to sell; what they could not do was sell to others.

[44] A Lenhoff, 'Development of the Concept of Eminent Domain' (1942) 42 *Columbia Law Review* 596, 603. 'An expropriatory change in the ownership of land by mere operation of law, that is without regard to the owner's will, was so foreign to all the technique and all the ideals of that purely individualistic doctrine that it could not be conceived except by tacking it to notions of purchase and sale.'

[45] Mann (n 1) 196–98; 1 Bl Comm 135.

[46] 1 Bl Comm 135.

[47] Mann (n 1) 196–98.

> they fulfil these or those conditions', 'All boroughs shall have these powers for widening their roads', 'All marriages may be dissolved if the wife's adultery be proved'. No, it deals with this and that marriage.[48]

He attributed this to jealousy of the Crown, as any general delegation of power to commissioners or boards would have allowed the Crown to increase its influence and patronage.[49] The consequence was the absence of any generalisation of principles and standards. Parliament's jealousy began to ease in the nineteenth century but even so, it is difficult to identify general principles from the thicket of detail. The Standing Orders and the consolidating legislation could be lengthy and detailed. The Land Clauses Consolidation Act 1845, for example, ran to 153 sections, excluding appendices, with a wide range of rules on the form of a compulsory purchase. Plainly not all the provisions would be considered constitutional, despite their repeated incorporation in a multitude of private bills. Moreover, some points that we would now consider as core constitutional principles were left to be resolved without legislative guidance. For example, the 1845 Act did not set out principles of valuation for determining compensation. Indeed, it did not even say that compensation should cover the owner's loss: it seems that this was assumed. Similarly, the Act's procedures provided an opportunity to consider the public interest but did not describe the nature of that interest. The consideration of the bill in committee would require proof of the public interest, but there was no overarching statutory guidance on what this might require. Indeed, Parliament enacted legislation across so many different areas that it must have seemed that there was no conceivable purpose that could never justify legislation. This is not to say that some bills were not debated at length.[50] However, there is no indication that Parliament attempted to lay down general principles for determining whether a bill satisfied a public interest test.

Finally, it is worth noting that other points were uncontroversial, but their basis was not clearly explained. For example, the Standing Orders covered the procedures for providing notice to affected parties and for proving consents where given. Notice was clearly important in constitutional terms, because it provided the opportunity to exercise the constitutional right to appear before the committee. The reason for requiring consents were not as clear. In very broad terms, constitutional theory acknowledge that property could not be taken without consent, but that property holders delegated the power to give consent to their representatives in Parliament. Hence, individual consents should not have been necessary. However, with enclosures, private bill committees required proof that consents had been given. Initially, the requirement was for unanimity. As Robert Tennyson

[48] FW Maitland, *The Constitutional History of England*, 1st edn (edited by HAL Fisher) (Cambridge University Press, 1908) 383.

[49] JAG Griffith, 'The Place of Parliament in the Legislative Process. Part I' (1951) 14 *MLR* 279, 282: the lack of interest in general principles is more easily explained as a product of Parliament's focus on foreign and colonial policy: 'the eighteenth as compared with the nineteenth century was not a time of extensive administrative reformation'.

[50] For example, on the cost of railway bill proceedings, see Jack and Jack (n 40).

says, Parliament probably followed the practice in Chancery, which would approve agreements for enclosure but only if supported by all interest-holders.[51] This provides an historical explanation, but it seems weak as a constitutional justification, as the scheme itself would be in the public interest whether landowners give their consent or not. In any case, by the middle of the eighteenth century, Parliament relaxed the requirement to four-fifths of the interest-holders by value and later to two-thirds of holders, but without explaining why consents were required at all.[52] With nationalisation, there has been no expectation that a minimum proportion of shareholders should consent before a bill can be passed. With the Churches (Scotland) Act 1905, Parliament authorised a commission to redistribute the property of two churches without consent from either, either in general or in relation to specific assets.[53] On the other hand, the compulsory buy-out provisions of company laws can only be invoked once the holders of 80 per cent of the share capital have accepted a takeover offer.[54] Clearly, there are differences across these areas. Perhaps there are valid reasons for these differences, but Parliament has not felt it necessary to explain them. Hence, they reflect practices, but describing them as constitutional standards is problematic.

III. Challenges to the Compensation Standards

By the late nineteenth century, the wider land reform movement raised questions about compulsory purchase, with valuation and compensation as the focus.[55] Municipalities and public authorities were increasingly involved in the provision of public services. As this often required the purchase of land, they were particularly concerned with the generosity of compensation.[56] This brought a number of constitutional issues to the fore, which we now consider: (i) compensation for value generated by illegal or unethical activity; (ii) public authorities and the 'willing seller' standard; and (iii) compensation for unearned value and the recovery of betterment.

[51] R Tennyson, 'From Unanimity to Proportionality: Assent Standards and the Parliamentary Enclosure Movement' (2013) 31 *Law and History Review* 199, 205–17.

[52] ibid and 6 & 7 Will IV c 115 s 1.

[53] See chapter six, section III.C.

[54] See A Johnston, 'Takeover Regulation: Historical and Theoretical Perspectives on the City Code' (2007) 66 *Cambridge Law Journal* 422. The provisions first appeared in the Companies Act 1929, s 155, following recommendations of the Greene Committee: see Company Law Amendment Committee, *Report* (Cmnd 2657, 1926) paras 84–85.

[55] See A Offer, *Property and Politics, 1870–1914: Landownership, Law, Ideology, and Urban Development in England* (Cambridge University Press, 1981); JA Yelling, *Slums and Slum Clearance in Victorian London* (Routledge, 1986); EF Biagini, *Liberty, Retrenchment and Reform: Popular Liberalism in the Age of Gladstone, 1860–1880* (Cambridge University Press 1992) 184–90; I Packer, *Lloyd George, Liberalism and the Land: The Land Issue and Party Politics in England, 1906–1914* (Royal Historical Society, 2001) 1–33; M Tichelar, *The Failure of Land Reform in Twentieth-Century England: The Triumph of Private Property* (Routledge, 2018) 11–42.

[56] See chapter four, section I.

A. Value Generated by Illegal or Unethical Activity

In the Victorian era, municipalities increasingly turned their attention to the improvement of slum conditions.[57] Legislation and local bye-laws imposed rules regarding sanitation, water supply, building standards, overcrowding and population density. In some cases, municipalities sought compulsory purchase powers to enable the acquisition of unfit housing, for either renewal or replacement. Not surprisingly, they objected to paying full compensation to landlords who were failing to observe housing standards. With overcrowding, for example, the usual rules of valuation for compensation depended on rental income, even if inflated by occupancy that exceeded the legal limit. Section 21 of the Housing of the Working Classes Act 1890 therefore required a reduction in compensation in three circumstances. The first dealt with overcrowding: in such cases, the value was calculated on the basis of lawful occupancy. Secondly, a deduction would be made to reflect the cost of abating a nuisance arising from the condition of the property. Finally, where the property was unfit for human habitation and not reasonably capable of being made fit, compensation would be limited to the value of the land and the materials of its buildings.

These provisions clearly undermined the practice that owners would be generously compensated for their loss. However, they were not contentious in Parliament. Indeed, the Act was introduced by the Conservative and Unionist Government and supported by the Liberal opposition. There was no suggestion that modifying the standard represented an attack on the constitutional rights of landowners. Charles Ritchie, the President of the Local Government Board, observed that

> I venture to think there is not a Member in the House who will not welcome any fair and reasonable scheme which will cut down to a minimum the money payable to owners of property who grossly neglect their duty in regard to their property.[58]

Nevertheless, Ritchie went on to say that the Government had 'gone as far as it is possible with justice' to reduce compensation, which suggests that reductions could not be used as a penalty, but only to stop landlords from benefiting from their own breaches of duty.[59] Compensation should still be fair, and that meant that it should counterbalance the loss, but fairness did not require compensation for value that had been gained by illegal or immoral methods. Accordingly, it was not always necessary to compensate at the rate that the owner might have obtained for the property on the open market or at the amount that would replace the lost income.

The provisions were incorporated in the Acquisition of Land (Assessment of Compensation) Act 1919 and remain part of the law. Throughout, there has been no suggestion that the provisions contravene constitutional rights. Moreover,

[57] See Yelling (n 55).
[58] HC Deb 24 June 1890, vol 354, col 1825.
[59] ibid; see also Ritchie on Third Reading: HC Deb 21 July 1890, vol 347, col 390.

the 1919 Act gave the principle general application. That is, it might have been argued that the reduction of compensation was only appropriate where the very purpose of the legislation was to address misconduct to the type that produced the enhanced value. It would be particularly unfair to the local authority to expect it to pay for illegal conduct that it sought to remedy. However, the 1919 Act was not based on such specific criteria, as it would apply to reduce compensation even where the purpose was not to remedy the illegal activity. Instead, the focus is more on the legitimacy of the claim to value, regardless of the purpose of acquisition.

B. Public Authorities and the 'Willing Seller' Standard

Local government bodies also challenged the 'unwilling seller' standard of valuation. It may have seemed fair where commercial enterprises sought to acquire land for projects that were expected to earn high profits, but this was not the case with public authorities. As the cost would be borne by their ratepayers, they began to ask whether the same generosity should apply to public authority purchases. The Housing of the Working Classes Act 1890 set the precedent. Not only did it allow for the deductions for breaches of duty but it also stated that compensation should be set at the 'fair market value', with no award of the solatium. The Small Holdings Act 1908[60] and the Housing Act 1909[61] provided that 'no additional allowance shall be made on account of the purchase or hiring being compulsory'. The question continued to receive attention and, during World War I, it was reviewed by the Committee on the Acquisition and Valuation of Land for Public Purposes (often called the Scott Committee, after Leslie Scott, the Chair). In its report to Parliament, submitted in November 1918, it stated that the 'unwilling seller' model was inappropriate for acquisitions by public authorities, as they could not be compared with 'speculative adventurers'.[62] Fairness only required payment of the price that could be obtained on the market. This was particularly important in the post-War period, where the cost of compensation threatened to undermine the development of housing by public authorities. Moreover, there was nothing about ownership itself that required such generosity:

> It ought to be recognised, and we believe that to-day recognised, that the exclusive right to the enjoyment of land which is involved in private ownership necessarily carries with it the duty of surrendering such land to the community when the needs of the community require it.[63]

[60] Small Holdings Act 1908, s 39(5) 'In determining the amount of any disputed compensation under any such order, no additional allowance shall be made on account of the purchase or hiring being compulsory.'

[61] Housing Act 1909, s 64(7) (the language is the same terms as in the Small Holdings Act).

[62] Scott Report (n 40) para 8.

[63] ibid.

The Committee's recommendations were reflected in the Acquisition of Land (Assessment of Compensation) Act 1919, which contained six 'rules' on compensation for land compulsorily acquired by a public authority.[64] The rules applied the 'willing seller' model of valuation and excluded both the solatium and the consideration of the impact of the acquiring authority's scheme on the value of the land.

These changes were significant. To be sure, they only applied to public authorities and they confirmed the principle that the owner should be compensated for its loss. Nevertheless, it is worth noting that, like the Housing of the Working Classes Act 1890, they did not raise constitutional objections in Parliament. Indeed, some MPs argued that the new rules were still too generous to landowners. Captain Bagley, a Conservative member, said:

> It seems to me that we are now passing a Bill which is going to stereotype the payment for the land we require at the highest possible price that can be fairly and reasonably imagined in the open market, and this is at a time when by the expenditure of scores of millions of pounds from the pockets of the taxpayer we have violently inflated the demand for this commodity whose supply is fixed.[65]

The Bill passed, but Bagley was certainly not alone in his mistrust of the market as a conclusive indicator of value or of the price that would be fair to all parties.[66] Indirectly, the cross-party agreement suggested that, if there were constitutional principles requiring compensation for loss, there was flexibility in terms of 'fair' compensation and the conception of the loss.[67]

C. Compensation for Unearned Value and Recovery of Betterment

The idea of recovering betterment has a long history in English law. Section 24 of the Act for Rebuilding the City of London (1666) noted that, due to the reconstruction plans, 'the Houses now remaining and to be rebuilt will receive more or

[64] Acquisition of Land (Assessment of Compensation Act) 1919, s 2.

[65] HC Deb 25 June 1919, vol 117, col 246.

[66] For eg, Sir R Thomas (Coalition Liberal) proposed an amendment fixing a maximum price for agricultural land: HC Deb 26 June 1919, vol 117, cols 395–96 (the Speaker ruled out debate on the amendment, on the basis that there had already been a debate and decision on market value as the standard). See also HC Deb 11 July 1919, vol 117, cols 2177–80: Major Entwistle (Liberal) argued that the proposed rules would be too generous to landowners.

[67] The one issue explicitly framed as a constitutional matter concerned rights of appeal. Clause 6 allowed an appeal on assessment to the High Court, but no further appeal. Henry Cautley (Coalition Conservative) proposed amendment to allow further appeal, by leave of the High Court, stating that 'I desire to give in such cases the constitutional right of every subject who is aggrieved to pursue the remedy which is given by our system of jurisprudence.' HC Deb 26 June 1919, vol 117, col 439. Sir G Hewart, the Attorney-General, said that there was no need, as the issues were narrowly concerned with questions of fact: HC Deb 26 June 1919, vol 117, cols 440–41.

lesse advantage in the value of their Rents by the liberty of Air and free recourse for Trade and other Conveniencies by such Regulation and Inlargements'.[68] Accordingly, the Chamberlain (who was also in charge of paying compensation) could request those with an interest in the property to contribute funds; failing agreement, a jury would assess 'such competent summe and summes of Money with respect to their severall Interests in consideration of such improvement and melioration as in reason and good conscience they shall thinke fitt'.[69] Funds raised in this way would be used in the payment of compensation on expropriation of other property. It seems that this was deliberately kept vague: 'reason and good conscience' might not necessarily require the benefiting parties to make a payment equal to their gains. What is more significant, however, is that a clear precedent for later laws on betterment was set before the end of the seventeenth century. Accordingly, various proposals for securing this value for the community have been made, such as the taxation of increments in the unimproved value of land, the imposition of betterment charges against increments attributable to specific public investments, or recoupment (buying land not needed for the project that would see an enhancement in value from it).[70] In a similar vein, the Housing of the Working Classes Act 1890 provided for the reduction of compensation on compulsory purchase if other property held by the same owner increased in value as a result of the project.[71]

In April 1894, a Select Committee of the House of Lords was appointed to consider whether increments in value due to the expenditure of public funds on local improvements should be recoverable from the landowners.[72] The Committee could see no principled objection to recovery: it was 'not in itself unjust' and the owners were 'equitably required' to contribute to the cost of improvements.[73] It recommended changes to the Standing Orders and that private bills should include provisions allowing special levies to compel contributions. Clauses were then included in the Manchester Corporation Act 1894: the Act authorised several improvement projects and stated that an 'improvement charge' would be placed on lands 'in respect or inconsideration of any substantial and permanent increase in value which is clearly shown to be derived from the improvement'.[74] The first national planning Act, the Housing Town Planning Act 1909, also allowed for betterment charges.[75]

[68] Rebuilding of London Act 1666, 19 Car II c 8, s 24; see Reddaway (n 27) and the Scott Report (n 40) app 3.

[69] Rebuilding of London Act 1666, ibid.

[70] See A Cox, *Adversary Politics and Land: The Conflict Over Land and Property Policy in Post-War Britain* (Cambridge University Press, 1984) and the material cited above in n 55.

[71] Housing of the Working Classes Act 1890, ss 38(8) and 41(1)(b); see also the Light Railways Act 1896, s 13.

[72] House of Lords Select Committee on Town Improvements (Betterment), *Report* (HC 1894, 292).

[73] ibid iii.

[74] Manchester Corporation Act 1894, s 22(1).

[75] Housing Town Planning Act 1909, s 58; see DG Hagman, 'Betterment For Worsenment: The English 1909 Act and Its Progeny' (1977) 10 *University of Queensland Law Journal* 29.

The Scott Committee considered the Select Committee's views and said that 'the justice of the principle has, we believe, been universally admitted'.[76] Requiring a contribution was in the public interest, especially given the great need to raise capital for improvements.[77] The Scott Committee also considered recoupment but rejected it. Its rejection was not, however, on the basis of constitutional principles, but on the ground that public authorities should not engage in land speculation and should limit their involvement in land management.[78] It did not suggest that recoupment amounted to an unjustified interference with property rights.[79]

The Government ultimately decided not to include provisions on betterment or recoupment in the Land (Assessment of Compensation) Act 1919. In the House of Lords, the Lord Chancellor stated that they were not included because they would have been controversial and would have delayed passage of the Bill. There was a vague promise to return to betterment and recoupment in future, and no suggestion that they were contrary to constitutional standards or economic policy.[80] The Lord Chancellor was probably correct in his estimation of the reaction to new provisions for betterment or recoupment. The battle over the land value tax of the People's Budget 1909 was still fresh in the minds of many MPs. As discussed in chapter five, the Budget would have enabled the valuation of land and imposed a tax of 20 per cent on increases in the value, on the basis that this would capture at least some of the gain that was generated by the community rather than the landowner.[81] It was, in some respects, a general betterment tax, although it did not depend on proof of any specific community investment or increment resulting from such investment. In practice, legislation did not address the issue until the Town and Country Planning Act 1947. The earlier attempts to capture unearned value were dropped: the Finance Act 1920 abolished the land value tax and, although Labour manifestoes called for the nationalisation of land, the Labour and National governments of Ramsay MacDonald took no steps to implement them.[82] Neither did the Attlee government of 1945–50: it stated that 'Labour believes in land nationalisation and will work towards it', but instead it

[76] Scott Report (n 40) para 32.

[77] The Committee recommended this apply also to 'private undertakings authorised in the public interest': ibid para 33.

[78] ibid para 54.

[79] ibid paras 51–58.

[80] HL Deb 22 July 1919, vol 35, cols 912–13.

[81] Chapter five, section IV.

[82] Labour had called for the nationalisation of land: see *Labour's Call to the People* (1918) 'land nationalisation is a vital necessity'; *Labour's Appeal to the Nation* (1929) 'The Land must therefore pass under Public Control'; *Labour's Call to Action* (1931) '... the land must be publicly owned' (the full paragraph seems confined to agricultural land); *The Labour Party's Call to Power* (1935) the Party 'has also declared for the public ownership of land'; and *Let Us Face the Future: A Declaration of Labour Policy for the Consideration of the Nation* (1945) 'Labour believes in land nationalisation and will work towards it, but as a first step the State and the local authorities must have wider and speedier powers to acquire land for public purposes wherever the public interest so requires.' The manifestos are reprinted in D Kavanagh, I Dale and I Dale Nfa, *Labour Party General Election Manifestos 1900–1997* (Taylor & Francis Group, 2000) vol 2. For the evolution of Labour policies, see Tichelar (n 55); K Manton, 'The Labour Party and the Land Question, 1919–51' (2006) 79 *Historical Research* 247.

opted to nationalise the owner's right to determine the use of land.[83] Under the Town and Country Planning Act 1947, owners could not change the use of land without a grant of permission from their planning authority. Payments for the loss of this 'right to develop' were made, but only to owners of land that was 'dead ripe' for development, and on the basis that they were ex gratia.[84]

Two further principles ensured that public authorities would control valuation and capture the betterment value. First, the Town and Country Planning Act departed from the principles of the Acquisition of Land (Assessment of Compensation) Act 1919, in that it excluded consideration of the market price in valuation on compulsory purchase. This, it was thought, would exclude values driven by speculation on the possibility of a grant of permission for a change of use. This was not contentious, given that there was cross-party support for denying compensation for speculation on decisions of public authorities.[85] This followed from the experience in World War II, when it was believed that the market was driven by speculation on the anticipation of policies on compensation for land acquired for reconstruction. In any case, there were precedents in earlier laws: in particular, the Tramways Act 1870 effectively excluded the impact of speculation on the continuation of licence to operate a tramway.[86] Accordingly, valuation for compulsory purchase would be based on the existing use of land as it stood in 1947, without recognition of any increase in value due to the hope of a grant of planning permission for a change of use.[87]

The taking of the right to develop also provided the framework for betterment, as the Act gave the Central Land Board the authority to set a charge for a grant of the right to develop. The Bill did not fix a level, but instead it allowed the Board to vary the charge over time and across regions. By this process, the Board could charge for betterment, at the point of the change of use. In Parliament, the idea of a development charge was not controversial, although the Conservatives did challenge several aspects of the proposals. In particular, they argued that the charge was a tax, and hence that the authority to charge should have been given under a finance bill. This would require parliamentary authority and hence it would remove the Board's discretion in setting the charge.[88] In addition, they argued that

[83] ibid, Labour Party, *Let us Face the Future* (1945).

[84] As explained in chapter five, section I, it was the Government's position that compensation was not paid as of right but ex gratia.

[85] See T Allen, 'Liberalism, Social Democracy and the Value of Property under the European Convention on Human Rights' (2010) 59 *International and Comparative Law Quarterly* 1055, 1061: 'The focus on existing use was also intended to iron out the fluctuations in the market for land. There was no direct control over the prices paid in private transactions, but the limitations on compensation in compulsory acquisition would, it was thought, impose some restraint on private speculation.'

[86] See chapter four, section I.

[87] The 10% solatium was therefore abolished as the general rule for all compulsory purchases. A version of it does, however, still apply in some specific contexts: see, eg, section 7(4)(b) of the Petroleum Act 1998, on compensation for the grant under section 8, Mines (Working Facilities and Support) Act 1966 of rights to enter land and extract oil. Note that the choice of 1947 as the base date was controversial: see Allen (n 85) 1060–61.

[88] See WS Morrison (Cons), HC Deb 29 January 1947, vol 432, cols 996–98.

there should be right of appeal from decisions of the Board, similar to rights of appeal for assessment of other taxes. The Government responded that the Board would hold the right to develop as one of its assets. Hence, the grant of development rights was akin to the disposition of any other commercially valuable asset. As such, it was not a tax. Accordingly, there was no need to set out fixed charges in a Finance Act; neither was it appropriate to allow for an appeal.[89]

So far as the constitutional aspects of compensation and betterment were concerned, there was very little controversy in Parliament.[90] Indeed, the Conservatives were more concerned that the Labour Government did not take credit for ideas that they saw as their own. For example, the Conservative MP Sir H Lucas-Tooth said that

> the great bulk of this Bill has been built on the Measures which have been introduced by Tory Governments during the last 20 to 26 years. It is on the work of those Governments that the good parts of this Bill have been brought forward today.[91]

The crucial point is that market prices could not be assumed to be fair. In addition, charging for a change of use and capturing betterment were accepted as legitimate measures.[92] To be sure, these points were not unprecedented, except that they were now part of a scheme that was far more comprehensive than anything that had gone before.

The Conservative support for the new system did not last. Conservative governments secured the enactment of the Town and Country Planning Acts 1953 and 1954, under which the development charge was abolished. However, compensation was still based on existing value, with the result that compensation on compulsory purchase fell further away from values that could be obtained on the market. The Town and Country Planning Act 1959 brought back the principles of the Acquisition of Land (Assessment of Compensation) Act 1919, although with provisions intended to reflect the planning system introduced in 1947.[93] There have been further legislative changes, with the Land Compensation Act 1961 consolidating much of the statutory framework for compensation. The Land Compensation Act 1973 also introduced further protections for landowners, in the form of compensation for depreciation due to public works and special payments for disturbance arising from displacement.[94] There has not been, however, any change

[89] See L Silkin, Minister of Town and Country Planning, HC Deb 1 August 1947, vol 441, cols 861–63.

[90] It was not controversial outside Parliament, with Commander Maitland, a Conservative MP, saying that 'The point about this Bill which has impressed me most is the astonishing lack of interest that a Bill of this importance has excited in the country during its passage.' HC Deb 20 May 1947, vol 437, col 2227.

[91] HC Deb 20 May 1947, vol 437, col 2272.

[92] As discussed in chapter five, section I, the Act also confirmed that there was no constitutional right to compensation for restrictions on the use of land.

[93] Town and Country Planning Act 1959, ss 2–9.

[94] Land Compensation Act 1973, Part I and Part III. There were also provisions regarding advance payments (s 52) and planning blight (Part V).

to the right to an independent valuation for the purposes of compensation. The 1961 Act provided that the Lands Tribunal would decide disputes over valuation and compulsory purchase, but this was consistent with the long-standing principle of independent valuation. It seems that, at least since the post-World War II era, the precedents have provided sufficient leeway for governments to pursue their policies relating to compulsory purchase.

D. Leasehold Reform

The land reform movement of the nineteenth century also considered landlord–tenant relationships. Reforms concerning the quality of housing, security of tenure, control over rent, compensation for improvements funded by tenants are covered in chapter five. This chapter considers compulsory purchase, in the form of leasehold enfranchisement. It raised public interest issues of allowing tenants to purchase the freehold and the compensation that should be paid for it. To a large extent, these issues were resolved with the Leasehold Reform Act 1967, when tenants were given the right to purchase the freehold at a favourable rate, but the process of reaching that point took nearly a century.

In England and Wales, parliamentary discussions of enfranchisement began well before the 1967 Act. The majority on the Royal Commission on the Housing of the Working Classes, 1884–85 considered it. One of its members, Henry Broadhurst, introduced a private member's bill that would have allowed it.[95] It was not, however, supported by the Government, with the Attorney-General objecting that it would not have been workable and would not have produced the desired benefits.[96] The Select Committee on Town Holdings, which was appointed in 1886 and published a report in 1889, saw some merit in enfranchisement but ultimately did not recommend it, except to the extent that local authorities might be given the powers of compulsory purchase with a view to resale to the tenants.[97] Some further reforms were made in the land reform legislation of the 1920s, with enfranchisement for trustees holding a long lease for place of worship purposes,[98] the conversion of leases for lives into leases of fixed terms[99] and the tenant's right to compensation for improvements that it funded.[100] However, except for the Places of Worship (Enfranchisement) Act 1920, there was no significant movement on enfranchisement, whether on the

[95] Royal Commission on the Housing of the Working Classes, First Report 1885 (C (2nd series) 4402, 1885) 59, 73–76; the bill was the Leaseholders (Facilities of Purchase of the Fee Simple) Bill, 1884. For a discussion of the Commission and Bill, see GLH Griffiths, 'The Hundred Years War – The Development of the Movement towards Leasehold Enfranchisement in Wales' (2003) *Conveyancer* 289, 293–95.

[96] HC Deb 19 March 1884, vol 286, col 238.

[97] Select Committee on Town Holdings, *Report* (HL 1889, 190) 39–40.

[98] Places of Worship (Enfranchisement) Act 1920.

[99] Law of Property Act 1925, s 149.

[100] Landlord and Tenant Act 1927, Part I.

Irish model of voluntary, subsidised transfers, or through compulsory purchase by local authorities for sale to tenants or the conferral of a direct right of compulsory enfranchisement on tenants.[101]

The absence of general enfranchisement legislation does not mean that enfranchisement had no precedents. Parliament was accustomed to enacting laws allowing one private person to acquire land of another private person without their consent. It had also enacted laws for redistributing rights amongst a group of interest holders. The earliest enclosure statutes date from the sixteenth century, although they were enacted infrequently until the eighteenth century. However, through the eighteenth and nineteenth centuries, enclosure bills were enacted with such frequency that the Enclosure Act 1801 became the first example of a model clause Act. Similarly, Parliament passed numerous estate bills in the eighteenth century, to make certain and redistribute interests amongst a relatively small group. With enclosure and estate bills, there was still a need to establish the public advantage.[102] However, it was not necessarily tied to a larger scheme, as the redistribution or resettlement of interests was a purpose in itself. There was an expectation that the bill would result in wider benefits: for example, an enclosure would indicate the specific land and give some indication of how it would be divided, but without going into the kind of detail seen in a canal or railway bill. Usually, the bill would appoint commissioners to survey the land and work out the details, but no plan was needed for enactment itself. It does not seem that it was particularly difficult to satisfy Parliament that an enclosure, or authority to deal in the assets of a settled estate, served an appropriate purpose. This would later be seen with leasehold enfranchisement: there were wider arguments that tenants would invest in the property if they held title, but Parliament did not require specific tenants to establish how or when they would invest or indeed that they would do so. The redistribution was, by itself, the aim of the legislation.[103]

[101] The Law of Property Act, s 153 provided a right of enfranchisement, although only in narrow circumstances (leases granted for a minimum of 300 years, with a minimum 200 years left, and only with no or token rent).

[102] On enclosures, see M Turner, *English Parliamentary Enclosure: Its Historical Geography and Economic History* (Dawson, 1980); M Turner, *Enclosures in Britain 1750–1830* (Macmillan Press, 1984); Sharman, 'An Introduction to the Enclosure Acts' (n 39); Mingay (n 38); S Lambert, *Bills and Acts: Legislative Procedure in Eighteenth-Century England* (Cambridge University Press, 1971) 129–49. On estate bills, see J Hoppit, 'Patterns of Parliamentary Legislation, 1660–1800' (1996) 39 *Historical Journal* 109, 110–28; K Dimitruk, '"I Intend Therefore to Prorogue": The Effects of Political Conflict and the Glorious Revolution in Parliament, 1660–1772' (2017) 22 *European Review of Economic History* 261.

[103] Beyond land law, the compulsory buy-out provisions of company legislation were in place when the Leasehold Committee considered enfranchisement in 1950: see Johnston (n 54). The provisions first appeared in the Companies Act 1929, s 155, following recommendations of the Company Law Amendment Committee, *Report* (Cmnd 2657, 1926) para 84–85. Johnston at 425, notes that 'Despite the controversial nature of statutory provisions that allow the compulsory purchase of property, they seem to have provoked little debate, and the proposal received no substantial discussion in Parliament', and that it was not until the Financial Services Act 1986 that minority shareholders were given the corresponding right to require a purchase of their shares.

In addition to enclosure and estate bills, there were also Irish precedents on enfranchisement.[104] The most important was the Land Purchase (Ireland) Act 1903 (the 'Wyndham Land Act'), which set up a scheme under which government provided tenants with loans to finance a purchase of the freehold. Alongside this, it supplemented the tenants' payments with additional payments to landlords, to make the price attractive to them.[105] To be sure, the Act did not provide a constitutional precedent for enfranchisement, because it did not give tenants compulsory powers to purchase the freehold. However, it did show that Parliament could take the view that general enfranchisement would produce a wider public benefit.

In England and especially in Wales, the issue became more acute after World War II, when many 99-year residential leases were approaching the end of their term. In 1948, the Lord Chancellor appointed the Leasehold Committee to consider the issue. It reported to Parliament in 1950.[106] By this point, the arguments for and against compulsory enfranchisement were well-rehearsed. The majority's primary constitutional objection concerned the degree of scrutiny regarding the use of compulsory purchase powers for private purposes. With a private bill, a parliamentary committee would check that the public benefit was sufficient to warrant the grant of compulsory powers. With public Acts that gave Ministers the power to issue compulsory purchase orders, there were procedures for Parliament to scrutinise the purposes of specific orders. With compulsory enfranchisement, there would be no such scrutiny for specific enfranchisements. Indeed, it was not clear that a tenant would be required to show, to anyone, that their own enfranchisement served some wider public interest beyond their private interest. The majority claimed that the moral case for general enfranchisement was not strong enough, as it could not be said that every landlord–tenant relationship was unjust or that putting land in the hands of tenants 'would be used to the greater benefit of the community than would have been the case if it had remained in the hands of the landlords'.[107] There might be a case for general enfranchisement if either one could be shown, but the majority did not accept that there was. In terms of general

[104] R Walsh and L Fox O'Mahony, 'Land Law, Property Ideologies and the British–Irish Relationship' (2018) 47 *Common Law World Review* 7, 7–19; P Bull, *Land, Politics & Nationalism: A Study of the Irish Land Question* (Gill & MacMillan, 1996); T Dooley, 'Land and Politics in Independent Ireland, 1923–48: The Case for Reappraisal' (2004) 34 *Irish Historical Studies* 175. There were also precedents from the colonies: see ED Steele, 'Ireland and the Empire in the 1860s. Imperial Precedents for Gladstone's First Irish Land Act' (1968) 11 *Historical Journal* 64; P Singh Aulakh, 'British Empire, Land Tenure and the Search for an Ideal Proprietor: 1868–1875' PhD thesis (York University, 2022). The Land Purchase Act 1875, SPEI 1875, c 32 of Prince Edward Island, which authorised compulsory enfranchisement of an absentee landlord class, was described by Sir Graham Montgomery in the House of Commons as a 'dangerous precedent' but James Lowther, the Undersecretary of State for the Colonies, pointed out that the Colonial Office had already given up its power of disallowance over legislation from Prince Edward Island: see HC Deb 23 July 1875, vol 225, cols 1954–56; Steele, ibid; and R Bitterman and M McCallum, 'Upholding the Land Legislation of a "Communistic and Socialist Assembly": The Benefits of Confederation for Prince Edward Island' (2006) 87 *Canadian Historical Review* 1.

[105] Bull, ibid 152–75.

[106] Leasehold Committee, *Final Report* (Cmd 7982, 1950).

[107] ibid para 76.

policy, it said that 'the leasehold system is a convenient – and even an essential – feature of our real property law'.[108]

Following the Leasehold Committee's report, the Conservative Government brought forward the Landlord and Tenant Bill, which passed into law in 1954. It provided greater security of tenure and compensation for improvements but left out enfranchisement. As enfranchisement was not part of the Bill, the constitutional aspects were not debated in Parliament. However, any constitutional objections to general schemes of compulsory enfranchisement were resolved by the Leasehold Reform Act 1967. Indeed, in the 1966 general election, both main parties supported enfranchisement schemes. The crucial difference between them concerned compensation: they both said that compensation should be 'fair' but disagreed on what this required. Labour won the election and set out its policy in the 1966 White Paper.[109] In essence, they took the view that the freeholder should only be entitled to the site value of the land, excluding the value of any buildings on the land: 'The price of enfranchisement must be calculated in accordance with the principle that in equity the bricks and mortar belong to the qualified leaseholder and the land to the landlord.'[110] This was reflected in clause 9 of the Bill, which became section 9 of the Leasehold Reform Act 1967. There was, of course, no legal or equitable title to the 'bricks and mortar', but only a moral claim arising from the tenant's obligation to maintain the building. In Labour's view, the tenant had paid for the buildings by the end of the lease and hence should not be required to pay for them again when acquiring the freehold.

The clause was attacked by the Conservatives in Parliament on a number of grounds, largely echoing the concerns of the majority in the Leasehold Committee's report of 1950: that this was confiscation; that it was taking from one individual for another; that it interfered with existing contracts; and that it was retrospective because it altered the laws in place at the time that the contracts were made. In the Lords, Lord Stow Hill for Labour argued that there were precedents on all points.[111] The Bill was not confiscatory as it was not unfair to deny compensation for unearned value. The point about expropriation between private parties was clearly not unprecedented, given the long history of private Acts authorising the same.[112] The modification of private contracts 'has been done over and over again

[108] ibid.

[109] Minister of Land and Natural Resources, *Leasehold Reform in England and Wales* (Cmnd 2916, 1966) para 11. For the Conservative policy, see I Dale, *Conservative Party General Election Manifestos, 1900–1997* (Psychology Press, 2000) 170, 172: the manifesto stated that a Conservative government would 'Legislate to allow ground leaseholders to buy or rent their houses on fair terms except where the property is to be redeveloped.'

[110] Minister of Land and Natural Resources, ibid.

[111] HL Deb 26 June 1957, vol 284, col 38. Lord Aberdare said that the precedents were not relevant because they did not allow one person to expropriate another, and because they were not retrospective: HL Deb 26 June 1957, vol 284, cols 66–69. Neither point really stands up to scrutiny in terms of statutory precedent but Lord Aberdare did not specifically raise the constitutional aspect.

[112] To be sure, a number of enfranchisement bills had been introduced but not enacted. Lord Shackleton (Minister without Portfolio) stated that 'Since 1884 there has been a series of

when Parliament thinks that a contract does not work fairly as between the two parties to it'. He cited the 'whole pattern of the Rent Restrictions Acts dating back to 1915' as well as the Moneylenders Act 1927, the Restrictive Trade Practices Act 1956 and the Landlord and Tenant Act 1954.[113] Given that there were precedents on many points, and that the Conservative Party had included enfranchisement in its manifesto, it was clear that the controversy was more one of policy than constitutional principle. Indeed, although some Conservative governments after 1967 secured amendments to the Act, they did not challenge the fundamental principles of enfranchisement and compensation. In addition, the Conservative Government successfully defended the Act before the European Court of Human Rights.[114] This suggests that the constitutional standards, such as they are, impose a very low threshold. They direct Parliament's attention to fairness, for which it may wish to consider questions such as the source of value, but the constitution does not specify an answer to those questions: only that Parliament may wish to consider them. Moreover, the public interest requirement need not be satisfied for every compulsory purchase. It seems that Parliament is satisfied if the scheme, taken as a whole, would be beneficial to the public.

E. Post-1967 Developments

Since the Leasehold Reform Act 1967, there have been no changes to the law of compulsory purchase that have stepped outside the existing precedents. The compensation scheme of the Town and Country Planning Act 1947 was repealed by the Town and Country Planning Act 1959, but instead of creating a new set of rules, it revived the rules of the 1919 Act. These are still in force (except for compulsory purchase under the Leasehold Reform Act 1967). In 2004, the Law Commission published a detailed review of the law on compulsory purchase and compensation.[115] However, it did not recommend radical change. In particular, it stated that 'fair compensation' should remain the fundamental principle.[116] Its recommendations were aimed more at achieving greater clarity in the law than changing the position of landowners or promoters of schemes.

Labour's 2019 manifesto, *It's Time for Real Change*, stated that 'Labour will set up a new English Sovereign Land Trust, with powers to buy land more cheaply for low-cost housing.'[117] In its Green Paper, *Housing for the Many*, it said that the Trust would 'work with local authorities to enable more proactive buying of land at

enfranchisement Bills: there were 14 between 1884 and 1929, but only one reached the Statute Book; that is, the Places of Worship (Enfranchisement) Act 1920': HL Deb 26 June 1967, vol 284, col 15.

[113] HL Deb 26 June 1957, vol 284, col 38.

[114] *James v United Kingdom* (1986) Series A no 98.

[115] Law Commission, *Towards a Compulsory Purchase Code* (Law Com Nos 286 and 291, 2004).

[116] ibid xiii.

[117] Labour Party, *It's Time for Real Change: The Labour Party Manifesto 2019* (Labour Party, 2019) 78.

a price closer to existing use value. As part of this we will consider changes to the rules governing the compensation paid to landowners.'[118] Payment of existing use value would have fallen within the scope of precedents set by the Town and Country Planning Act 1947. However, as a political matter, it is likely that applying the existing use value would be much more controversial than when it was first introduced in 1947. Nevertheless, it is worth noting that the Conservative Government was also considering changes that would have restricted compensation. In an independent report commissioned by the Chancellor, Sir Oliver Letwin proposed that local planning authorities could insist on diversity (a minimum proportion of affordable housing) for large housing developments, with the intended effect that this would limit compensation to around 10 times the existing use value.[119] The report stated that compensation would be for 'perhaps as little as 5% of the current residual development value of a straightforward site with unconstrained development permission and no major infrastructure requirements in an area of high housing demand'.[120] This would still be far more generous to owners than Labour's plan but nonetheless it would be considerably less generous than the current rules, as they require consideration of all potential uses of land for which planning might have been granted. The Government set out its position on Letwin's report in a written statement to the House of Commons. James Brokenshire, the Secretary of State for the Ministry of Housing Communities and Local Government, noted that 'many in the housing-building industry are sceptical of this approach' but nonetheless agreed that 'the costs of increased housing diversification should be funded through reductions in residual land values'.[121] He did not commit the Government to any specific action and there have been no legislative proposals along the lines of the Report's recommendations. Nevertheless, he did not rule out the recommendations on the basis that they would be so unfair as to be unconstitutional. It appears that there is at least some common ground that the current rules sometimes provide more compensation than what is needed to be fair, and that they can also obstruct developments that serve important public interests.

IV. Conclusion

Compulsory purchase raises matters of principle: landowners should be entitled to fair compensation for their loss, and to challenge both the valuation and the legitimacy of the purpose of the acquisition before an independent body. None of these principles have been subject to a serious challenge in Parliament. There

[118] Labour Party, *Housing for the Many: A Labour Party Green Paper* (Labour Party, 2018) 22, available at https://labourhousing.org/wp-content/uploads/2019/05/Labour-Party-Green-Paper-Housing-for-the-Many.pdf.
[119] Sir Oliver Letwin, *Independent Review of Build Out: Final Report* (CM 9270, 2018) para 4.4.
[120] ibid para 4.17.
[121] HC Deb 13 March 2019, vol 656, col 20WS.

have, of course, been re-examinations of them. Valuation has been adjusted and re-adjusted, and the process of assessing compensation and the case for compulsory purchase is now handled by administrative bodies with rights of appeal to the Lands Tribunal.

The surprising aspect of the development of the law is the extent of agreement between government and opposition, even over fairly controversial issues. Party politics did not arise in the consideration of private bills (and still does not arise, in the trickle of bills that still come before Parliament). The modifications to compensation in the Acquisition of Land (Assessment of Compensation) Act 1919 had cross-party support, as did the Town and Country Planning Act 1947. Both Labour and Conservative members had reservations on leasehold enfranchisement until the 1960s, when both parties favoured it. The compensation provisions of the Leasehold Reform Act 1967 were controversial, but ultimately the Conservatives did not repeal them when in power and defended them before the European Court of Human Rights in 1986.[122] In private law, they backed the Landlord and Tenant Act 1954, which brought in rent controls and greater security of tenure for tenants. The proposals for more radical reforms, such as land nationalisation or the redistribution of land for peasant ownership, did not occur, but it seems that they did not hold strong support in the Labour party in any case. At most, they were seen as a distant goal rather than an immediate objective. In the long evolution of land law, there has been sufficient common ground that reforms can be accommodated within the constitutional standards.

[122] *James v United Kingdom* (n 114).

4

Nationalisation

The nationalisation of an industry is a relatively modern activity. It was not until the nineteenth century that governments sought powers to nationalise industries by the compulsory purchase of private enterprises. Before then, the Crown or Parliament did create or authorise the creation of monopolies over specific sectors, and many of these enterprises had characteristics of both public and private enterprises, as we would understand them now: the Post Office and chartered companies such as the East India Company are the leading examples. However, the first modern example of Parliament authorising the acquisition of enterprises for the purpose of creating a state monopoly did not arise until the Lighthouses Act 1836. Since then, there have been many other examples. The debates on these bills raised constitutional standards, especially in relation to the provision of compensation for owners. This chapter therefore considers the development and relevance of these standards. It adopts a chronological structure, beginning with the nationalisations of the Victorian period through to World War II. In most of these cases, it was a Conservative Government, or at least a government dominated by Conservatives, that introduced the nationalisation bill. The nationalisation programme of the Attlee Government is then considered. It departed from the earlier precedents, in that nationalisation was intended to restructure the economy: it was not merely a means to save an ailing sector or enterprise. The Attlee Government's legislation produced very contentious debates, but there was a remarkable degree of cross-party agreement that owners should receive 'fair compensation' or 'fair and equitable compensation'. The chapter then considers the interpretation of 'fair compensation' in relation to the Callaghan Government's nationalisation of the aircraft and shipbuilding industry, before a discussion of Labour's 2019 election manifesto. The final section departs from the focus on the position of owners, as it considers the position of third parties – especially employees – who may suffer loss as a result of the nationalisation.

I. Nationalisations before 1945

Public enterprises played a significant role in the United Kingdom (UK) long before the Attlee Government's nationalisation programme. Indeed, the road network and the Post Office were established before the division between public and private sectors was as sharp as it is now. The early chartered companies (especially those operating overseas) combined elements of modern commercial companies, state enterprises and local government. By the Victorian period and through to World War II, many municipalities were engaged in a wide range of activity, including ports, water and sewerage works, local passenger transport, telephone networks, electricity, schools, and local medical services and hospitals.[1] Many of these municipal enterprises were nationalised during the twentieth century. Local public bodies were not compensated, except to relieve them of debts associated with the assets.[2] Hence, the valuation of property or recourse to independent arbitration did not arise in at least some cases.

For most nationalisations, however, central bodies did make significant acquisitions from private owners. In some cases, acquisitions were from both local authorities and commercial companies. The Central Electricity Board and the National Health Service were examples, as both municipalities and commercial companies were active in the sectors.[3] The local authorities did not receive compensation (except to relieve their financial obligations) but the companies did. In other cases, acquisitions were primarily or entirely from the private sector. This was true of the most important nationalisations prior to the Attlee programme, including the Post Office's acquisition of the telegraph industry under the Telegraph Acts 1868 and 1869 and the telephone network under the Telephone Transfer Act 1911. In the capital, the Metropolis Water Act 1902, the Port of London Act 1908 and the London Passenger Transport Act 1933 transferred the water supply network, the port and then the passenger transport networks from private operators to new public sector bodies.[4] Unworked coal was nationalised from private owners under the Coal Act 1938.[5] The railways were not nationalised until after World War II, but a compulsory amalgamation was carried out under the Railways Act 1921.[6]

[1] S Webb and B Potter Webb, *English Local Government: Statutory Authorities for Special Purposes* (Longmans, Green, 1922); KD Tennent and others, 'Blending Public and Private: British Municipal Trading c. 1889–1975' (2020) 2020 *Academy of Management Proceedings* 20352; JR Kellett, 'Municipal Socialism, Enterprise and Trading in the Victorian City' (1978) 5 *Urban History* 36. On specific sectors, see JL Kieve, *The Electric Telegraph: A Social and Economic History* (David and Charles, 1973); AN Holcombe, 'The Telephone in Great Britain' (1906) 21 *Quarterly Journal of Economics* 96; D Foulkes, 'The Post Office and Its Services' (1980) 11 *Cambrian Law Review* 11; WM Stern, 'Water Supply in Britain: The Development of a Public Service' (1954) 74 *Journal of the Royal Sanitary Institute* 998.

[2] M Bell Cairns, 'Some Legal Aspects of Compensation for Nationalized Assets' (1951) 16 *Law and Contemporary Problems* 594, 611.

[3] The Central Electricity Board was created under the Electricity (Supply) Act 1926, to acquire and manage the national grid. The National Health Service Act 1946, National Health Service (Scotland) Act 1947 and the Health Services Act (Northern Ireland) 1948 created the structures for the health service in each country.

[4] See F Trentmann and V Taylor, 'From Users to Consumers: Water Politics in Nineteenth Century London' in F Trentmann (ed), *The Making of the Consumer: Knowledge, Power and Identity in the Modern World* (Berg, 2006) 55.

[5] Coal Mines Act 1930 also included provisions on compulsory amalgamation, but they were subject to conditions that made it virtually impossible to apply in practice.

[6] See G Crompton, 'The Railway Companies and the Nationalisation Issue 1920–50' in R Millward and J Singleton (eds), *The Political Economy of Nationalisation in Britain, 1920–1950*, 1st edn

The production of beet sugar was nationalised in 1937 under the Sugar Industry (Reorganisation) Act 1936[7] and the British Overseas Airways Act 1939 nationalised the airlines.[8]

With acquisitions from private owners, negotiations regarding compensation were often completed before the introduction of the bill in Parliament. The bill therefore merely stated the agreed price without setting out the principles that guided negotiations. Parliament had little opportunity to question or amend the terms of compensation.[9] Nevertheless, if asked, Ministers invariably justified the price, on the basis that it was a fair price for both sides. Furthermore, if agreement had not been reached with some of the targets, the bill would include specific provisions on valuation and arbitration. In some cases, the legislation incorporated the principles for the compulsory purchase of land.[10] Where there was no reference to land acquisition, the legislation would be based on the principle of fair compensation. An early example was the nationalisation of lighthouses in 1836, which provided that compensation (if not agreed) would be set by a local jury, which would hear witnesses and give a verdict 'for the true, fair and just Value of such Lighthouse … having regard to the Rights, Benefits, and Advantages resulting to the Proprietors from the Enjoyment thereof'.[11] The price was usually set as the average annual net maintainable revenue of the enterprise over a set period, multiplied by the 'years of purchase'. As discussed in chapter three, 20 years' purchase had become a fairly standard measure for land and hence it was often the figure used for nationalisation.[12] In most cases, payment took the form of interest-bearing securities issued by the new public enterprise. In the abstract, this appeared to be a good bargain on both sides. In practice, however, valuations were often quite

(Cambridge University Press, 1995); DCH Watts, 'On the Causes of British Railway Nationalisation: A Re-Examination of the Causes, 1866–1921' (2002) 16 *Contemporary British History* 1.

[7] Sugar Industry (Reorganisation) Act 1936; see PE Hart, 'Competition and Control in the British Sugar Industry' (1953) 5 *Oxford Economic Papers* 317. It was the processing of raw sugar from sugar beet that was nationalised.

[8] RDS Higham, 'The British Government and Overseas Airlines, 1918–1939' (1959) 26 *Journal of Air Law and Commerce*; AJ Quin-Harkin, 'Imperial Airways, 1924–50' (1954) 1 *Journal of Transport History* 197.

[9] See JL Kieve, *The Electric Telegraph: A Social and Economic History* (David and Charles, 1973) 174: 'The direct negotiation between the Post Office and the companies, by-passing parliament, and, in fact, presenting it with a virtual fait accompli, was damaging to the control it had over the spending of public money.' See below, text to n 21, on the negotiations for the acquisition of the telephone network from the National Telephone Company: Parliament did approve negotiation principles by resolution before the final agreement was reached.

[10] See, eg, Telegraph Act 1869, s 10(3).

[11] Lighthouses Act 1836, s 7; see J Taylor, 'Private Property, Public Interest, and the Role of the State in Nineteenth-Century Britain: The Case of the Lighthouses' (2001) 44 *Historical Journal* 749.

[12] Chapter three, text to n 25. It was, however, less generous than the Railway Regulation Act 1844, section 1, which provided that railway lines established after its enactment would be subject to a purchase option in favour of the Treasury, exercisable 21 years from 1 January after the passing of the Act, at 25 years' purchase of the average profits in the three years preceding the exercise of the option. On the Act in general, see M Bailey, 'The 1844 Railway Act: A Violation of Laissez-Faire Political Economy?' (2004) 12 *History of Economic Ideas* 7.

generous to the owners. In theory, the determination of the revenue and years' purchase were questions for experts, but in practice, government negotiators could be sympathetic to arguments that poor financial years or forecasts should be excluded from consideration. The cautionary example was provided by the nationalisation of the telegraph network. The Act set compensation at 20 years' purchase, with additional amounts in some cases.[13] It is not clear how this formula was reached. In the Commons, William Fowler, a Liberal MP, claimed that the terms were 'improvident', as they were based on highly optimistic projections of revenue and insufficiently pessimistic views of the actual value of the existing assets.[14] The claims proved to be correct, as the telegraph business subsequently recorded very poor financial results over a long period. Indeed, in 1895, the Postmaster-General identified the burden of paying for the acquisition as one of the causes of the Post Office's financial difficulties.[15] However, the generosity of compensation did not raise constitutional issues. For the governments that introduced the bills, the gravity of interfering with rights of property required any questions over valuation to be resolved in favour of the owner.

The principle of generosity did not go entirely unchallenged. As discussed in chapter three, new rules in the Acquisition of Land (Assessment of Compensation) Act 1919 reflected a more balanced system for acquisitions of land by public authorities. This was also seen in some nationalisation Acts. An early expression of these principles appeared in the Tramways Act 1870. At that time, local authorities were authorised to grant 21 year concessions to private promoters for the construction and operation of street tramways. If the local authority did not renew the concession, and it wished to continue some or all the service, it could require the tramway company to sell such assets as it wished to acquire, at their existing value. The Act specifically provided that the price would not include 'any allowance for past or future profits of the undertaking, or any compensation for compulsory sale, or other consideration whatsoever'.[16] This followed from the expiry of the concession: without it, the tramway business could not operate. As there would be no future profits, there was no reason to compensate for lost income, and hence to calculate net maintainable revenue or set a figure for the years of purchase. Clearly, this was considerably less generous to the owners than the usual mode of valuation.

[13] The monopoly was later held to include the telephone, although it was not invented until after the 1869 Act: *Attorney-General v Edison Telephone Company of London Ltd* (1880–81) LR 6 QBD 244.

[14] HC Deb 26 July 1869, vol 198, col 747 (W Fowler); see also Kieve (n 1) 161–75 and S Fari, *Victorian Telegraphy Before Nationalization* (Springer, 2015) 189–90.

[15] Holcombe (n 1) 134; but see Sir E Murray, *The Post Office* (GP Putnam's Sons, 1927) 71: writing in 1927, he agreed that prices were excessive (especially as some companies received additional payments for specific purposes) but 'it is a fallacy to suppose that the existing telegraph deficit is attributable to the excessive price paid for the system'. Other factors, such as the subsidy to the news media, were more significant.

[16] Tramways Act 1870, s 43.

The debates on the Tramways Bill 1870 shows that the terms were not particularly controversial, despite being much less favourable to the companies.[17] So long as promoters were aware of the conditions on a concession before acceptance, there would be nothing unfair about the arrangement.[18] In effect, to the extent that there was a constitutional standard, it was the same as for negotiated compensation: consent is sufficient assurance that the constitutional rights of a property owner have been respected. In practice, however, 'tramway terms' were only used nationally for the takeover of the telephone network in 1911. The Post Office already held a monopoly over the telephone services, but it allowed private companies and municipalities to operate their own networks under licence.[19] By 1901, the Government had decided that it would nationalise the sector. The task was relatively simple because, by this time, the National Telephone Company had acquired virtually all the licences held by other operators. However, all of them would expire by 1911.[20] The Post Office opened negotiations with the company in 1904 and reached an agreement in 1905. Throughout, it negotiated on the basis of tramway terms. Parliament approved this approach by resolution in 1905 and then later when it enacted the Telephone Transfer Act 1911.[21] In 1911, when the Postmaster-General argued that there was nothing unfair about refusing payment for goodwill, past or future profits, or for the compulsory nature of the purchase 'because the company's business, as I say, existed solely by virtue of the licence held from the Postmaster-General, and if things were left to take their course, the whole business would come to a sudden stop on 31st December, 1911'.[22] This was not a controversial point. There were precedents for compensating for lost earnings on the termination of a licence, but it seems that they did not establish a parliamentary standard.[23]

A variation on this argument was made in relation to the takeover of the London water system. Various failings in the sector led to pressure for nationalisation,

[17] They were certainly less favourable that the terms that had been applied to other acquisitions on the expiry of a licence or similar grant of authority. The East India Stock Dividend Redemption Act 1873 provided shareholders with generous compensation on the expiry of the charter of the East India Company (the Act honoured the terms set out in the Government of India Act 1833 (later titled the St Helena Act 1833) regarding the termination of its monopolies).

[18] Instead, MPs focused on the practical impact on tramway development. The Government acknowledged that the terms might make it more difficult for some promoters to raise capital, but that that would be counter-balanced by allowing them a free hand in setting fares and dividends: see, eg, George Shaw-Lefevre (Parliamentary Secretary to the Board of Trade), HC Deb 1 March 1870, vol 199, cols 1083–84.

[19] In *Attorney-General v Edison Telephone Company of London Ltd* (1880–81) LR 6 QBD 24, the High Court held that the monopoly under the Telegraph Act 1869 already extended to the telephone network, but rather than take over the existing networks, the Post Office allowed them to continue under licence.

[20] See generally Holcombe (n 1); A Hazlewood, 'The Origin of the State Telephone Service in Britain' (1953) 5 *Oxford Economic Papers* 13, 17.

[21] See Murray (n 15).

[22] HC Deb 19 June 1911, vol 27, col 48.

[23] See the East India Company, above n 17.

with the London County Council (LCC) petitioning for private bills allowing it to take over the private water companies on several occasions in the 1890s.[24] Parliament did not enact the bills; instead, it authorised nationalisation under the Metropolis Water Act 1902, which provided that compensation would be agreed with the target companies, or failing agreement, by a Court of Arbitration.[25] The Court had authority to resolve matters referred to it, 'on such terms and in such manner as most just and fit'.[26] In relation to compensation, the Court was directed to apply 'with necessary modifications, the law of compensation for the purposes of the Lands Clauses Acts', but excluding the allowance for a compulsory sale and the impact of the Act on the market.[27] In this case, compensation would provide an income to shareholders equivalent to what they had been receiving from their companies. This was not without controversy, however. By this point, it was clear that generous compensation could cripple the new public enterprise. When the 1902 bill was introduced, the LCC and sympathetic MPs argued that compensation would be excessive, for several reasons. In relation to tramway terms, the LCC noted that the companies were operating under a statutory regime that granted them valuable rights, such as rights of access and pricing, that might be withdrawn by Parliament. The LCC therefore argued that their businesses were not as secure as ordinary private property, and that should affect their valuation. They proposed that valuation should be on 'special terms of arbitration', which would have directed the Court of Arbitration to take the political risk of a change of law into account. In formal terms, this was clearly not the same as tramway terms, where the expiry of the rights and licences would be certain without legislative intervention. Nevertheless, the idea of political risk reflected a broadly similar view of valuation. In effect, the LCC was arguing that, if tramway terms are legitimate in circumstances where a concession or licence expires, a similar principle should apply to any situation where there is real possibility of a significant change in the statutory regime. Or, put differently, the LCC was taking the view that there is no reason to compensate for value gained by the conferral of special statutory privileges. The LCC was dominated by Progressive councillors, and this view was consistent with the Liberal thinking that there should be no obligation to compensate on a compulsory purchase of land for value that had been created by the community rather than the owner. Prior to the 1902 Act, there were various bills presented to Parliament by the LCC or sympathetic MPs with clauses reflecting these ideas. For example, one of the proposals would have directed the 'arbitrators to take into account the probability of some legislative interference with the existing statutory rights of the companies which would affect their income'.[28] The Royal

[24] See generally Stern (n 1); Trentmann and Taylor (n 4).
[25] Metropolis Water Act 1902, s 2(2).
[26] ibid s 23(5).
[27] ibid s 23(8).
[28] Royal Commission on Water Supply within the Limits of the Metropolitan Water Companies, *Final Report of the Commissioners* (C (2nd series) 25, 1899) para 22.

Commission that made recommendations on the London water sector rejected this argument:

> It appears to us that any arbitration, to ascertain the value of these companies, must proceed upon the basis of these statutory rights; and, that the arbitrator should not take upon himself to consider whether Parliament would, or might, curtail them, and, therefore, to assign to the companies a lower compensation, on the ground of the probability of such interference with existing statutory rights.[29]

Ultimately, the 1902 Act followed this principle. Indeed, there have been no cases since then where the possibility of a change in the statutory regime has been used to justify a reduction in compensation.

The refusal to consider political risk highlights another point about valuation. That is, fair compensation in these cases did not necessarily follow the market or accounting measures of value. Political risk might lower these values, but compensation was not simply aimed at providing a financial equivalent, but at recognising the interference with individual rights.

There could be circumstances in which fairness might require more than the financial equivalent. Equally, it might justify something less than the equivalent. This had already arisen in relation to the compulsory purchase of land. As noted in chapter three, under the Housing of the Working Classes Act 1890, Parliament allowed lower compensation in cases of residential housing that did not meet the statutory standards.[30] The LCC raised similar questions of conduct and moral entitlement in relation to the water companies. It argued, firstly, that the average income to shareholders was inflated because the companies had been paying out unsustainable dividends. Hence, compensation would also be inflated. Secondly, the companies were guilty of serious under-investment, with the result that the new Water Board would find that the cost of basic catch-up maintenance would make it impossible to invest in the required improvements. Again, they saw these as valid reasons for 'special terms of arbitration'. These arguments were also rejected by Parliament, just as they had been rejected by the Royal Commission that was appointed to investigate the situation. Very little was said in Parliament about the terms of compensation, but the Royal Commission acknowledged that special terms of arbitration would not have been unprecedented, as departures from the ordinary rules had already been permitted under the 1890 and 1894 Acts. However, the Commission did not think the situations were comparable, as the housing legislation dealt with owners who had allowed their property to become a danger to public health. Here, 'The companies have, upon the whole, performed their duties to the public satisfactorily and well.'[31] There was evidence that this was not the case, but clearly the Commission and the Government took the view that it would be unfair to modify the standard unless the misconduct was extreme.

[29] ibid para 46.
[30] See chapter three, section III.A.
[31] Royal Commission Report (n 28) para 48.

A final point concerning fair compensation and the pre-World War II nationalisations arose in the negotiations for the acquisition of the National Telephone Company's assets. The Government acknowledged that it might have been able to obtain better terms if it had pressed its negotiating position. However, it clearly believed that it would be inappropriate, and perhaps not constitutionally permissible, to negotiate beyond the point of fair treatment. In the 1905 debate on the agreement, Austen Chamberlain, Chancellor and previous Postmaster-General, explained the Government's policy to Parliament as follows:

> The Post Office agreed to buy on the terms which were known as 'tramway terms,' which were the fairest terms that had yet been devised to meet the case of a transfer of private property to the public. Those terms provided that the Post Office should pay only on the value of the property as it existed at the transfer. *Less than those terms would not be fair to the company; and therefore less than those terms they ought not to ask the company to accept.* They were the fairest terms that the Post Office could possibly secure (emphasis added).[32]

The Company's position was not necessarily that weak, because without its equipment, the Post Office would have been forced to acquire new assets from other sellers, potentially at a higher cost. At least at first glance, the negotiation was between two parties of equal strength and the Post Office should have sought the lowest possible price.[33]

This concern with fairness was most obvious in the debates on the London Passenger Transport Act 1933, which transferred transport undertakings to the new London Passenger Transport Board. For most of the target companies, the Bill merely stated the price of acquisition, as it had already been agreed in negotiations with the target companies. Indeed, in many of these cases, the price was agreed before the economic depression of the early 1930s, which had significantly reduced the value of the undertakings. One might have thought that the Government would have re-negotiated or abandoned the agreements to reflect the changed economic conditions before asking Parliament to approve their terms. The Marquess of Londonderry, as Secretary of State for Air, introduced the Bill in the Lords and sought to refute such arguments:

> Finally, I would ask any who are tempted to question the settlements made with the existing undertakings, on the ground that they were made before the present depression, whether they consider that it would be either fair or reasonable to claim that these vast enterprises, in which great amounts of capital have been sunk, should be forcibly bought out on the basis of their earning capacity in a time of extreme depression. Surely that would be confiscatory action of the most unjustifiable description, a course to which no Government commanding the support of Conservative opinion would be a party.[34]

[32] HC Deb 9 August 1905, vol 151, col 860.

[33] Although an article in the National Telephone Company's journal stated that 'the Postmaster-General drove the Company to make what it thought was a very hard bargain' and 'the terms were very favourable to the State': A Anns, 'The History of the National Telephone Company: Part III' (1911) 6 *National Telephone Journal* 208, 218.

[34] HL Deb 1 March 1933, vol 86, col 925.

The Marquess did not explain why paying a price that reflected the value of the assets at the point of vesting would be 'confiscatory action'. His concern might have been fairness of equality as between owners, given that negotiations had already been concluded regarding some undertakings, on the basis of revenues prior to the depression.[35] In any case, not surprisingly, there was very little opposition from the companies or Conservative backbenchers. Indeed, for the companies, it is difficult to imagine a better deal.[36] For Conservative MPs, only a generous compensation package would counterbalance the intrusion on fundamental rights that was inflicted by a compulsory purchase.

Overall, in the pre-Attlee period, there was general agreement on that Parliament should be guided by a principle of 'fair compensation' on nationalisation. This took into account both fairness in terms of counterbalancing the loss of a specific owner and the equity of treatment across owners in general. In addition, there were signs that Parliament agreed that Ministers and civil servants should apply a principle of 'fair negotiation'. It was also reasonably clear that, for many MPs, fairness was something more than financial equivalence. Accounting and market measures of value were relevant, but they did not necessarily capture the impact of the loss of consent; neither would they capture serious misconduct by the owner. Both of these were factors that Parliament might wish to take into account. However, it was not settled how the different factors might come into play. At least for Conservative MPs, it seemed that choices in valuation should be exercised in favour of the owner, so that market and accounting measures represented a minimum that might be increased in some cases.

II. The Post-World War II Nationalisation Programme

The Labour manifesto for the 1945 election, *Let Us Face the Future*, set out an ambitious programme for nationalisating the fuel and power industries, inland transport, the iron and steel industries and the Bank of England.[37] Labour's programme departed from previous nationalisations, as it was aimed at

[35] See London Passenger Transport Act 1933, s 14(2): the arbitration tribunal should 'have regard to the nature and value and the consideration paid for the transfer of any other undertaking or part of an undertaking (other than as aforesaid) transferred by this Act, whether that consideration is fixed by this Act or by agreement under this Act.' In the Commons, Labour criticised the provision as unclear and likely to favour the companies; the Attorney-General defended it as fair and equitable: HC Deb 5 December 1932, vol 272, cols 1323–39.

[36] Although Lord Banbury, a shareholder of one of the companies to be nationalised, complained that it was not generous enough: HL Deb 1 March 1933, vol 86, cols 938–39.

[37] D Kavanagh, I Dale and I Dale Nfa, *Labour Party General Election Manifestos 1900–1997* (Taylor & Francis Group, 2000) vol 2, 51–60. See generally R Kelf-Cohen, *British Nationalisation 1945–1973* (Springer, 1973); NV Joy, 'Fair Compensation Under the British Labor Government' (1950) 65 *Political Science Quarterly* 538; Cairns (n 2); FRD, 'British Nationalization of Industry. Compensation to Owners of Expropriated Property' (1949) 97 *University of Pennsylvania Law Review* 520; WS Buckingham, 'Compensation and Profits in British Nationalized Industries' (1953) 8 *Journal of Finance* 422.

restructuring the economy rather than supporting sectors that were struggling and faced structural issues that could not be resolved. Hence, the post-War programme made it clear that there was no general constitutional principle that it was limited to these cases. Rather, it was seen as a political choice.

The manifesto provided very little detail on the process or terms of nationalisation, except that the targets would be 'taken over on a basis of fair compensation'.[38] As noted in the previous section, this reflected the practice going back to the Lighthouses Act 1836, and earlier, in relation to the compulsory purchase of land. Indeed, so far as the terms of acquisition were concerned, very little about the post-War nationalisation programme was novel. To be sure, all parties believed that there was much more at stake than with the preceding nationalisations. Nevertheless, despite the political stakes, the post-War legislation followed the legislative models used by Conservative and Conservative-dominated governments of the pre-World War II era. This was largely a pragmatic decision, as it allowed the Government to prepare bills quickly. There had, of course, been extensive discussions within Labour circles about nationalisation long before the 1945 election, but they focused on identifying targets for nationalisation and their subsequent governance rather than the process of acquisition or the constitutional standards that might be relevant.[39] Emanuel Shinwell, the Minister of Fuel and Power, who led on the nationalisation of the coal industry in 1946 and electricity in 1947, explained that 'I had believed, as many other members had, that in the Party archives a blue-print [for nationalisation] was ready' but instead he found that 'nothing practical and tangible existed'.[40]

Accordingly, once the Government accepted the principle of fair compensation, the earlier legislation could be used as models for the Labour legislation. One of the most important features of early models concerned the mode of payment: with earlier acquisitions, it was provided in the form of interest-bearing securities issued by the new public enterprise. In theory, there would be no cost to the Treasury, as the debt would be that of the new public enterprise, which it could cover the cost from its revenue. It is worth noting, however, that it was not a foregone conclusion that Labour would accept 'fair compensation' as the general standard. Indeed, in the debates on the Coal Bill 1938, a number of Labour MPs strongly opposed the provision of any compensation for the nationalisation of unworked coal.[41] In the House of Commons, Shinwell acknowledged

[38] Kavanagh, Dale and Nfa, ibid 56.

[39] See also Kelf-Cohen (n 37) 19–20.

[40] E Shinwell, *Conflict Without Malice* (Odhams Press, 1955) 172–73.

[41] See, eg, J Griffiths, HC Deb 22 November 1937, vol 329, col 926: 'I believe that if the State or an individual purchases something from a man or a corporation which has produced that thing, compensation is due. Compensation should only take place when a man or a body of men sells something which they have produced to somebody else. The royalty owners have not produced the coal. They have no moral claim to it. They have no social claim to it. I make no bones about it. What we would like is a Bill saying that on and after a certain date the coal would revert to its real owners, the nation.' See also Joseph Batey, HC Deb 22 November 1937, vol 329, col 955: 'I do not think royalty owners should receive a penny from the Government or from industry.'

that the policy of 'fair compensation' had met opposition within the party, as he explained:

> We have sought to be fair in this matter [compensation]. I have been under pressure from certain quarters not to afford compensation at all. Hon Members opposite must not be under any illusion; there is a substantial body of opinion in this country which is opposed to compensation .... indeed there was a time in the Labour Movement when compensation was regarded as a mistaken policy. We are much more reasonable nowadays, but we must not be too generous with public money.[42]

Although the manifesto said very little, it was clear that 'fair compensation' was intended to cover the owner's loss. At no point did the Labour leadership suggest that owners should not be compensated for their loss. Moreover, the legislation did not distinguish value generated by the enterprise's own investment from value generated by government subsidy or the community as a whole. The idea of community-generated value would be central to the land acquisition and betterment policies under the Town and Country Planning 1947, and it was reflected in the land tax scheme of the People's Budget of 1909. However, it was not part of the valuation principles of the nationalisation of industry. Nevertheless, the manner of calculating the loss proved controversial with many of the nationalisation bills.

Where a new state corporation took over the corporate entity, valuation was based on the willing buyer–willing seller model.[43] If the shares were listed, the average Stock Exchange price was set over a fixed reference period.[44] This followed the precedent set by the Emergency Powers (Defence) Act 1939 and Regulations 55 and 78 of the Defence (General) Regulations, 1939, with the price for shares set at the average Stock Exchange price over a fixed reference period or periods.[45] Where the new corporation took over assets instead, the prices were set at the market value; if the acquisition destroyed a business, there could also be compensation for the loss of goodwill.[46] Other methods were also used. With the Bank of England, compensation was in the form of interest-bearing government stock, with the amount of stock providing an income equal to the average gross dividend in the 20 years prior to 31 March 1945.[47] With the coal nationalisation, there was an elaborate process of valuing all assets across the industry to obtain a global value, which was then apportioned across the companies.[48] This method of setting a global figure was not novel: it was applied in the nationalisation of coal reserves under the Coal Act 1938.[49] In all cases, compensation was payable in the form

[42] HC Deb 13 May 1946, vol 422, col 1542.
[43] Cable and Wireless Act 1946, s 2; Gas Act 1948, s 31.
[44] Transport Act 1947, s 17; Electricity Act 1947, s 20; Gas Act 1948, s 25; Iron and Steel Act 1949, s 15 (with arbitration in anomalous cases).
[45] On Regulations 55 and 78, see *Short v Treasury Commissioners* [1948] AC 534.
[46] Transport Act 1947: railway wagons were purchased at market value (s 30); the same applied to road haulage assets, with an additional allowance in some cases for loss of goodwill (s 47).
[47] Bank of England Act 1946, s 1.
[48] Coal Industry Nationalisation Act 1946, s 10.
[49] See JHA Lang, 'The Coal Act, 1938' (1939) 2 *MLR* 301; Cairns (n 2) 598–99.

of securities, rather than cash (except for the acquisitions of assets, where the amounts were small). The securities were not freely transferable or redeemable for set periods, to avoid flooding the market. For example, the securities provided to Bank of England shareholders were not redeemable until 1966.

All of these schemes, according to the Government, provided 'fair compensation' to the owners. It was variety itself that was the point of criticism. As Ned Vernon Joy explains,

> Nearly all of the criticism of the government's compensation policies, both in the press and in Parliament, appears to be based on an assumption that there exists a simple, almost mechanical device for arriving at an objectively valid 'fair price' for the assets of the nationalized industries. Had the Labor Government but been willing to apply this device, the argument runs, then the owners of the socialized industries could have been compensated accordingly and the pledge of fair compensation would have been fulfilled.[50]

Joy concluded by saying that 'The trouble with this argument is that no such device exists.'[51] Indeed, this was the view of the Government. When explaining the compensation provisions of the Bank of England Bill, the Chancellor, Hugh Dalton, said that:

> I desire to emphasise that, though these terms of compensation … are fair and appropriate in this particular case, they are not to be regarded as a precedent for any subsequent measure of nationalisation. The terms of compensation must vary from one instance to another, according to the merits of each case.[52]

But even the Conservative MPs who accepted that the principles had to accommodate the circumstances were suspicious that valuation methods were chosen with a view to minimising the cost. Instead, they argued in favour of Conservative pre-War nationalisations, where the choice of valuation method favoured the owners.

There were several points of criticism aimed at specific methods of valuation. The first concerned the use of markets, especially the Stock Exchange, as a measure of value. In the debates on the Iron and Steel Bill, Sir John Anderson stated that 'The Stock Exchange value reflects human weakness and error. It is essentially subjective and not objective.'[53] Anderson did not reject share prices for all companies: if, for example, the shareholder only held their shares with a view to making a profit on a sale, with no real interest in the underlying assets, it would be appropriate to use Stock Exchange prices to value their interest.[54] Indeed, Stock

[50] Joy (n 37) 553.
[51] ibid.
[52] HC Deb 29 October 1945, vol 415, cols 47; see also Joy (n 37) 541.
[53] HC Deb 16 November 1948, vol 458, cols 268–69.
[54] He did not explain how valuation could distinguish between these interests, except that he said that shareholders in some companies (such as the Bank of England) were not interested in the underlying assets, but shareholders in others (such as iron and steel companies) were.

Exchange valuation could be very generous, as shown by the terms of the Bank of England nationalisation, where former shareholders received compensation in the form of stock issued by the Bank and backed by a Treasury guarantee. The effect was to give the shareholders a capital gain, in addition to equivalent income with the Treasury guarantee.[55] However, it would not be appropriate when it was the underlying assets and business, rather than the shares, that were the real object of investment. The Government's response was that this would become impossibly complex to administer: not only would it be very difficult to determine the motivations of each shareholder, but it would be unfair to compensate them on different scales.[56] From the perspective of the opposition, this is where the principle of generosity came into play: the Government should choose the method of valuation that would be most generous to the shareholders, so as to ensure that none of them were under-compensated.

The second line of attack concerned the impact of the regulatory scheme on the valuation of a company. For example, during the War, the Government sought to persuade companies to keep dividends low, so as to increase the funds available for reinvestment. It was argued that this reduced share prices, and hence that they should not be used as a measure of value. The social democrats also challenged the liberal notion that there is a 'true' value of property that exists in the absence of regulation. For example, with the railways, there was general agreement that valuation should be based on profits or 'reasonable net maintainable revenue', but little agreement on the relevant period.[57] Profits before the War had been low but rose during the War, but were expected to be very poor in future without state support. Indeed, some companies would not have survived. The problem was that there was no unregulated state of affairs in the railway industry that might have provided a valuation. Ultimately, valuation was determined by Stock Exchange prices over a reference period.

The post-War Labour nationalisations ultimately provided little in the way of further elaboration of constitutional standards, despite their scope. Perhaps the most significant point was Labour's acceptance of the principles of fair compensation and independent valuation. The plethora of valuation methods suggests that 'fair compensation' gives a great deal of scope to governments and Parliament. Labour did not accept the Conservative arguments in favour of generosity, but neither did they accept the arguments of some Labour members that there was no obligation to provide any compensation, or even that there is some kind of trust-like or fiduciary obligation requiring governments to apply the method that would be most favourable to the taxpayer.

[55] See Joy (n 37) 540; Cairns (n 2) 602.

[56] HC Deb 16 November 1948, vol 458, cols 307–308, 309, 310.

[57] G Crompton, '"A Very Poor Bag of Assets": The Railway Compensation Issue 1921–47" (1996) 6 *Accounting, Business and Financial History* 73; T Allen, 'Liberalism, Social Democracy and the Value of Property under the European Convention on Human Rights' (2010) 59 *International and Comparative Law Quarterly* 1055, 1059–60.

III. Aircraft and Shipbuilding Industries Act 1977

Labour's manifesto for the February 1974 election stated that it would 'take shipbuilding, shiprepairing and marine engineering, ports, the manufacture of airframes and aeroengines into public ownership and control'.[58] It won the election and, on 31 July 1974, the Secretary State for Industry (Tony Benn) announced that a White Paper would be released later that year. Whilst there were few details, it did say that 'legislation will provide for fair compensation for the interests to be taken into public ownership'.[59] Labour did not secure a majority in the February election and a second election was called without a bill being put through Parliament. In its manifesto for this election, held on 10 October 1974, it repeated its commitment to public ownership.[60] Labour won the election and introduced a bill in November 1975.[61] There then followed a tortuous progress through Parliament. The first Bill was rejected by the House of Lords and then re-introduced in November 1976. This Bill was eventually passed as the Aircraft and Shipbuilding Industries Act 1977, but only after the Government reached an agreement with the Conservative leadership to leave out the nationalisation of the ship repair sector.[62]

As in the post-World War II nationalisations, compensation proved to be highly contentious. For companies with shares traded on a recognised stock exchange, compensation was based on the average price over a 'reference period' prior to the vesting date.[63] As noted above, this was the method used for several of the earlier nationalisations.[64] For companies without listed shares, compensation would be based on a 'hypothetical share price', which would be the value that shares would have had if they had been listed on an exchange in that period.[65] This was calculated as the company's average earnings over the reference period, multiplied by the typical price-earnings ratio of traded shares over that period.[66] In some cases, where companies held assets across sectors, the assets were acquired directly. Finally, the Act declared that valuation should ignore the impact of past and potential future financial support from the Government, even if the ordinary market would have taken that into account.

[58] Kavanagh, Dale and Nfa (n 37) 189.

[59] Department of Industry, *The Regeneration of British Industry* (Cmnd 5710, 1974).

[60] Kavanagh, Dale and Nfa (n 37) 201.

[61] A bill was introduced in April 1975, but there was insufficient time for it to be enacted before the end of the parliamentary session.

[62] The controversy over the applicability of the hybrid bill procedures is discussed in chapter two, section III.

[63] Aircraft and Shipbuilding Industries Act 1977, s 37; the reference period was between 1 September 1973 and the general election of 28 February 1974.

[64] Above text to nn 43–45.

[65] Aircraft and Shipbuilding Industries Act 1977, s 38(10).

[66] See the description in *Lithgow v United Kingdom* (1986) Series A no 106 para 36; see also M Mendelson, 'The United Kingdom Nationalization Cases and the European Convention on Human Rights' (1987) 57 *British Yearbook of International Law* 33.

On the face of it, the compensation provisions were broadly consistent with those of earlier nationalisations. The use of a price-earnings ratio was new, but arguably not substantially different to valuation based on net maintainable revenue and more likely to bring equity as between shares listed on the Stock Exchange and unlisted shares. Nevertheless, there were strong criticisms, especially in relation to unlisted shares.[67] These covered many different points. In particular, MPs argued that the reference period was long before the vesting date, which was contrary to the usual principle that property is valued as at the point of transfer.[68] The Government conceded the general point, but in response it stated that the reference period had to end before the 1974 general election, as that was the point at which nationalisation became a real possibility. If the reference period extended past the election, share prices would reflect speculation on nationalisation. The owners also argued that the hypothetical share price model for unlisted shares excluded the premium usually obtained on the sale of a controlling block.

As with the Attlee programme, the criticisms reflected a belief that the Government focused on reducing the cost of nationalisation at the expense of ensuring fairness. Taken in isolation, the rules may have appeared fair, but their cumulative effect could be quite harsh. For example, in some cases, shareholders received less than the company's cash reserves.[69] The opposition in the Lords, with its Conservative majority, was so strong that they returned the Bill with numerous amendments, most of which were aimed at increasing compensation for the owners. The Government and Commons rejected most of the amendments but ultimately made the key concession of dropping the ship repair business from the scope of nationalisation. Once that was done, the House of Lords agreed to let the Bill through.

The protracted length of the debates suggests that there was very little common ground between the parties. However, there were several points on which there was at least some agreement. The first is that compensation is only 'fair' if it is fair to both sides of the transaction. Precisely what this means is unclear, but at face value appears to reject the maximisation model, as implicitly advocated by some Conservative MPs, as it could be unfair to the acquiring body to apply principles that yield the highest possible price. It also reflects the importance of achieving equity across the owners. Lord Selsdon, for example, argued that compensation would not be 'fair' if some owners were treated more favourably than others.[70]

[67] This applied to most of the companies.

[68] The reference period closed 28 February 1974 but vesting was not until 29 April 1977 for the aircraft industry and 1 July 1977 for the shipbuilding industry.

[69] This seemed to be due to several factors. Companies with low earnings and low price-earnings ratios would receive a relatively low valuation, irrespective of their cash reserves. Moreover, the cash position did not reflect liabilities or advance payments received on contracts (see *Lithgow v United Kingdom* (n 66) paras 38 and 174). Finally, cash reserves were high at the point of vesting because the Government imposed restrictions on dividend payments and because companies were reluctant to invest their reserves pending vesting. In Parliament, these points were debated at length in the committee stage in the House of Lords: HL Deb 20 October 1976, vol 375, cols 1343–1463.

[70] See HL Deb 20 October 1976, vol 375, col 1425.

This focused largely on the valuation of unlisted shares. Share price valuation would be generous for holders of listed shares because Stock Exchange prices in general had fallen since the close of the reference period. However, the combined effect of the valuation assumptions for unlisted shares meant that many (but not all) holders of these shares, especially the holders of controlling blocks, felt that their treatment would be harsh. There was a precedent: regulations in World War II allowed the Government to appoint a controller to take over an undertaking. If necessary, the controller could transfer the shares to specified transferees. The Regulations provided that the Treasury could set the price by order, provided it was no lower than a willing buyer–willing seller valuation.[71] The Treasury relied on Stock Exchange prices in valuing one undertaking; this was later challenged by shareholders, who argued that valuation should have been on the basis of a takeover of the entire company at one point in time. This would have been higher than Stock Exchange prices, because Stock Exchange transactions were usually for small holdings rather than full control of the company. This did not lead to any objections in Parliament, and the judicial challenges were dismissed in the courts.[72]

It is worth noting that compensation was only one of a number of points of conflict concerning the Bill. There were lengthy debates on the hybridity of the Bill and the responsibilities of the House of Lords in the light of the Salisbury–Addison agreement and the Parliament Act 1949.[73] Some of the provisions on the powers, governance and management of the new enterprises were also very controversial. Moreover, perhaps surprisingly, the debate on compensation was not framed in terms of constitutional standards or precedents. Hence, there is some doubt whether there is a constitutional standard at all, given both the lack of agreement and the indifference to constitutional argument. To be sure, there were discussions that were clearly focused on the meaning of 'fair compensation' and whether the Bill would ensure that it would be provided. However, where MPs sought to show that the provisions either did or did not do so, they tended to refer to valuation practices in the financial world rather than prior legislation or parliamentary debate. There is a clear contrast with the contemporaneous debates on retrospection and tax avoidance, where there was a practice of interpretation from precedent that was missing in the debates on the 1977 Act.[74] In constitutional terms, the debates took the issues no further than the Attlee Government's nationalisations.

[71] Regulations 55 and 78 of the Defence (General) Regulations 1939 (enacted under the Emergency Powers (Defence) Act 1939).

[72] Cairns (n 2) 599. The House of Lords held that there was no interpretive principle against the Treasury's valuation: see *Short v Treasury Commissioners* (n 45).

[73] For a full discussion, see chapter two, section III.

[74] See chapter six, section III.C.

The controversy over the Act had an unexpected conclusion. The Conservatives won the 1979 election on a manifesto that included a promise to privatise the nationalised enterprises.[75] However, before starting privatisation, it completed the nationalisation on the terms of the 1977 Act. Despite its criticisms of the compensation terms when in opposition, and again when it formed the Government after the general election of 1979, it did not modify them. As explained by Sir Keith Joseph, Secretary of State for Industry, establishing 'new compensation terms retrospectively would be unjust to the many people who sold shares on the basis of the previous terms'.[76] Fairness still governed, although in this case it was fairness as across the class of shareholders.

A number of owners of shares not traded on the Stock Exchange applied to the European Commission of Human Rights for a declaration that the terms violated their rights under the European Convention on Human Rights (ECHR).[77] The Government therefore found itself in the unusual position of defending legislation against arguments that it had put forward in Parliament when in opposition. It succeeded, as the Court held that states are required to strike a fair balance between the various interests at stake, and in particular not to impose a disproportionate burden on the owners.[78] Furthermore, states have a very wide discretion to determine how it should be applied, especially with legislation aimed at restructuring the economy.[79] Put differently, there is no human rights obligation to maximise compensation by adopting the method of valuation that is most favourable to property owners. In essence, the Government's position under the Convention mirrored that taken by the Labour Government in Parliament. If there is a constitutional standard, it is very flexible.

IV. Labour Manifesto of 2019

Labour's manifesto for the 2019 election stated that it would bring 'rail, mail, water, energy, bus networks and broadband-relevant parts of BT into public ownership'.[80] It did not set out compensation terms or principles in the manifesto, although its policy document on energy, *Bringing Energy Home*, stated that

[75] Conservative Party (Great Britain), *Conservative Manifesto, 1979* (Conservative Central Office, 1979).

[76] HC Deb 7 August 1980, vol 990, col 290W; he also said the Government had considered offering the shares back to former owners, but it would prove too complex, especially as the assets and liabilities of the companies had changed, in some cases irreversibly.

[77] Convention for the Protection of Human Rights and Fundamental Freedoms (Rome, 4 November 1950).

[78] *Lithgow v United Kingdom* (n 66) para 120.

[79] ibid para 121.

[80] Labour Party, *It's Time for Real Change: The Labour Party Manifesto 2019* (Labour Party, 2019) 7); see also 19: 'Labour will ensure that councils can improve bus services by regulating and taking public ownership of bus networks' and 53: 'We will bring the broadband-relevant parts of BT into public ownership'.

'The UK legal framework is clear that the level of compensation should be decided by Parliament.'[81] *Clear Water*, its policy on the nationalisation of water companies, was similar.[82] By contrast, the Labour manifestoes issued in 1945 and then again in 1974 specifically stated that property would be taken on the basis of 'fair compensation'. As Labour lost the 2019 election, there were no white papers, bills or debates elaborating on the meaning of its pledge. In *Bringing Energy Home* and *Clear Water*, it said that it would nationalise the companies rather than the assets, and that shareholders would be compensated with bonds.[83] However, neither the policy documents nor the manifesto said whether compensation would cover the owner's loss, and they did not promise 'fair compensation' or 'fair and equitable compensation' as seen with all prior nationalisations.

The manifesto did not suggest how these issues would have been resolved, but the energy and water policies identified factors that might be relevant. They said, in particular, that 'Parliament may seek to make deductions for compensation on the basis of: pension fund deficits; asset stripping since privatisation; stranded assets; the state of repair of assets; and state subsidies given to the energy companies since privatisation.'[84] No more information was provided, and hence it cannot be said whether specific measures would have departed from precedent.[85] For example, in the post-World War II acquisitions, the state of repair of assets would have been relevant in an acquisition of assets, but not where a traded company was acquired on the basis of Stock Exchange prices.

The range of factors gives a strong sense that a Labour government would have considered excluding compensation for unearned or undeserved value. This would be novel in a nationalisation, but there are precedents in the Leasehold Reform Act 1967 and, earlier, the compulsory purchase provisions of the Town and Country Planning Act 1947 and the land tax measures of the People's Budget 1909.[86] With the Leasehold Reform Act, residential tenants exercising the right to

[81] Labour Party, *Bringing Energy Home: Labour's Proposal for Publicly Owned Energy Networks* (Labour Party, 2019) 18, available at www.labour.org.uk/wp-content/uploads/2019/03/Bringing-Energy-Home-2019.pdf.

[82] Labour Party, *Clear Water: Labour's Vision for a Modern and Transparent Publicly-Owned Water System* (Labour Party, 2019) 6, available at www.labour.org.uk/wp-content/uploads/2018/09/Conference-2018-Water-pamphlet-FINAL.pdf.

[83] Labour Party, *Bringing Energy Home* (n 81) 18. Labour Party, *Clear Water* (n 82) 6. In other sectors, asset acquisitions might have been more sensible. In particular, Labour stated that it would not acquire the railway franchisees but allow them to lapse. At that point, it might have considered terms along the lines of the Tramways Act 1870 for any assets it did wish to acquire.

[84] Labour Party, *Bringing Energy Home* (n 81) 18. It was implicit that compensation would be initially calculated without these deductions.

[85] For example, a company with a substantial pension fund deficit is carrying a risk that, ordinarily, would be reflected in the share value. Similarly, one would expect the price of traded securities to reflect the liabilities or write-downs of stranded assets and the true value of assets in a poor state of repair. If the intention was to ensure that such points were reflected in valuation, and not to set aside market value, it could have been consistent with the additional of terms of valuation as seen in the Banking (Special Provisions) Act 2008, as discussed in the following section.

[86] See the discussion in chapter three, section III.

buy the freehold were not required to pay the landlord for the value of the building, on the basis that, by honouring the maintenance obligations over the course of a long lease, the tenants would have already paid the landlord the full value of the building. With nationalisation, the argument would be that there should be no entitlement to value that the public had already paid for, through subsidies. One might argue that the value of subsidies cannot be traced so directly, or that the subsidies were granted and received without a claim to the value they might generate. However, similar points were made against the compensation provisions of the Leasehold Reform Act, both in the parliamentary debates and before the European Court of Human Rights, without success.[87] There are therefore both constitutional and human rights precedents for taking the source of value into account. However, consistency with those precedents would have depended on the detail of any such provisions.

The bigger question from the manifesto and the policy documents is whether the precedents on compensation are still relevant. The concerns focused on legal rather than constitutional standards. The sentence from *Bringing Energy Home* that was quoted above, which referred to the 'UK *legal* framework', was immediately followed by the statement that 'This was confirmed in 2012 by the UK Appeal Court and the European Court of Human Rights in relation to the nationalisation of Northern Rock.'[88] This is not correct if it is intended to say that there were no Convention standards on compensation. States do have considerable discretion to determine the principles on which compensation is assessed, especially on nationalisation, but those principles are still subject to a human rights review. However, more important at this point is the suggestion that the Convention is the only relevant source of standards. There was no reference to UK constitutional standards or precedent.

V. The Valuation Process

In most cases, the process of nationalisation starts with negotiations between the relevant department or public body and the owners. If a price is agreed, it is put into the bill, without reference to the principles that guided the negotiators on the public side. Whilst this limits the opportunity for parliamentary debate, Ministers have always been willing to explain and defend the basis on which the price was negotiated. If a price has not been reached, the legislation invariably provides that the price should be referred to independent arbitration. In this respect, the public bill procedure is similar to that of private bills for the compulsory purchase of land: Parliament sets the general principles but the final figure (if not determined by consent) is set by an independent tribunal operating in a judicial manner.

[87] See the discussion in chapter three, section III.D.
[88] Labour Party, *Bringing Energy Home* (n 81) 18.

However, precedents show that the degree of discretion can vary considerably, to the point that there is no consistent practice or standard that requires either broad or narrow discretion. Moreover, this does not emerge from parliamentary indifference. Indeed, the scope and terms of discretion has been very contentious in a number of cases. This is demonstrated by three cases in which discretion has been particularly controversial.

The first concerned the question of 'special terms of valuation' which arose in debates on the Metropolis Water Act 1902. The Act stated that compensation would be agreed with the target companies, or failing agreement, by a Court of Arbitration[89] 'on such terms and in such manner as most just and fit'.[90] It also directed the Court to apply 'with necessary modifications, the law of compensation for the purposes of the Lands Clauses Acts', excluding the allowance for a compulsory sale and the impact of the Act on the market.[91] As noted above, it was proposed that the Act should direct the Court to apply 'special terms of arbitration' requiring the consideration of risk of a change in the law.[92] The Conservative majority in Parliament followed the Royal Commission recommendations and rejected the proposal, on the point that it would be unfair to consider political risks in valuation. However, the focus of debate was on substantive fairness, rather than the scope of discretion. In other words, it was not suggested that Parliament could not enact 'special terms' because there were constitutional standards requiring unfettered discretion to arbitrators. Parliament would want to review any restrictions on the arbitrators, but restrictions were not objectionable as such.

The converse situation arose with the nationalisation of the aircraft and shipbuilding industries in 1977. Lord Selsdon put forward an amendment that would have allowed the arbitration tribunal to adjust compensation wherever it considered that an owner would not receive 'fair compensation' under the general statutory principles. His amendment would have required 'such amount as the tribunal shall determine to be fair compensation'.[93] His amendment was passed by the Lords but rejected by the Commons and did not become part of the Act itself. Lord Melchett, Minister of State, responded that the formula itself was fair and would be applied by an impartial and independent tribunal and hence there was no need for some further discretion to modify compensation.[94] In the Government's view, the amendment would undermine fairness and equality, by allowing some property owners to plead that they deserved special treatment. In effect, the Labour Government accepted the general principle of fairness across owners, but not necessarily in relation to specific outcomes under the

[89] Metropolis Water Act 1902, s 2(2).
[90] ibid s 23(5).
[91] ibid s 23(8).
[92] See above, text to n 28.
[93] HL Deb 20 October 1976, vol 375, col 1425.
[94] ibid cols 1445–46.

nationalisation programme. As in 1902, the focus fell on the substantive principles of valuation; the principle that legislation could restrict the discretion of the tribunal was not itself in doubt.

The final example concerns the takeover of the Northern Rock bank in 2008. During the credit crisis, the bank became unable to raise the funds it needed to finance its business. It only avoided a complete collapse by obtaining 'lender of last resort' funding from the Bank of England. The Government decided to take it over after failing to find a suitable private sector buyer for it. Authority for the acquisition came from the Banking (Special Provisions) Act 2008, which provided that the Treasury could issue an order for the acquisition of a bank or other authorised deposit-takers on specified conditions. The Treasury issued the order in February 2008.[95]

The provisions of the Act and the Order were carefully written to limit the amount of compensation payable to a bank that would have collapsed without emergency support. They followed precedent, in that they stated that shareholders would receive the value of the shares immediately before vesting, as determined by an independent valuation. However, they also provided that valuation would proceed on the basis that the Bank of England or Treasury had not provided financial assistance and would not do so in future.[96] The statutory order regarding compensation for the Northern Rock went further, as it both directed the valuer to follow the principles of the Act, with the additional assumption that Northern Rock was 'unable to continue as a going concern' and 'is in administration' at the point of valuation.[97] As expected, the valuer ultimately determined that the shares were worthless. A group of shareholders later challenged the valuation assumptions under the ECHR, but the Court of Appeal dismissed their claim, on the basis that the valuation principles of the legislation and statutory order fell within the UK's margin of appreciation.[98]

The compensation and arbitration provisions were not controversial in Parliament, not only in relation to the content of the directions to the valuer but also to the more general principle that directions could be given that, at least in

[95] The Northern Rock plc Transfer Order 2008, SI 2008/432; The Northern Rock plc Compensation Scheme Order 2008, SI 2008/718 dealt with the determination of compensation.

[96] Banking (Special Provisions) Act 2008, s 5(4) 'In determining the amount of any compensation payable by the Treasury by virtue of any provision in an order under this section, it must be assumed—

(a) that all financial assistance provided by the Bank of England or the Treasury to the deposit-taker in question has been withdrawn (whether by the making of a demand for repayment or otherwise), and
(b) that no financial assistance would in future be provided by the Bank of England or the Treasury to the deposit-taker in question (apart from ordinary market assistance offered by the Bank of England subject to its usual terms).'

[97] Northern Rock plc Compensation Scheme Order 2008, SI 2008/718 para 3(2).

[98] *R (on the application of SRM Global Master Fund LP) v Treasury Commissioner* [2009] EWCA Civ 788; NJ Calamita, 'The British Bank Nationalizations: An International Law Perspective' (2009) 58 *International and Comparative Law Quarterly* 119.

this case, would virtually determine the outcome.[99] As in 1977, Parliament set very narrow principles of valuation, in this case without dissent that the substantive principles were appropriate, and that it was legitimate to set terms of arbitration that effectively dictated the outcome.

As a final observation, it is worth noting that no government has asked Parliament to overturn or modify the outcome of an arbitration. Indeed, as discussed above, the Aircraft and Shipbuilding Industries Act 1977 led to the odd result in which the subsequent Conservative Government completed the acquisition of the shares without modifying the terms of arbitration, despite its intense opposition to the Bill in Parliament. In their view, valuation was unfair, but a change in direction would be unfair to those for whom the acquisitions had been completed.

VI. Employees of Nationalised Enterprises

A final aspect of nationalisation concerns the rights of those who suffer indirect loss from the expropriation of the property of others. As discussed in other chapters, there is no constitutional standard requiring compensation at large for everyone who suffers loss from expropriation. Nationalisation is no different: compensation is given to the expropriated owners, but not others.[100] There is, however, a regular practice of providing some compensation for the employees and officers of targeted enterprises who lose their position or suffer financially as a result of nationalisation. The Lighthouses Act 1836 allowed for pensions for 'officers and servants' whose employment ended on nationalisation.[101] The Telegraph Act 1868 provided that officers and clerks of nationalised companies whose employment did not continue would receive compensation in the form of an annuity. It was quite generous: those in employment for 20 years received two-thirds of the former salary annually, diminishing by one-twentieth for each year under 20.[102] The Local Government Act 1888 was, plainly, not a nationalisation statute, but it included provisions on compensation for any 'direct pecuniary

[99] George Osborne, the Shadow Chancellor, agreed that the shares were worthless: HC Deb 19 February 2008, vol 472, col 182. Other points about structure and accountability of nationalised bank and place in the banking sector were more controversial: see, eg, HC Deb 19 February 2008, vol 472, cols 236–98 and HC Deb 21 February 2008, vol 472, cols 629–54.

[100] To be more precise, it must be a direct interference that causes an ascertainable loss: see the discussion of the Petroleum (Production) Act 1934 in chapter three, n 12. The Act vested subsurface petroleum in the Crown without compensation, on the basis that reserves were unknown and hence there was no loss to any specific land.

[101] Lighthouses Act 1836, s 29 gave the power 'to such reasonable Pension, by way of annual or quarterly Payments, as to them shall seem proper'. It could not exceed the public civil service pensions, and was in the discretion of the 'Master, Wardens, and Assistants' and only payable out of the tolls of the lighthouse.

[102] Telegraph Act 1868, s 8(7).

loss' suffered by officers as a result of anything done under the Act, such as an amalgamation of local authorities.[103] This was then applied under the Metropolis Water Act 1902, in addition to provisions which guaranteed continuity of terms for those continuing in the same work.[104] The Telephone Transfer Act 1911 might appear to be a counter-example as it did not include similar provisions, but successive Postmasters-General assured the House of Commons that staff members on less than £700 a year would be taken into service by the Post Office after the takeover.[105] The London Passenger Transport Act 1933 provided for the transfer of employment to the new body and compensation for those whose employment was not continued.[106] The Sugar Industry (Reorganisation) Act 1936 and British Overseas Airways Act 1939 protected against reductions in wages following the takeover.[107] The post-World War II nationalisation laws also included provisions for the protection of employees, with very similar terms in the Electricity Act 1947, the Transport Act 1947, the Gas Act 1948 and the Iron and Steel Act 1949.[108] The provisions were changed slightly for the Aircraft and Shipbuilding Industries Act 1977, but the substance was very similar.[109]

The legislative record therefore shows that Parliament consistently sought to protect employees and officers from the consequences of nationalisation. More recently, standards for the transfer of undertakings and compulsory redundancies have been set by European law, for both the public and private sectors.[110] If a government decided to repeal the European laws, Parliament might consider the earlier legislation as setting constitutional standards, at least in cases where a public body takes over a private enterprise. It is quite clear that the standard is narrow, as it only applies to employees and officers rather than all consequential losses, but nevertheless the evidence for a standard is present.

VII. Conclusion

There is a consistent practice of providing 'fair' or 'fair and equitable' compensation for nationalised property. Opposition MPs have often argued that a bill does not in fact promise anything like 'fair' or 'fair and equitable' compensation.

[103] Local Government Act 1888, s 120.

[104] Metropolis Water Act 1902, s 47; subs (5) incorporates s 120 of the Local Government Act 1888.

[105] See HC Deb 13 March 1905, vol 142, cols 1185–86 (Lord Stanley); HC Deb 9 August 1905, vol 151, cols 829–30, and 846 (Lord Stanley); and HC Deb 1 March 1911, vol 22, cols 359–60 (Herbert Samuel).

[106] The London Passenger Transport Act 1933, ss 73–80.

[107] Sugar Industry (Reorganisation) Act 1936, s 23; British Overseas Airways Act 1939, schs 5 and 6.

[108] Electricity Act 1947, ss 54, 55; Transport Act 1947, Part VII (especially ss 101 and 102); Gas Act 1948, ss 58, 60; Iron and Steel Act 1949, ss 40, 41.

[109] Aircraft and Shipbuilding Industries Act 1977, ss 49 and 50.

[110] See the Transfer of Undertakings (Protection of Employment) Regulations 2006, SI 2006/246, implementing Council Directive 2001/23/EC, replacing Transfer of Undertakings (Protection of Employment) Regulations 1981, SI 1981/1794, implementing Council Directive 77/187/EEC (1977).

In some cases, they have argued that compensation is too generous and will cripple the new enterprise: in effect, the terms are not fair to the public. This also has a procedural aspect, as legislation has invariably required independent valuation or arbitration where there is no agreement on price. Again, opposition members have sometimes argued that the legislation does not give the valuers or arbitrators enough scope to do justice, but there is still agreement that an independent body should set the price. On that basis, a case can be made for saying that there is a parliamentary constitutional standard for the provision of fair compensation for owners who lose their property on a nationalisation. There is considerable dispute over its interpretation in a specific situation but that is often the case with constitutional standards, whether parliamentary or legal in nature.

This raises the question posed in chapter one regarding the necessary degree of precision for constitutional standards. Arguably, 'fair compensation' is simply too vague to be treated as a standard. This might not be said of the practices on independent valuation and arbitration, but 'fair compensation' does not have, for example, the clarity of standards relating to retrospection. Here, Parliament has consistently shown an interest in the precedents and has sought to extract general principles from them. Moreover, MPs have successfully employed constitutional arguments to persuade governments to amend retrospective provisions of bills. To be sure, this is not a frequent occurrence, but there are still no comparable examples in relation to nationalisation. Precedent seems much less important than economic and social policy.

Finally, human rights may have become more relevant as the source of standards on compensation. This was reflected in the Labour manifesto of 2019: it stated that its proposals satisfied the 'legal framework' without making any reference to parliamentary constitutional standards.[111] For Labour, the role of Parliament was less about ensuring compliance with standards derived from parliamentary practice and more about anticipating legal challenges in the courts.

[111] Labour Party, *Bringing Energy Home* (n 81) 18; see also Labour Party, *Clear Water* (n 82) 6.

5

Regulatory Laws

This chapter considers legislation that affects rights of property without a transfer of the full interest to another person. Most cases involve regulatory controls that diminish the value of property or authorise its destruction or confiscation. The question for this chapter is whether there is any general right to compensation for losses in such cases, or even to fair treatment. Losses may be severe, as with the destruction or confiscation of property, but compensation is not necessarily required. One might argue that, as the impact on the owner is the same as it is for expropriation, the entitlement to compensation should be the same. However, this is not the general position. Various explanations for the distinction are possible: with expropriation, the acquiring body takes over the asset for its own use. In addition, the impact of expropriation is usually much more selective than regulation, in that only a small number of owners face expropriation at any time. Conversely, the effects of regulation are usually too varied and diffuse to calculate the net loss or gain of every property owner with accuracy. Nevertheless, most states recognise that there may be situations where the impact and distribution of regulatory burdens is so harsh on some property holders that it cannot stand, unless compensation is provided. Hence, it is worth asking where there is an overarching principle of fairness that explains why compensation is provided in some cases and not others.

A quick comparative analysis suggests that there are two possibilities. First, there may be a general constitutional standard. For example, in France, the constitutional principle of equality extends to the distribution of the burdens of taxation and other public charges.[1] A general standard also applies under the European Convention on Human Rights.[2] Under Article 1 of the First Protocol to the Convention, compensation is normally required for expropriation and nationalisation but not for controls on the use of property or the taking of property in satisfaction of liabilities or the enforcement of other laws.[3] However, all cases are subject to the overriding requirement of proportionality. Accordingly, there have

[1] Déclaration des Droits de l'Homme et du Citoyen de 1789, Arts 6 and 13.

[2] Convention for the Protection of Human Rights and Fundamental Freedoms (Rome, 4 November 1950).

[3] Protocol to the Convention for the Protection of Human Rights and Fundamental Freedoms (Paris, 20 March 1952).

been situations where compensation has not been required for an expropriation[4] and, conversely, where it has been required for regulatory controls on property.[5] In addition, the European Court of Human Rights has issued judgments regarding the selectivity of taxes or other measures: where some people face an unusually heavy or arbitrary burden, there may be a case that the interference is disproportionate.[6] In some areas – especially in relation to the setting of rates – Parliament has shown a similar concern, although they usually frame it in terms of a standard of 'fair' treatment or 'fair and equitable' treatment, rather than proportionality.

Alternatively, the United Kingdom (UK) constitution may be similar in structure to the Fifth and Fourteenth Amendments to the United States (US) Constitution. The Fifth Amendment states that 'No person shall be … deprived of life, liberty, or property, without due process of law; nor shall private property be taken for public use, without just compensation.'[7] The Fourteenth has similar language.[8] The 'due process' guarantee has very broad application, but it does not include a substantive guarantee of fairness. Instead, its focus is on procedural fairness. The 'takings clause' does guarantee compensation, but the constitutional jurisprudence does not allow the clause to be applied to ordinary regulation or taxation.[9] This is not to say that American legislators have no interest in the substantive fairness or proportionality of regulatory laws or taxation, but only that they are not constrained by the constitutional guarantees of property rights. A similar pattern is found in the rights to property found in the independence constitutions drafted by the British for former colonies. As in the US, the constitutions included a general due process clause requiring lawful authority for the deprivation of rights of property, as well as a specific guarantee of compensation for the expropriation of property.[10] This followed the American formula, except that the drafters included long lists of situations where property may be taken or regulated without compensation.[11] These constitutions did not, however, make any mention of a general substantive standard, such as fairness or proportionality, that would apply to all deprivations of property, including those for which compensation was not required. It seems that there were only two possibilities in the minds of the constitutional drafters of that period: an interference with property either required compensation, or it did not.

[4] See, eg, *Jahn v Germany* ECHR 2005-VI.

[5] See, eg, *R (on the application of Mott) v Environment Agency* [2018] UKSC 10.

[6] See, eg, *Hentrich v France* (1994) Series A no 296.

[7] US Constitution, Fifth Amendment.

[8] US Constitution, Fourteenth Amendment extends the guarantee to the States: '… nor shall any State deprive any person of life, liberty, or property, without due process of law …'.

[9] See *Eastern Enterprises v Apfel* 524 US 498 (1998): there may be exceptions, although the Supreme Court did not speak with one voice on the issue.

[10] See T Allen, *The Right to Property in Commonwealth Constitutions* (Cambridge University Press, 2000). The most recent constitutions base their rights to property on Article 1 of the First Protocol to the European Convention on Human Rights, rather than the earlier Commonwealth models: see, eg, The Pitcairn Constitution Order 2010, SI 2010/244, sch 2, s 21.

[11] For example, in the Constitution of Zambia, the list of deprivations of property that do not require compensation runs to nearly 1000 words.

Arguably, the UK constitution follows the same pattern, with 'fair compensation' required only for compulsory purchase and nationalisation. As in the US, MPs and Parliament are not indifferent to questions of fairness, but in deciding whether compensation should be provided, they focus on principles relating to the bill – for example, whether measures in a money bill would conflict with general principles of tax policy – without looking to constitutional precedents or standards.

This chapter shows that Parliament has not recognised a general constitutional standard, but there is evidence that it observes a principle of substantive fairness in specific areas. The rest of the chapter therefore considers some of the most important areas of regulatory law and the extent to which they are governed by standards of fairness. It begins with regulatory losses arising from restrictions on the use of land and other property. These losses may be serious and yet, if owner retains title, there is usually no expectation of compensation or other measures to counterbalance the loss. This is also true of the destruction of assets and the extinction of rights of property. From the owner's perspective, the loss is the same as it would be for an outright expropriation. However, as with regulatory losses, there is no general constitutional right to compensation or other similar measures. It concludes by considering rates, taxation and other compulsory contributions. At least with the rates, there has long been an expectation that the distribution of the burden should be 'fair'. There is also some evidence, although weaker, that fairness is a constitutional requirement for taxation and other burdens.

I. Restrictions on the Use of Property

The impact of planning and environmental regulations often arises in constitutional and human rights law. Usually, the question is whether a property holder should be compensated for losses arising from regulatory controls; or, as the corollary, whether uncompensated regulation has a disproportionate impact on the property holder. There may be other issues: for example, whether the costs and benefits are fairly distributed or whether officials are given too much discretion in their implementation. In practice, however, compensation and proportionality are usually the primary concern. Parliament has taken the view that there is no constitutional requirement to compensate for regulatory losses. There are cases where it has provided compensation, but they are isolated and have been prompted by policy reasons – usually, the need to secure voluntary compliance – rather than constitutional standards.

Historically, local bodies and the Crown often enacted and enforced general regulations controlling matters such as building standards, sanitation, the obstruction of public rights of way and nuisances.[12] Most legislation focused on

[12] For descriptions of nuisance in the medieval period, see: HM Chew and W Kellaway, 'Introduction', *London Assize of Nuisance, 1301–1431: A Calendar* (London Record Society, 1973); JR Spencer, 'Public

the enforcement of customary and legal obligations. For example, many statutes authorised justices of the peace or local officials to clear obstacles to river navigation and public roads, but the obligation not to create the obstacles already existed at common law.[13] Parliament might also authorise the imposition of levies or contributions of building materials or human or animal labour to maintain local works; or, it might prohibit conduct that interfered with the rights of individuals or towns, such laws against the forestalling of markets.[14] In both cases, the underlying obligations were already in existence, and the statutes merely provided machinery to aid their enforcement.[15] In some cases, Parliament did impose new legal obligations, but with a view to enforcing morals or the preservation of the social order: sumptuary laws were one example;[16] the early regulation of market prices was another.[17]

In many cases, Parliament conferred these powers on local officials such as mayors, deans, or justices of the peace. Or, as in the case of the Statute of Sewers (1427), it might authorise the appointment of commissioners with broad powers to act.[18] Often, the delegees were granted the power to enact local rules defining the types of conduct that would be proscribed or the level and allocation of rates and contributions. The statutes granted a discretion, but it was not unlimited. Usually, it required the holders of powers to act honestly and without a view for their own interests. For example, under Henry VIII, Parliament enacted legislation charging sewers commissioners to 'make and ordeyne statutes ordenauncves and pvysions frome tyme to tyme as the case shale require … after the laws and customes of Romney Marsh … or otherwise by any ways or meanes afteyr your owne wisedomes and discrecions'. By their oath of office, they promised to make 'holsome juste equall and indifferent lawes and ordynaunces'.[19] Later, Parliament granted extensive power to enclosure commissioners, but subject to an oath that they act 'faithfully, impartially and honestly, according to the best of my skill and

Nuisance. A Critical Examination' (1989) 48 *Cambridge Law Journal* 55; J Loengard, 'The Assize of Nuisance: Origins of an Action at Common Law' (1978) 37 *Cambridge Law Journal* 144.

[13] See, eg, 25 Edw III stat 3 c 4 (1350–51); 45 Edw III c 2 (1370–71); 12 Ric III c 13 (1388); 21 Ric II c 18 (1397–98); 1 Hen IV c 12 (1399); 9 Hen V stat 2 c 11 (1421); 9 Hen VI c 9 (1430–31).

[14] See, eg, 6 Rich II stat 1 c 11 (1382); 5 & 6 Edw VI c 14 (1551–52); 21 Ric II c 19 (1397–98); 2 Hen VI c 12 (1423).

[15] See, eg, 6 Hen VI, c 5, 1427; 1 Hen VIII c 9 (1509–10); 9 Hen V stat 2 c 11 (1421–22); 22 Hen VIII c 5 (1530–31); 24 Hen VIII c 11 (1532–33); 25 Hen VIII c 8 (1533–34).

[16] M Hayward, '"Outlandish Superfluities": Luxury and Clothing in Scottish and English Sumptuary Law from the Fourteenth to the Seventeenth Century' in G Riello and U Rublack (eds), *The Right to Dress* (Cambridge University Press, 2019).

[17] J Davis, 'Baking for the Common Good: A Reassessment of the Assize of Bread in Medieval England' (2004) 57 *Economic History Review* 465.

[18] 6 Hen VI, c 5, 1427; WB Stoebuck, 'A General Theory of Eminent Domain' (1971) 47 *Washington Law Review* 553, 565–66.

[19] 23 Hen VIII c 5 (1531–32). Other examples of this period include 1 & 2 Phil & Mar c 14 s 2 (1554–55), 1 Mary c 5 (1554). The custom of Romney Marsh was often used as the basis for legislation: see HG Richardson, 'The Early History of Commissions of Sewers' (1919) 34 *English Historical Review* 385; AEB Owen, 'The Custom of Romney Marsh and the Statute of Sewers of 1427' (1996) 116 *Archaeologia Cantiana* 93.

judgment'.[20] Paul Craig's review demonstrates that this was the general pattern: Parliament often conferred generous powers on officials, but subject to constraints on their use. Moreover, the courts gave effect to these clauses, which was significant in itself:

> the very fact that Parliament enacted very many statutes that conditioned regulatory intervention on proportionability is indicative of the fact that the legislature was mindful of the concept's utility, and it did so knowing full well that the courts would adjudicate on its meaning and application.[21]

So far as compensation was concerned, these laws dealt with obligations that already existed and hence there was no interference with rights of property and no compensation was provided. This carried through to the modern era: the Great Fire legislation did not compensate landowners for the stricter building regulations that were enacted.[22] The legislation incorporated a plan for reconstruction, including the widening of streets and new building standards, with special Fire Courts to implement the plan and enforce the standards. The usual rules on compensation for compulsory purchase applied where land was acquired but not for losses that may have been caused by more restrictive building controls. None of this raised serious questions in Parliament.

This continued with the urban reforms of the eighteenth and especially the nineteenth century. This was seen in the work of the Improvement Commissions, whom the Webbs described as the 'progenitors of nearly all the activities of our present municipalities'.[23] The Commissioners were concerned with both the prevention of harm and regulation for the enhancement of the area. Their powers could be quite broad and it was clear that they could regulate without compensation. As with the Great Fire legislation, expropriation was compensated but regulation was treated as a different matter. Similarly, the Public Health Act 1848 set new building and sanitary standards and created local boards of health to enforce them. It also empowered the local boards to enact bye-laws on different aspects of housing and public health.[24] In Parliament, the substantive rules were seen as no more than an elaboration of the common law of nuisance.[25] There was no discussion of constitutional standards relating to regulation or compensation, or whether there was a general principle of fairness or other protections for property and liberty.

[20] FA Sharman, 'An Introduction to the Enclosure Acts' (1989) 10 *Journal of Legal History* 45, 59–67; GE Mingay, *Parliamentary Enclosure in England: An Introduction to Its Causes, Incidence and Impact 1750–1850* (Longman, 1997) 57–58.

[21] P Craig, 'Proportionality and Judicial Review: A UK Historical Perspective' in S Vogenauer and S Weatherill (eds), *General Principles of Law: European and Comparative Perspectives* (Hart Publishing, 2017) 160.

[22] TF Reddaway, *The Rebuilding of London After the Great Fire* (Jonathan Cape, 1940).

[23] S Webb and B Potter Webb, *English Local Government: Statutory Authorities for Special Purposes* (Longmans, Green, 1922) 236.

[24] Public Health Act 1848, ss 37, 62, 105–106.

[25] See, eg, D Urquhart, HC Deb 21 February 1848, vol 96, col 1022 and HC Deb 5 May 1848, vol 98, col 713, where he described the centralisation of implementation as 'un-English and unconstitutional'.

The constitution of the new bodies and their relationship with central government was controversial, but not the idea that standards could be set or that property owners would not be compensated.

The denial of compensation did not mean that Parliament was not concerned with the impact of regulation on owners. Indeed, in some cases, it has required compensation for regulatory losses. The Housing, Town Planning, etc. Act 1909 is an example.[26] The Act enabled towns to adopt a planning scheme for their area and to set housing standards. With minor changes, the provisions were carried forward to the Town Planning Act 1925[27] and then again, with some modification, in the Town and Country Planning Act 1932.[28] The 1909 Act allowed landowners to claim for 'injurious affection' caused by the making of a scheme, in addition to any claims arising from expropriation.[29] In addition, the Act addressed a general concern with any form of compensation for regulation: that the cost would inhibit governments and local authorities from enacting regulatory schemes that would benefit the public. This was addressed by a betterment charge, as the Act allowed the responsible authority to recover any resulting increase in the value of property from the owner. As a sound plan should produce a net increase in property values, the betterment charges should have covered the liabilities for injurious affection. This not only offered more fairness, but in principle it would be at little or no cost. Indeed, the responsible authority should have realised a gain from planning.[30]

The provisions of the 1909 Act were rarely applied in practice. It seems that the uncertainty in determining the net cost of compensation discouraged many towns from developing plans. However, the debates show that Parliament did not consider either the compensation or betterment charges to be particularly controversial.[31] Planning itself was not as controversial, probably because there were many precedents. In any case, many landowners were happy with the new planning laws, as they reduced the risk of new developments that might reduce the value of their own land. Providing compensation for their own losses due to injurious affection helped win them over. To be sure, there were debates over points of detail, especially in relation to accountability and governance by the Local Government Board, but the idea that compensation and betterment might be part of a legislative scheme for planning was not challenged. It does not appear that MPs thought

[26] P Booth and M Huxley, '1909 and All That: Reflections on the Housing, Town Planning, Etc. Act 1909' (2012) 27 *Planning Perspectives* 267.

[27] Town Planning Act 1925, s 10(3).

[28] Town and Country Planning Act 1932, ss 6–9.

[29] In any case, there could be no claim for injurious affection if the provisions of the plan could have been passed by bye-laws, or if the loss of value was caused by rules setting standards on height and character and density of buildings: Housing, Town Planning, etc. Act 1909, s 58.

[30] Housing, Town Planning, etc. Act 1909, s 58; it was originally set at 100% of the increment, but later reduced by amendment to 50%. Booth and Huxley (n 26) 277: 'The evident desire to capture that increment for the benefit of the country at large had then its counterpoint in the belief that landowners who were prevented from developing their land because of a planning scheme, might be reasonably entitled to compensation.'

[31] Booth and Huxley (n 26) 273–76.

there was any kind of constitutional obligation to spread the burden by compensating for planning losses. It was a pragmatic measure to gain agreement and it complemented the betterment charges, which reflected views that planning gains should be recovered by the community.

In a world without administrative costs, the 1909 Act might have provided the fairest solution. The practice, however, proved different. Towns had the power to adopt plans but very few did. The Town and Country Planning Act 1947 therefore extended the planning system to the entire country and introduced a new system for addressing the losses and gains from planning. The 1947 Act transferred the owners' right to develop land through a change of use to the Central Land Board, without compensation. The Minister of Town and Country Planning, Mr Silkin, said that, as there was no expropriation, there was no obligation to compensate for the transfer.[32] Nevertheless, he also explained that payments would be made in cases of 'hardship', and he explained that that would address the potential for 'inconsistent treatment as between individuals'.[33] In particular, owners of land 'dead ripe' for development under the old system did receive payments when the 1947 Act took away permission, as these owners may have incurred expenditure in the expectation that they could proceed with a development. Arguably, this might be seen as an acknowledgement of a constitutional right, although only in the narrower grounds of equal treatment. However, even here, the Government was clear that these payments were made *ex gratia*: there was no constitutional right to compensation and no indication that the earlier planning Acts or the 1947 Act set a precedent. There is no indication MPs thought that constitutional standards were relevant to the questions of planning gains and losses. Indeed, as noted in chapter three, the discussion on constitutionality was limited because there was a high degree of consensus on the key issues, and both leading parties accepted that no compensation was required for the taking of the right to develop in 1947.[34] Fairness, it seems, is relevant in the same way that it is relevant to tax policy: the perception of fairness may be important in making the law effective, but it is not a constitutional requirement.

II. Destruction of Property

Public bodies occasionally order the destruction or confiscation of property as part of the enforcement of regulatory standards. For the individual, the loss may be the same as it would be for an expropriation, and yet compensation is not normally provided. Arguably, the severity of the loss should support a case for compensation. Clearly, this would not be a universal rule, as there is often good

[32] HC Deb 29 January 1947, vol 432, cols 974–75.
[33] ibid col 974.
[34] See chapter three, section III.C.

reason not to compensate. For example, the forfeiture of property obtained by criminal activity is, for obvious reasons, not subject to an obligation to indemnify the holder. Similarly, an order for the destruction of a building that was erected contrary to planning or public health laws should not require compensation. As noted above, there were many early statutes authorising justices of the peace to remove nuisances in towns and obstacles to navigation, without compensation.[35] There were also related statutes allowing officials to compel owners to repair or rebuild dwellings that had decayed. The concern was that the lack of dwellings would cause labourers to move off the land.[36] Again, there was no expectation of compensation.

However, where there is no suggestion of wrongdoing on the part of the property owner, Parliament sometimes does authorise compensation or other forms of financial support. A recent example is the various forms of support provided to businesses and employees subject to restrictions during the COVID-19 pandemic. Nevertheless, although there are examples of compensation and support, there is no overarching constitutional standard requiring Parliament to enact such laws. Even where Parliament does seek to alleviate hardship, it does not necessarily provide full compensation. With the COVID-19 restrictions, the support schemes were not intended to cover all losses, but to enable businesses to survive.[37] An earlier illustration arose in World War II in relation to war damage caused by British forces overseas. During the War, Ministers took the view that support for reconstruction and repair should be offered to those who suffered loss as a result of lawful military action overseas.[38] The aim was not to compensate for all losses, but to support the recovery of the individual or enterprise. For the denial damage suffered by British companies in Burma, the British made *ex gratia* payments to the companies of about one-quarter to one-third of the value of their losses.[39] As noted in chapter six, in *Burmah Oil v Lord Advocate*, the House of Lords found that there was a specific obligation to compensate for the damage, which the companies argued should be more generous than support or 'rehabilitation'.[40] Strictly speaking, the case concerned prerogative rather than statutory powers. Nevertheless, Parliament's views became clear when it reversed the judgment by enacting the War Damage Act 1965. The retrospective aspect of the bill was very controversial but there was no challenge to its prospective aspect.

[35] Above nn 12 and 13.

[36] See, eg, 4 Hen VII c 19 (1488–89); 6 Hen VIII c 5 (1514–15); 7 Hen VIII c 1 (1515); 26 Hen VIII c 8, 9 (1534); 32 Hen VIII c 18, 19 (1540); 35 Hen VIII c 4 (1543–44); 39 Eliz c 1 (1597–98). Similar laws required the restoration of land to tillage: 39 Eliz c 2 (1597–98).

[37] For a summary, see M Sandford and others, 'Coronavirus: Support for Businesses' (2022) House of Commons Library Briefing Paper Number 8847.

[38] HC Deb 18 February 1943, vol 386, col 1942 (Sir Kingsley Wood, Chancellor of the Exchequer).

[39] See HC Deb 3 February 1965, vol 705, cols 1091–99 on the background.

[40] *Burmah Oil v Lord Advocate* [1965] AC 75. It is not clear that they would have succeeded in this argument: if the case had proceeded to the assessment of damages, the award might have been considerably less generous than the offer of rehabilitation: see Lord Reed.

The most extended discussion of compensation has arisen in relation to the control of contagious disease in animals.[41] Compulsory slaughter dates back to the outbreak of cattle plague in 1714. The Privy Council ordered the destruction of infected cattle, with compensation set at half of the value of a fully grown animal.[42] Given the mortality rate of cattle plague, this was thought to be sufficient to induce farmers to report the disease rather than take the risk that it would spread to their other animals. A similar programme of slaughter and compensation was applied to the outbreak of 1745–57. The plague proved more difficult to control than in 1714, and so a 1753 Act increased the inducement to full compensation for the first three animals.[43] It was clear, by this point, that the level of compensation could be an important factor in controlling disease. Indeed, in some areas, landlords and local authorities supplemented the compensation in order to secure voluntary compliance with the controls.[44]

In these early responses, compensation was aimed at encouraging voluntary compliance with the law.[45] There is no evidence that it was thought that there was a constitutional right to payment, even where the hardship could be attributed to state action.[46] A further outbreak in 1865–66 led to closer parliamentary consideration of the compensation question.[47] The Home Secretary, Sir George Grey, told the House of Commons that the compensation scheme of the previous century led to 'much fraud and recklessness' and 'should operate as a warning rather than an encouragement to repeat the experiment'.[48] Again, this confirms that there was no constitutional obligation to provide support, for if there had been such an obligation, compensation would have been required even if it did little to induce compliance. With the 1865–66 outbreak, the Liberal Government's initial response was simply to empower local authorities to slaughter animals and pay compensation, but not to require them to do so.[49] When pressure for action mounted, the Government introduced the Cattle Disease Prevention Act 1866. The debates

[41] CF Mullett, 'The Cattle Distemper in Mid-Eighteenth-Century England' (1946) 20 *Agricultural History* 144; AB Erickson, 'The Cattle Plague in England, 1865–1867' (1961) 35 *Agricultural History* 94; J Broad, 'Cattle Plague in Eighteenth-Century England' [1983] *Agricultural History Review* 12; JR Fisher, 'British Physicians, Medical Science, and the Cattle Plague, 1865–66' (1993) 67 *Bulletin of the History of Medicine* 651; A Woods, 'The Construction of an Animal Plague: Foot and Mouth Disease in Nineteenth-Century Britain' (2004) 17 *Social History of Medicine* 23.

[42] There were other measures, such as quarantining infected cattle.

[43] Cattle Distemper, Vagrancy, Marshalsea Prison, etc. Act 1753 26 Geo II c 34 (1753); see Mullett (n 41) 158–59; Broad (n 41) 106–10.

[44] Broad (n 41) 108.

[45] See ibid 107.

[46] Indeed, John Broad observed that 'Parliament played a minor and subsidiary role, although briefly in 1746 the Privy Council deferred to its collective wisdom. After the Commons had spent a month in fruitless discussions, a simple enabling bill passed responsibility back to the Privy Council. Later legislation rarely did more than provide statutory authority for existing Orders in Council.' Broad (n 41) 105.

[47] See generally Erickson (n 41); Fisher (n 41).

[48] HC Deb 12 February 1866, vol 181, col 378.

[49] See Erickson (n 41) 96–97. On the first Orders in Council, which were intended to enable but not require local authorities to compensate owners.

on the Act went into more depth about compensation than any other debate on the control of animal disease, before or since. Was compensation provided out of constitutional obligation, or as a pragmatic encouragement to report disease, or as support for those facing hardship, or as a political response to the power of landed interests in Parliament? Of these, it is reasonably clear that hardship was not seen as requiring compensation. Benjamin Disraeli argued that, but for the need to check the disease, a public subscription would have been the correct response.[50] This was the usual response to such events at that time, as Parliament did not authorise compensation for losses due to disaster or calamity. Indeed, neither the 1866 Act nor any of the preceding Acts authorised compensation for animals that simply died of the disease: it was only paid where slaughter was required by the legislation.

Some MPs did say that there was a constitutional case for compensation, on the basis that the owners' losses were caused by government action rather than the plague itself. Mr Newdegate argued that 'If you deprive a man of the exercise of his own judgment in the disposal of his own property, you must compensate him.'[51] However, most MPs justified compensation as the price of securing compliance for a measure of high public interest. Sir George Grey, introducing the Bill, said that the losses arising from slaughter

> ought to be borne to a certain extent by the whole community, because the whole consuming and producing population are interested in checking the disease; but that a special burden may be fairly thrown upon those on whom the loss primarily and immediately falls.[52]

The 'whole consuming and producing population' would be harmed if the disease were not checked; hence, it was legitimate to use public funds to do so.[53] The rights of cattle owners was not central to his argument. By this reasoning, compensation should be no higher than the amount that would secure compliance. Indeed, William Gladstone, as Chancellor, secured an amendment to the rate to one-half from the initial proposal of two-thirds of the value of a healthy animal. As compliance could be bought for a lower price, there was no need to pay more.[54]

Parliament frequently extended the authority of the earlier legislation, with a series of enactments known in the nineteenth century as the Contagious Diseases of Animals Act and in the twentieth century as the Diseases of Animals Act. The Animal Health Act 1981 consolidated the earlier laws, with subsequent

[50] HC Deb 15 February 1866, vol 181, col 556.

[51] HC Deb 12 February 1866, vol 181, col 405. See also Mr Neville-Grenville: compensation was required when the government ordered the slaughter (rather than just for animals that died from disease): HC Deb 14 February 1866, vol 181, col 501.

[52] HC Deb 12 February 1866, vol 181, col 379.

[53] A number of MPs cited both fairness to owners and the need to provide an incentive to report: see, eg, Mr Lowe, HC Deb 14 February 1866, vol 181, cols 483–87; Mr J Stuart Mill, HC Deb 14 February 1866, vol 181, cols 488–90.

[54] HC Deb 15 February 1866, vol 181, col 541.

legislation in 1984 and the Animal Health Act 2002. Throughout, the principles on compensation remained substantially the same. It might be argued that the repeated practice of providing at least some compensation for the destruction of animals has become a constitutional principle. However, the focus throughout has been on securing compliance with the law. Where payments would have no effect on compliance, there is no compensation. Indeed, Parliament has not extended compensation to cover consequential losses to the cattle owner or to labourers or third parties who suffered as a result of the outbreak and compulsory slaughter. As long as the purpose is to incentivise compliance, there is no need to compensate those who are not responsible for reporting the disease. In effect, they have no compliance to buy. This was also seen in the 2001 outbreak of foot and mouth disease, where farmers were compensated for animals that were destroyed, but not for losses caused by strict movement controls. Rural and tourist businesses received very little support despite the impact of the controls on their profits.[55] Jonathan Shaw, the Parliamentary Under-Secretary of State for Marine, Landscape and Rural Affairs, reiterated the position in relation to the 2007 foot and mouth outbreak: 'It is a long established principle that the Government does not meet the costs of consequential losses, which must be borne by the industry.'[56] Compensation may be sought and welcomed by the owners of cattle that are destroyed, but from Parliament's perspective, this is more a matter of ensuring compliance or economic support rather than the protection of individual rights.

In conclusion, Parliament has not recognised a constitutional right to compensation or even financial support in cases where it orders or authorises the destruction of property. This is true even in cases where the owner is not at fault. They are likely to have a stronger political case for compensation or support especially if, as in the case of animal disease, COVID-19 or wartime losses, they are also a victim. However, the constitutional case is weak.

III. Extinction and Termination of Rights of Property

In his famous article, 'The New Property', Charles Reich argued that many of the different forms of licences, permits, concessions and other privileges that confer rights should be treated as property under American constitutional law.[57] These

[55] See Sir Iain Anderson, *Foot and Mouth Disease 2001: Lessons to be Learned Inquiry Report* (HC 2002, 888) 2: 'Farmers were compensated for animals that were culled for disease control purposes and for welfare reasons. Rural and tourist businesses however received very little recompense. Farmers whose stock was not culled, but who were subject to strict movement controls, received no compensation at all.' See also the discussion in Robert G Lee, 'The (Not So) Great Escape: The Legal and Moral Responsibility for the Foot and Mouth Outbreak 2007' in I Kenway, Dr J Gunning and Professor S Holm (eds), *Ethics, Law and Society* (Taylor & Francis Group, 2009) vol IV, 382–87.

[56] HC Deb 24 October 2007, vol 465, col 309WA.

[57] C Reich, 'The New Property' (1964) 73 *Yale Law Journal* 733.

rights may be as important to the holder's security and autonomy as ordinary property. The licence to use assets in a particular way often enhances the value of the asset: agricultural land can increase in value many times over if permission is granted to develop it as residential land. Or, in the case of railways operating under public licence, the withdrawal of the licence may cause its assets to lose most of their value. Reich's question is whether the constitutional protections for property apply to the withdrawal or modification of licences and other administrative rights, even without a taking of a physical asset. In particular, should compensation be paid on the withdrawal of a licence? There is also the case of extinctions of types of property to consider, as in cases where holding specific assets becomes illegal.

Parliament has not articulated an overarching principle on compensation and the withdrawal of 'new property' or extinctions of types of property. Several situations can arise. First, the legislation may both extinguish valuable rights or licences relating to specific assets and authorise a public body to acquire the assets for its own use. In such cases, should compensation reflect the pre- or post-extinction value of the assets? Secondly, the extinction may cause a loss in the value of the assets, but no acquisition follows. Is there any obligation to compensate for the loss? There are examples of the extinction of types of property where owners were very generously compensated. The most notorious is probably the Slavery Abolition Act 1833, which guaranteed compensation for the slaveowners. The East India Company was very generously compensated when its commercial privileges came to an end in 1873, probably far in excess of any reasonable valuation, especially as no positive action was needed to terminate them. The Company's privileges were only granted for a specific period and they were simply allowed to expire.[58] In principle, there was no loss of property to compensate. Similarly, the private Acts constituting railway companies normally granted the promoter a licence to operate for a 21-year period, with compensation at 25 years' purchase if the licence were not renewed.[59] A further example is the Licensing Act 1904, which required compensation for the loss of value to a public house on non-renewal of a liquor licence.[60] Finally, there are also situations where legislation requires compensation for withdrawal of valuable licences, but only for wasted expenditures, rather than the loss of value.[61]

These examples suggest that Parliament has followed a practice of providing compensation for the abolition of a form of property or the extinction of a valuable licence or permit. However, they must be set against cases where it did not

[58] The company's charter was extended by 20 years and its dividend by 40 years, by the Government of India Act 1833. The payment was authorised by the East India Stock Dividend Redemption Act 1873. See N Robins, *The Corporation That Changed the World*, 2nd edn (Pluto Press, 2012) 184–87.

[59] Railway Regulation Act 1844.

[60] Licensing Act 1904, s 2; compensation was '... the difference between the value of the licensed premises ... and the value which those premises would bear if they were not licensed premises'.

[61] See B Denyer-Green, *Compulsory Purchase and Compensation*, 11th edn (Routledge, 2018) 362–75.

require compensation. The Tramways Act 1870 allowed municipalities to grant 21-year concessions to promoters to construct and operate local tramways, but it also provided that compensation would not be paid for goodwill on the expiry of a licence. The municipality could seek a compulsory purchase of the company's assets, but at their break-up value rather than the value of the company as a going concern. In effect, there was no compensation for the expiry of the concession.[62] 'Tramway terms' were also applied to the nationalisation of the telephone network in 1911. The Postmaster-General argued that there should be no compensation for goodwill, or future profits, or for the compulsory nature of the purchase because the business would be worth nothing without the licence.[63] Similarly, under the current legislative schemes, the Office of Rail and Road (ORR) may grant an indefinite licence to an operator. However, licences are subject to revocation without compensation, within the terms of the legislation and the licence. The ORR's practice is to include provisions on revocation in the licence. With passenger services, for example, the ORR's standard form licence allows it to revoke a licence without compensation on 10 years' notice, any time after the licence has been in effect for 25 years.[64] In effect, the current system is a version of 'tramway terms'.

Reich also considered the withdrawal and extinction of social welfare benefits or subsidies for businesses. These benefits and subsidies fall into many different categories. Some seem so far from proprietary rights that their modification or withdrawal would not raise issues under constitutional or human rights to property. Access to public health services or public roads are examples. However, others, such as accrued social welfare benefits or state pension entitlements, are closer to ordinary property. For these, it could be argued that they should be given the same weight as proprietary interests, given their importance to the security of the holder. It does not seem, however, that there are any constitutional limits in the UK on their adjustment or withdrawal. If the changes are prospective, the situation would be similar to that of licences or permits that expire at the end of the term, for which Parliament has not adopted a practice of compensation. There may be a stronger case where benefits have already accrued, as an ascertained statutory entitlement should be closer to a proprietary right.[65] However, the example of the Jobseekers (Back to Work Schemes) Act 2013 suggests that the evidence is weak.[66]

[62] See chapter four, section I.

[63] HC Deb 19 June 1911, vol 27, col 48.

[64] Office of Road and Rail, 'Template Passenger Train Licence', Part IV, available at www.orr.gov.uk/sites/default/files/2023-07/template-passenger-train-licence_0.pdf. No compensation for assets is required on revocation for cause, or after the 25/10 year notice period (note that the ORR would not seek to acquire the business in any event). See also Railways Act 1993, s 31: there is no security of tenure for the franchisee for leases.

[65] In human rights law, social welfare benefits may qualify as 'possessions': see I Leijten, 'From Stec to Valkov: Possessions and Margins in the Social Security Case Law of the European Court of Human Rights' (2013) 13 *Human Rights Law Review* 309; I Leijten, 'The Right to Minimum Subsistence and Property Protection under the ECHR: Never the Twain Shall Meet?' (2019) 21 *European Journal of Social Security* 307.

[66] See chapter six, section III.C.

The Act retrospectively extinguished benefits that had already accrued and were confirmed by the courts. The Constitution Committee expressed concerns regarding the retrospective aspect of the Act, but the Government did not concede that there were any constitutional issues.

From this discussion, it seems that there is no constitutional principle regarding compensation or other support for losses due to the extinction of licences or similar assets. There is no consistency in the practice. In addition, the cases where compensation is provided are more easily explained as the product of political bargaining: compensation for the abolition of slavery is an example. As a final observation, it is worth noting that these issues are often not addressed in Parliament, because it usually delegates decisions to a statutory authority or the relevant Minister. There are exceptions: for example, the legislation on the destruction of animals has specified compensation levels for different diseases. There was a pragmatic reason for this, as the control of disease often requires a national effort and hence national standards are appropriate. More generally, there does not appear to be a constitutional requirement that levels must be set out in the legislation. Parliament is often concerned with fairness, but it does not appear that its concern has been formulated with the clarity of a constitutional standard. There is no discussion of precedent, as in the case of retrospection, compulsory purchase or nationalisation. Often, the crucial question was whether the terms would attract sufficient investment or affect compliance. For example, with the Tramways Act 1870, George Lefevre, the Parliamentary Secretary to the Board of Trade, acknowledged that the terms might make it more difficult for some promoters to raise capital, but that that would be counter-balanced by allowing them a free hand in setting fares and dividends.[67]

IV. Rates, Taxes and Other Charges

This section considers taxes, rates and other liabilities or contributions that public bodies may impose. In the common law world, constitutional rights to property do not typically extend to taxes or other compulsory contributions. In these systems, the right does not apply unless there is a direct interference with specific property. The imposition of a tax or other liability may affect wealth, but the constitutions protect property specifically rather than wealth in general.[68] This is not to overlook the importance of the fiscal constitution, but to recognise that many of its principles are not directly concerned with rights of the individual. For example, the distribution of power between the executive and Parliament and the relationship

[67] HC Deb 1 March 1870, vol 199, cols 1083–84.

[68] Note that: (i) there may be no impact on wealth, if a third party satisfies the liability; (ii) the imposition of a liability is within the scope of the right to the peaceful enjoyment of possessions under the European Convention on Human Rights (see, eg, *Hentrich v France* (1994) Series A No 296-A).

between the two Houses of Parliament is clearly important, but it is not aimed at protecting the rights of the individual. The question for this section is whether there are standards – specifically, substantive standards – regarding the rights of the individual. In particular, is there a constitutional standard of fairness regarding the distribution of the burdens of taxation and other contributions?

There is ample evidence of a long-standing concern with fairness in taxation. John McDonald has shown that it was important in the tax system of the eleventh century.[69] Edwin Cannan, in his study of the rates and early taxes, found that they were tied to the benefits received from expenditure or the ability to pay, both of which reflected ideas of fairness. For example, with liabilities imposed to pay for the maintenance of sewers and sea defences, the burden fell on those whose land would be at risk of flooding if the work was not carried out.[70] It probably seemed fair to most MPs and constituents that the burden should be heavier on those who held more land at risk. Indeed, as it depended on the extent of holdings, it reflected both the benefit received and the ability to pay. Where benefits were more diffuse, as in the relief of the poor or the construction of a jail, the burden would be more widely distributed, on the basis that everyone in the community benefited in some way.[71] In these cases, the ability to pay became more important. For example, the poll taxes of the fifteenth century were graduated by the social rank and wealth of individuals.[72] The poor rates had their origins in voluntary almsgiving, by which each should contribute by their ability.[73] Well into the nineteenth century, the tension between benefit and ability to pay remained controversial at the local level.[74]

Parliament has frequently debated whether the tax base should fall on capital, wealth, income or consumption, and the fairness of the measures of each. Generational equity has also been raised: in debates on the introduction of income tax in 1799, the Solicitor-General argued that taxation was preferable to borrowing, as borrowing would unfairly shift the burden to posterity.[75] Chantal Stebbings refers to Sir William Pulteney in the same debate, who, like many others, argued that taxation was not fair unless it was voluntary. Hence, taxation should be restricted to consumption, with the exception of necessaries (the 'direct and

[69] J McDonald, 'Tax Fairness in Eleventh Century England' (2002) 29 *Accounting Historians Journal* 173.

[70] See E Cannan, *The History of Local Rates in England, Five Lectures* (Longmans, 1896) 29: 'It is evident that the general principle of the early sewers rates or taxes for sea defence was that they should be levied in respect of all kinds of property liable to danger, in proportions determined by the extent or value of that property.'

[71] eg 14 Edw III Stat 1, c 20; see generally P Harris, *Income Tax in Common Law Jurisdictions: Volume 1, From the Origins to 1820* (Cambridge University Press, 2006) ch 1.

[72] Cannan (n 70) 18.

[73] ibid 67, 102.

[74] James Hanley provides a detailed study of the difficulties faced in finding the appropriate base for rates for funding local sewers in the early 19th century: see chapter 2 of JG Hanley, *Healthy Boundaries: Property, Law, and Public Health in England and Wales, 1815–1872* (Boydell & Brewer, 2016).

[75] *Cobbett's Parliamentary History of England*, XXXIV, 92 (1798).

immediate articles of life') such as bread, milk and vegetables.[76] The 'voluntary' aspect of consumption taxes still arises: chancellors often see 'luxury' or 'sin' taxes as a useful and relatively acceptable source of revenue; conversely, taxation on consumption that is not seen as voluntary can come under heavy criticism.[77] A further aspect of fairness was raised in the debates on the People's Budget of 1909, which would have imposed a tax of 20 per cent on increases in the value of land, at the point of a transfer. The Government's intention was to recover at least some of the unearned increment in value. In both Houses, the opposition raised fears of 'class legislation': that legislation should not favour one class at the expense of another.[78] For example, in the Commons, Arthur Balfour said that 'this special attack upon a special class will undoubtedly inflict, has inflicted, and is inflicting a great injury upon the particular owners of a particular class of property'.[79] It was a constitutional issue in the widest sense, in that it threatened to upset a balance in social, economic and political power; moreover, to the critics, state power was targeted at a narrow class. There was, of course, vigorous debate regarding the conventions on money and supply bills. More generally, many MPs focused on the efficacy of the new tax, as they doubted that it would raise the desired funds. Nevertheless, the selectivity of a tax raised basic questions of fairness for some MPs. For the Liberals, it was entirely fair to tax unearned increments in land; for the Conservative-Unionist opposition, it was manifestly unfair. In any case, the 1909 budget fell, but following the general election in 1910 the Government re-introduced the land tax and it passed into law. As a precedent, the 1910 budget confirmed that the choice of tax base was constitutional.

From this brief review, it is apparent that fairness is a regular point of debate in the annual budget rounds. There is therefore some evidence in favour of a constitutional standard that taxes must be fair to individuals. However, the argument against a substantive standard is stronger, for two reasons: the purported standard is too vague to be meaningful, and in any case the practices are more

[76] ibid 135; C Stebbings, 'Consent and Constitutionality in Nineteenth-Century English Taxation' in J Tiley (ed), *Studies in the History of Tax Law*, (Bloomsbury, 2009) vol 3; C Stebbings, 'The Equity of the Executive: Fairness in Tax Law in Nineteenth-Century England' in PG Turner (ed), *Equity and Administration*, 1st edn (Cambridge University Press, 2016) 260–64.

[77] For a recent application of the voluntariness principle, see HM Treasury, 'Tampon Tax Abolished from Today' (*GOV.UK*), available at www.gov.uk/government/news/tampon-tax-abolished-from-today. The voluntariness argument arguably lay behind the controversy over the rise in Vehicle Excise Duty (VED) in 2006 and Airline Passenger Duty (APD) in 2007: in theory, the VED and APD are imposed on voluntary consumption, but the increases came at a point where the choice to consume or not would have seemed illusory to many. The debate was framed in terms of retrospection, but (as discussed in chapter six), the changes were not retrospective. However, the concerns were quite clear: people were subject to a consumption tax that they could not reasonably avoid.

[78] For a discussion of 'class legislation', see D Schneiderman, 'A. V. Dicey, Lord Watson, and the Law of the Canadian Constitution in the Late Nineteenth Century' (1998) 16 *Law and History Review* 495, 501–10.

[79] HC Deb 30 June 1909, vol 7, col 458. For a similar view, see HC Deb 5 July 1909, vol 7, col 844 (Sir Philip Magnus) and in the Lords, see HL Deb 23 November 1909, vol 4, col 880 (Marquess of Londonderry).

easily explained as the product of tax policy than constitutional norms. Taking the point about vagueness first, it is argued in the chapters on compulsory purchase and nationalisation that there is a parliamentary constitutional standard regarding compensation. There is clear evidence of a long-standing, consistent practice, and that the practice was sufficiently precise to provide a focus for debate. To be sure, valuation methods of land and enterprises can vary considerably, but there is agreement on several important points. In particular, the purpose of compensation is to cover the owner's loss. MPs would demand justification of a legislative standard that openly disregarded the owner's loss as the measure of compensation. In addition, the valuation of the loss falls to an independent body; as such, it is not solely for government officials to determine. These details provide the points of reference for the culture of justification and support the existence of a constitutional standard. With taxation, there is no common basis for understanding what substantive fairness requires. An MP's conception of fairness might focus on the benefits received from taxation, the comparative sacrifices of taxpayers, their ability to pay, generational fairness, consent and voluntariness, the selectivity of a tax, the relative burdens of the classes, methods of implementation and perhaps still others. Indeed, when the Treasury Committee adopted the *Principles of Tax Policy* in 2011, it put forward fairness as one of two core substantive principles (along with growth) but did not explain it in any detail.[80] It gave no indication of the specific points that an inquiry into fairness should consider or what fairness should achieve. MPs are clearly concerned with the fairness of taxation, but it is not clear what they mean by it. As such, it adds little to a culture of justification, as far as it relates to the individual's right to property.

Secondly, and perhaps more important, the practice can be explained without any reference to constitutional standards. Again, the contrast with compulsory purchase and nationalisation is instructive. In those cases, MPs have debated compensation provisions on the basis that they protect individuals, as they moderate the impact of the interference with rights of property. In other words, they frame the purpose of fairness in terms of the rights of the individual in the face of state power. With taxes and rates, the concerns of the Treasury and Parliament are usually with the cost of collection and shortfalls due to evasion or avoidance, rather than the need to protect an individual's wealth. Pragmatically, an unfair tax is likely to be ineffective or very costly to enforce, as voluntary compliance is likely to be low and may lead to the loss of political support (or even rebellion or violent resistance, as in the case of Wat Tyler's rebellion and the poll tax riots of the 1980s). Hence, regardless of any constitutional standards, governments are likely to enact taxes that are perceived to be fair. Indeed, MPs raise fairness but do not frame it as a matter of individual rights, as in the case of compulsory purchase and nationalisation. Rather, it arises as a general value for all legislation and, specifically, in relation to its impact on voluntary compliance and the efficacy of tax legislation.

[80] House of Commons Treasury Committee, *Principles of Tax Policy* (HC 2010–11, 753).

The absence of a commitment to fairness as a constitutional standard weakens arguments in its support.

One possible counter-example can be seen in the changes made to the rates by the Government of Margaret Thatcher under the Local Government Finance Act 1988.[81] These changes followed years of discussion after World War II, when the expansion of local services put increasing pressure on the resources of local authorities. To alleviate the pressure, Parliament authorised central grants to the authorities. At the same time, the incidence of the rates became increasingly controversial, due to the failure to re-value property for rate assessments in the years after World War II. Land values had become, at best, an imperfect measure of both the ability to pay or the benefits received from local authority expenditure. There were also questions over accountability, as there were frequent complaints that some local authorities provided services without a view to cost, because the governing party had been elected by voters who paid little or nothing in rates.[82]

The Thatcher Government's solution was to depart entirely from the ability to pay as the basis for determining rates, in favour of a basic head tax. In response to criticisms, the Government argued that, firstly, local rates were already regressive, as the failure to re-value had shifted the burden to those on lower incomes in many areas.[83] However, instead of pushing through a new valuation, the Government abandoned it as the basis for setting rates. Instead, the new system was based almost entirely on the benefits received, and on the theory that the benefits of local government were roughly equal for all of its residents.[84] There was also the pragmatic objection that progressive taxation at the local level would have adverse consequences for all, as higher rate individuals would avoid rates by moving to areas with lower rates, which were likely to be those with a higher proportion of higher value properties.[85] Ability to pay, by this reasoning, was simply not sustainable. Progressive taxation could only work at the national level, where avoidance would be more difficult. As the new system abandoned the link to property values, and in particular the link to the ability to pay (however flawed it had become), the 'poll tax' was seen as abandoning one of the long-standing principles of fairness.

As is well-known, objections to the poll tax were so strong that the Conservative Government of John Major repealed it in 1992.[86] Although not labelled as 'rates', the new council tax tied assessments to the value of 'dwellings' and the burden

[81] See J Gibson, 'The Presentation of the Poll Tax' (1989) 60 *Political Quarterly* 332, and the speeches of Nicholas Ridley, Secretary of State for the Environment, HC Deb 16 December 1987, vol 124, cols 1115–16 and Earl of Caithness (who introduced the Bill in the Lords), HL Deb 9 May 1988, vol 496, cols 826–33.

[82] See N Ridley, Secretary of State for the Environment, HC Deb 16 December 1987, vol 124, cols 1115–16.

[83] ibid.

[84] There were some exceptions: see, eg, Local Government Finance Act 1988, s 13 (students).

[85] Nicholas Ridley, Secretary of State for the Environment, HC Deb 16 December 1987, vol 124, col 1125.

[86] Local Government Finance Act 1992.

fell on residents.[87] Arguably, the repeal of the poll tax confirms that there is a constitutional principle that rates cannot be set without consideration of the ability to pay, and perhaps other factors relating to fairness. However, although many MPs referred to fairness in the debates on the poll tax and its repeal, there was no explicit claim that it was a constitutional standard.[88] Clearly, the Conservative Government thought it was politically wise to reintroduce property values and the broader principle of the ability to pay, but from its perspective, it was a matter of political and economic judgement rather than adherence to a constitutional standard. Moreover, none of the other parties in Parliament suggested that the Government was constitutionally obligated to reintroduce the ability to pay as a criterion in rate-setting. Ultimately, the poll tax saga demonstrates that there would be strong political objections to movement away from ability to pay based on wealth. However, it is not at all clear that the objections would be constitutional in nature. Fairness has a pragmatic, political aspect that does not always equate with a constitutional standard.

V. Conclusion

Is there a substantive rule regarding losses from regulation, taxation and the imposition of other compulsory contributions? Arguably, there is one for the rates, but there is slim evidence for a general substantive standard in other areas. Instead, political concerns have been directed at the delegation of power and the risk of an abuse of power by the delegee. This, however, has been addressed by circumscribing the scope of the power and by the courts through the growth of judicial review of the exercise of a power. In addition, with many schemes, there are both judicial and administrative appeals: for example, with planning, the Secretary of State hears final appeals on many issues; with revenue, there are defined routes to the tribunals. It seems that, between judicial and administrative reviews and appeal, the control over localised decision-making has been sufficient to allay concerns of abuse.

[87] ibid ss 1–9.

[88] In the House of Lords, the constitutionality of rejection or amendment of the bill was discussed, as it raised questions regarding the Government's electoral mandate and the status of the bill as a matter of taxation; it was not, however, discussed in terms of a constitutional standard of fairness: see HL Deb 9 May 1988, vol 496, cols 839–42 (Lord Jenkins) and cols 913–15 (Lord Beloff).

6

Retrospection

In the debates on the War Damage Bill 1965, the Attorney-General, Sir Elwyn Jones, said that retrospective laws are 'in general wrong and contrary to the rule of law' but there may be 'exceptional circumstances which make it just and equitable to depart from that rule'.[1] There was nothing novel in this statement: Bracton, Coke and Blackstone all spoke against retrospective laws.[2] Neither is it surprising that retrospection should be widely condemned. As noted in chapter one, the Constitution Committee's first report states that 'The Rule of Law, encompassing the rights of the individual' is one of the five basic tenets of the UK constitution.[3] Retrospection undermines the stability that the rule of law should offer individuals, so that they can plan their affairs. Moreover, it is contrary to basic ideas of fairness to penalise those who acted within the law. However, as this chapter shows, retrospection is used with such regularity in civil matters that one may question whether it is exceptional. Indeed, in *Philips v Eyre*, Willes J remarked that 'it would fill a long chapter in history to enumerate all the instances of retrospective legislation'.[4] Willes J spoke in 1870; the use of retrospective legislation has certainly not declined since then.

This chapter is concerned with retrospection that affects rights of property. It begins by considering the meaning of retrospection, where it shows that Parliament has used a narrow construction when considering the scope of the standard. It then moves to uncontroversial uses of retrospection, such as curative and remedial legislation and measures to discourage forestalling of changes in taxation or regulatory schemes. The chapter then considers retrospection where legislation responds to or anticipates judgments that are contrary to the wider public interest. It first examines cases where the state has no direct interest in the outcome. These situations are rare, as Parliament is usually content to allow judgments to remain in force. However, as discussed below, there have been cases where the threat of disruption justifies action. The discussion then moves to legislation aimed at plugging loopholes in regulatory schemes. This is a particularly important category, because retrospection has been used so frequently there have been attempts at codification of the statutory precedents.

[1] HC Deb 12 May 1965, vol 712, col 600.

[2] EE Smead, 'The Rule against Retroactive Legislation: A Basic Principle of Jurisprudence' (1936) 20 *Minnesota Law Review* 775, 775–77.

[3] House of Lords Constitution Committee, *Reviewing the Constitution: Terms of Reference and Method of Working* (HL 2001–02, 11) paras 21, 51.

[4] *Philips v Eyre* (1870) LR 6 QB 1, 25.

I. 'Retrospection' and the Scope of the Constitutional Standard

Governments have consistently taken a narrow and technical view of the constitutional standards applicable to retrospection. There are two key points to consider. First, the standards do not apply to procedural matters. This has been contentious in relation to criminal law but not with rights of property or civil claims.[5] The second is substantive, as it limits the constitutional standard to changes in the law that take effect as of a prior date.[6] Accordingly, a law may extinguish or modify rights that have already vested without necessarily being retrospective. Tenancy laws, for example, may restrict or extinguish rights contained in an existing lease, but provided that the restriction only operates from the date that the Act comes into effect, it is not retrospective.[7] Similarly, changes in taxation are not retrospective if they only increase the burden in future, even if they negate the intended effects of prior tax planning arrangements.

Some MPs have argued that the constitutional standard should apply to any law that frustrates expectations arising from prior transaction. By this view, the standards on retrospection would apply where individuals would have arranged their affairs differently if they had known that the law would be changed. No government has accepted that retrospection is this broad. For example, in the debates on the replacement of Personal Equity Plans and Tax-Exempt Special Savings Accounts with Individual Savings Accounts would be retrospective because taxpayers had made plans in the expectation that the tax advantages of PEPs and TESSAs would be continued indefinitely, Ross Cranston, Labour MP and subsequently Solicitor-General, countered that:

> It [retrospective legislation] makes unlawful something that was lawful at the time or, in the tax context, renders a past transaction subject to tax that was not applicable at the time. At the most, one could say here that expectations have been disappointed. But I do not think that anyone who deals in the area of taxation can have any such expectations. ... One has to expect different Chancellors to change taxation regimes. No one can proceed on the basis that regimes will remain unchanged for ever. No one could have had a legitimate expectation that the existing tax regime would remain unchanged.[8]

Similar questions arose in relation to anti-avoidance measures introduced in 2004, increases in the Vehicle Excise Duty (VED) in 2006 and the Airline Passenger Duty

[5] SN McMurtie, 'The Constitutionality of the War Crimes Act 1991' (1992) 13 *Statute Law Review* 128, 143–46.

[6] On the different ways that laws may have retrospective or retroactive effect and the distinctions between them, see N Duxbury, 'Ex Post Facto Law' (2013) 58 *American Journal of Jurisprudence* 135; CS Bobbett, 'Retroactive or Retrospective? A Note on Terminology' (2006) 1 *British Tax Review* 15.

[7] Although note that the Leasehold Committee's report on leasehold reform regarded compulsory enfranchisement as retrospective, because it would modify rights under existing contracts: Leasehold Committee, *Final Report* (Cmd 7982, 1950) 29; at 144, the minority disagreed.

[8] HC Deb 3 March 1998, vol 307, col 894.

(APD) in 2007. With the Finance Bill 2004, the focus fell on schemes under which individuals transferred assets to others but continued to use them, with a view to reducing the inheritance tax that would ultimately be payable on their estate. The new measures subjected the transferor to an income tax charge for value of the use of the assets. As this would apply to assets that had been transferred in the past, Conservative and Liberal Democrat Members argued that the changes were retrospective.[9] In fact, the charge would not apply until April 2005, and even so, it would only apply to beneficial use after that date; previous beneficial use would not be taxed. Nevertheless, it was said to be retrospective because individuals had made decisions in the expectation that they would avoid tax. Had they known that the transfers would not remain effective to avoid tax, they might have done things differently. Dawn Primarolo, the Paymaster-General, did not accept the argument.[10] Neither did the Joint Committee on Human Rights, which considered the measures and concluded that they were not retrospective.[11]

With the VED and the APD, the Government proposed to increase the duty on higher emission vehicles, but from the next tax point.[12] There would be no increase of the VED for prior years. With the APD, an increase was announced that would not take effect until legislation was in force, although it would apply to departures after that date that had already been booked by and paid for by passengers before the Bill was introduced. In both cases, MPs argued that the measures were retrospective because individuals had entered transactions in the expectation that the tax or duty would not increase, and they were not in a position to adapt to the new rules. For example, with the VED, some MPs argued that owners of older vehicles could not avoid the increase by trading in their vehicles, because many of them were on lower incomes and the cost of a newer vehicle would be prohibitive. With the APD, passengers had already booked flights. In principle, they could cancel their booking and avoid the increase, but this was not a practical choice for most of them.[13] Ultimately, in the debate on the APD, Helen Goodman (Labour) acknowledged that the increase may have upset expectations, and that some individuals would not be able to re-order their affairs for the new regime, but that was

[9] HC Deb 7 July 2004, vol 423, cols 890–91 and 898–99 (John Gummer).

[10] HC Deb 7 July 2004, vol 423, col 890: 'We are not backdating the provision. Under the Bill, either there will be a charge to income tax on people's new arrangements or they can revert to inheritance tax and pay what is due.'

[11] Joint Committee on Human Rights (JCHR), *Twelfth Report of 2003–04, Scrutiny of Bills: Fifth Progress Report*, HL Paper 93/HC 603, paras 1.48–1.51. Note that the JCHR was only concerned with compatibility with the European Convention on Human Rights, rather than the parliamentary constitutional standards.

[12] The debates on the VED can be found at HC Deb 2 July 2008, vol 478, cols 902ff; for the APD, they are at HC Deb 1 May 2007, vol 459, cols 1416ff.

[13] In any case, it was the airline, rather than the passenger, that was liable for the duty, although it may not have been obvious to the passenger because most airlines routinely added the duty (and the increase) to the cost of a ticket. John Healey, Financial Secretary to the Treasury, reported that at least two airlines had decided not to pass on the increase to passengers who had already paid for their flights: see HC Deb 1 May 2007, vol 459, col 1437.

not unusual. As she put it, the increase was 'not significantly different from all sorts of taxes that we must pay. For example, the same applies to council tax – when the local council issues a bill, one does not have time to move house'.[14]

The meaning of retrospection has been central to the controversy concerning the Loan Charge controversy, which was introduced in the Finance Act (No 2) 2017. It was aimed at schemes by which payments for services were channelled to offshore intermediaries, which then paid the individual in the form of a loan. The aim was to avoid tax, as the intermediary would not demand payment of the loan. HM Revenue & Customs (HMRC) had long taken the view that these schemes were not effective to avoid employment tax and National Insurance Contributions, but nonetheless they continued to be popular. The Loan Charge was seen as a simple means of ensuring that earnings would be taxed, as it required individuals to include the value of any loans made since 5 April 1999 that were still outstanding on 5 April 2019 in their taxable income for that year.[15] Individuals therefore had the choice: include the loan as income and pay tax on it, or repay the loan and pay no tax on it. They could not, however, retain the loan *and* avoid the tax, as they had hoped.

The Finance Act (No 2) 2017 did not re-open closed assessments and its provisions did not take effect for two years after Royal Assent. Hence, it was not retrospective. However, it clearly upset expectations that had been formed in respect of past conduct.[16] As in the case of the pre-owned assets charge and the changes to PEPs, TESSAs, the VED and the APD, the critics felt that that should be enough to make the law retrospective. Indeed, when the first Loan Charge bill was introduced in the Commons, Mel Stride, the Financial Secretary to the Treasury, appeared to acknowledge that it was retrospective.[17] However, the Government subsequently stated that the Loan Charge was not retrospective after all. In the House of Lords Economic Affairs Committee, Lord Young, Chief Whip and Parliamentary Secretary to the Treasury, stated that the Loan Charge was a new charge on outstanding loan balances and as such 'It does not change the tax position of any previous year or the outcome of any open compliance checks.'[18] This was also the view taken by John Glen, Economic Secretary to the Treasury, in a Westminster Hall debate: 'The legislation is not retrospective because it sets out Parliament's intention: payments subject to the loan charge should always have been, and will be, subject to tax.'[19]

[14] ibid col 1420.

[15] As discussed below, the date was changed from 5 April 1999 to 9 December 2010: see text to n 156.

[16] HMRC has not conceded that schemes were ever effective.

[17] PBC Deb (Finance Bill) 19 October 2017, col 101 'She [Annelise Dodds, Shadow Financial Secretary] raised the issue of the retrospection or otherwise of these measures. We will certainly be looking at individuals who may have entered into these kinds of arrangements as far back as 1999.'

[18] HL Deb 29 April 2019, vol 797, col 811.

[19] HC Deb 20 November 2018, vol 649, col 293WH. See also the position taken by Jesse Norman, Financial Secretary to the Treasury: PBC Deb (Finance Bill) 4 June 2020, col 37. It is not clear if the Government was arguing that the law was not retrospective because the scheme users were already

Ultimately, the Government did make changes to the legislation in response to the criticisms. However, except for Mel Stride's apparent concession at the beginning of the debate, it has not accepted that the Loan Charge is retrospective. The MPs attacking the Loan Charge have taken the line that the constitutional standard should apply whenever there is a change in the tax burden relating to decisions that cannot be easily reversed, even if the change only takes effect from a point in the future. This is not supported by precedent. Indeed, it goes beyond saying that legislation should not interfere with vested rights, as there were no vested rights at stake. That is not to say that the constitution is incapable of change or that a wider view will not take hold at some point: arguably, some MPs are dissatisfied with the technical approach to retrospection that emerges from the precedents. For them, the real issue is fairness, especially when a small group faces unusual hardship as a result of changes in the tax regime. Retrospectivity is still useful because it provides an indication that specific measures should be given closer scrutiny, but it should not operate as a filter that frees government or Parliament of the burden of closer scrutiny where legal changes have a serious impact on a select minority.

In conclusion, there is clearly some support for widening the standard to include the interference with settled expectations, especially where it appears that legislation would undermine the stability associated with the rule of law. Clearly, Parliament should consider whether the disruption of any proposed law would be greater than the benefits. However, this seems more a matter of social and economic or criminal policy, rather than constitutional standards. Indeed, reasonable people also make plans on the basis of government promises of action. The failure to carry through on plans therefore upsets expectations and might even lead to claims against the Government.[20] However, it is only contrary to the rule of law if those promises were given the force of law, which most governments are careful to avoid.

II. Procedural Standards

The *Cabinet Manual* states that 'the Law Officers' consent is required for legislative provisions that have a retrospective effect'.[21] In theory, a Minister may introduce a bill without consent, but the Cabinet Office's *Guide to Making Legislation* indicates that the Parliamentary Business and Legislation Committee of the Cabinet would not allow the bill's introduction without it.[22] These are strictly executive

liable for tax on the income or if it was not retrospective because the Loan Charge did not re-open closed assessments and would not apply until a future point.

[20] See A Lidbetter and J Randhawa, 'Developments in Judicial Review of Decisions That Are Wholly or Substantially Commercial' (2016) 21 *Judicial Review* 105.

[21] Cabinet Office, *Cabinet Manual* (Cabinet Office, 2011) para 6.7. See also Cabinet Office, *Guide to Making Legislation* (Cabinet Office, 2022) paras 3.10, 3.42, 12.2, 22.6.

[22] Cabinet Office, *Guide to Making Legislation*, ibid para 20.11.

rather than parliamentary conventions, but in any case, there are no other conventions or procedural rules specific to retrospective measures. In the debates on the APD, Paul Goodman, the Shadow Minister for Business, Innovation and Skills and a spokesman for Treasury matters, put forward an amendment that would have enacted 'Principles of good practice for retrospective taxation legislation'.[23] The amendment was modelled on section 19 of the Human Rights Act 1998, as it would have required the Minister in charge of the bill to make a statement before the Second Reading that any retrospective tax provisions were compatible with the Principles or that no such statement could be made but the Government wished to proceed with the bill nonetheless. Goodman's Principles would have required the Minister to confirm:

i. that it appears, whether as a result of a judgment given by a court or otherwise, that some part of the law relating to taxation no longer conforms to the reasonable expectations about its effect previously held by taxation practitioners and that it is necessary to restore the position retrospectively in order to protect the interests of the general body of taxpayers;
ii. that HMRC becomes aware of a new tax avoidance scheme and it is necessary, in order to prevent a significant loss of tax revenue, to amend the law retrospectively.[24]

This would have been a novel principle. When the Government introduced the Immigration Bill 1971, it did not specifically bring the House's attention to the retrospective element of some provisions, despite their impact on liberty. In a later debate, the Opposition argued that it should have done so, but the Government responded that the responsibility lay with MPs to review bills properly.[25] In relation to Goodman's proposal, John Healey, the Financial Secretary, said that section 19 of the Human Rights Act 1998 already required a Ministerial statement and hence no further statement was required. Section 19 is, of course, concerned with human rights rather than the constitutional standard, but in any case the amendment did not pass. Even if it had, the Principles would not have applied to the changes to the APD, as they only applied prospectively.

The guidance on seeking consent of the Law Officers assumes that Parliament will have the opportunity to review retrospective legislation. Section 75 of the Banking Act 2009 raises a further issue, as it gives the Treasury the power to make orders to change the law so as to enable its other powers under Part 1 of the Act to be used effectively. Not only does section 75 grant this power, but subsection 3

[23] HC Deb 25 June 2007, vol 462, col 48.

[24] ibid col 45.

[25] See HC Deb 26 June 1973, vol 858, col 1409 (Shirley Williams) and HC Deb 26 June 1973, vol 858, col 1416–20 (Secretary of State for the Home Department (Robert Carr)). Another example is section 43 of the Pensions Act 2004, which gave Regulator power to Financial Support Directions in respect of conduct occurring before the Act came into force (confirmed in *Granada UK Rental & Retail Limited and others v The Pensions Regulator and another* [2019] EWCA Civ 1032). This was not highlighted in the debates.

specifically provides that the order may have retrospective effect, 'in so far as the Treasury consider it necessary or desirable'. Lawmaking by order is controversial in any context, but this was highly exceptional. The Constitution Committee asked the Government if there were any precedents for conferring such a power; none were provided.[26] But going further, the Government argued that the Act included sufficient safeguards, because any use of the power under section 75 would be subject to the Human Rights Act 1998.[27] This was essentially the same argument that John Healey made when rejecting the proposals for requiring Ministerial statements to be made in relation to retrospective tax measures.

III. Substantive Standards

This section looks at substantive aspects of retrospective laws. The laws exist in such volume that the analysis is clearer if they are put into categories, from least to most contentious, and to analyse them in that order.

A. Curative Measures

Some retrospective laws do not have adverse consequences for individuals. If so, it is unlikely that MPs would object to them.[28] Other laws do have adverse consequences but minimise the impact on some individuals. This is often the case where legislation overturns a judgment. Many such laws exempt those who have received a final judgment. By safeguarding the position of the successful claimants, the Government hopes to lower the threshold for justification and minimise the interference with the judicial process. Hence, in 1991, David Mellor, the Chief Secretary to the Treasury, stated that 'If the Revenue loses a case, it does not seek to take back from the litigant the benefit that has been gained.'[29] This is borne out in a number of cases where statutes reversed judgments with retrospective effect, such as the War Charges Act 1925 (reversing *Attorney-General v Wilts United Dairies*[30]), Wireless Telegraphy (Validity of Charges) Act 1954 (reversing *Davey Paxman v Post Office*[31]), the Finance Act 1987 (reversing *Padmore v Inland Revenue Commissioners*[32]) and the Finance Act 1991 and Finance (No 2)

[26] House of Lords Constitution Committee, *Banking Act 2009: Supplementary Report on Retrospective Legislation* (HL 2008–09, 11) 5–8.

[27] ibid 7.

[28] This was the case with the Charitable Trusts (Validation) Act 1954, discussed below in the text to n 84ff. For other examples, see the discussion in JW Bridge, 'Retrospective Legislation and the Rule of Law on Britain' (1967) 35 *University of Missouri Kansas City Law Review* 132, 138–39.

[29] HC Deb 30 April 1991, vol 190, cols 185–86.

[30] *Attorney-General v Wilts United Dairies* (1922) 38 TLR 781.

[31] *Davey Paxman v Post Office* The Times, 16 November 1954.

[32] *Padmore v Inland Revenue Commissioners* (1987) STC 36 affirmed by the Court of Appeal (1989) STC 493.

Act 1992 (reversing the *Woolwich* cases, to which Mellor was referring[33]): in all of these cases, the legislation protected the position of the successful litigants. In some cases, legislation has also protected the position of those who commenced claims before the bill was introduced, or those who would have been entitled to do so.[34] This occurred with the Wireless Telegraphy (Validity of Charges) Act 1954,[35] which provided exemptions for anyone who would have been entitled to make a claim before the Government announced its intention to legislate. It turned out that no other claims had been started before the announcement, but the suggestion was that they would have been honoured.[36]

However, there appears to be no constitutional requirement to minimise the impact in this way. The Indemnity Act 1920,[37] the War Damage Act 1965[38] and the Jobseekers (Back to Work Schemes) Act 2013[39] are examples of laws that did not provide exemptions, even for those holding judgments in their favour. In these cases, the Government was protecting public revenue. In addition, it argued that the impact on judgment holders would be slight in any event, because they only lost an unearned or unexpected windfall. In effect, the litigant was seeking better treatment that those in a similar position, and fairness to the rest of the class justified the deprivation. This point arose under the Finance Act 1985 and associated regulations, in relation to changes in the taxation of interest earned in building society accounts. In *R v Inland Revenue Commissioners ex p Woolwich Equitable Building Society*, the House of Lords held that these provisions created a

[33] *R v Inland Revenue Commissioners ex p Woolwich Equitable Building Society* [1990] 1 WLR 1400 and *Woolwich Building Society v Inland Revenue Commissioners* [1993] AC 70.

[34] eg, Enemy Property Act 1953, s 17(1). This was not done with the Compensation Act 2006, s 3, which reversed the effect of *Barker v Corus* [2006] UKHL 20 with retrospective effect to the date of the judgment. This was justified by Bridget Prentice (Parliamentary Under-Secretary of State for Constitutional Affairs) on two grounds: (1) the degree of retrospection was limited because the courts had suspended cases on the relevant point in anticipation of legislation, and hence the period of retrospection was 'barely seven or eight weeks', and restricted to the specific aspects of the case; (2) it would be unfair to claimants with claims still unresolved to be subject to the holding where future claimants would not be (see HC Deb 17 July 2006, vol 449, cols 47–48). The Constitution Committee decided that the Bill did not raise significant constitutional issues: see House of Lords Constitution Committee, *Final Progress Report* (HL 2005–06, 255) app 2.

[35] Earl de la Warr, the Postmaster-General, stated that 'Any new action started after the date of my announcement on November 11 will be invalidated.' HL Deb 16 November 1954, vol 189 col 1487; see also Sir Harry Hylton-Foster, the Solicitor-General, HC Deb 17 December 1954, vol 535 col 2293. The intention to legislate was announced in the House of Commons by the Assistant Postmaster-General, but he said nothing about the impact on claims that had been commenced (or would be commenced by November 16th): HC Deb 11 November 1954, vol 532, col 1406–1407.

[36] Jocelyn Simon (Conservative, and later Solicitor-General and a Law Lord) argued that the announcement was not sufficiently clear and that claims filed after the announcement should have been honoured, but as no proceedings were commenced, it was a moot point in any event: HC Deb 10 December 1954, vol 535, cols 1274–75 and HC Deb 17 December 1954, vol 535, cols 2295–96 (it was not clear, at this point, whether any claims had been started after the announcement).

[37] The Act was general in scope but made no exemption for existing judgments or proceedings including, controversially, *Newcastle Breweries v R* [1920] 1 KB 854; this was cited as a precedent by the Attorney-General in the War Damage Bill debates, at HC Deb 12 May 1965, vol 712, col 606.

[38] See below text to n 62ff.

[39] See below text to n 167ff.

'gap period' in which interest was not taxable.[40] The Treasury had not intended to allow the gap period and, pending a decision from the courts, it collected the tax during that period. Then, in *Woolwich Equitable Building Society v Inland Revenue Commissioners*, the House of Lords held that the Woolwich should have restitution of the amounts that it had paid.[41] Other building societies then commenced claims for restitution of the amounts they had paid, but Parliament extinguished their claims by the Finance Act 1991 and the Finance (No 2) Act 1992.[42] The legislation made an exemption for the Woolwich but not the other building societies. From the Treasury's perspective, the Woolwich had gained an unearned windfall from the litigation, but this did not entitle others to a similar windfall.[43] More generally, as discussed in chapter three, the idea that unearned or unjustified gains may be taken without compensation was accepted in legislation on compensation for land, when ideas of community value were prominent in political thinking.[44] In the case of windfall gains in the form of tax savings, the 1991 and 1992 Finance Acts show that there is no general constitutional principle that says governments and Parliament are under an obligation to ensure that everyone who is similarly placed must get the same windfall.

B. Forestalling

Even the most efficient parliamentary procedures leave a gap between the announcement of the intention to legislate and the date that the law comes into force. This can raise concerns over forestalling, where people bring transactions forward, before the effective date of the legislation, or delay them until after the date, solely to put themselves under the rules that are the most advantageous to them. In many cases, the impact on the legislative aims is not significant.[45] Indeed, Ministers may have reasons to induce people to bring forward transactions.[46] However, forestalling can also undermine the legislative policy. It is a regular concern in the annual budget round, as changes are announced well before the Finance Act comes into force. Hence, the practice arose that the changes are backdated to Budget Day.[47]

[40] *R v Inland Revenue Commissioners ex p Woolwich Equitable Building Society* [1990] 1 WLR 1400.

[41] *Woolwich Equitable Building Society v Inland Revenue Commissioners* [1993] AC 70.

[42] Finance Act 1991, s 53 and Finance (No 2) Act 1992, s 6.

[43] HC Deb 30 April 1991, vol 190, cols 185–86 (David Mellor, Chief Secretary to the Treasury).

[44] See chapter three, section III.

[45] P Mathews, 'Forestalling Ahead of Property Tax Changes' [2016] OBR Working Paper no 10. Mathews reviews six examples in detail from December 2009 to March 2016 and the ways in which forestalling is accounted for in financial forecasts.

[46] ibid. Mathews notes that there are cases where governments wish to encourage forestalling. The recent stamp duty holiday during the COVID-19 outbreak is an example: it was intended to bring forward activity that might have been delayed, or not occurred at all, even though it resulted in a loss of revenue over the longer term.

[47] Ordinarily, a resolution would not be sufficient to impose a tax. However, budget resolutions can do so, under the Provisional Collection of Taxes Act 1968 or under the Finance Act 1973, s 50;

Laws aimed at forestalling are retrospective, but the practice is an accepted exception to the usual principles.[48] The alternatives are not attractive. For example, Parliament could enact laws before meaningful debate could occur, or delegate authority to Ministers to make changes without further parliamentary authority.[49] The current system does less violence to the rule of law than the alternatives, and less than the rules that previously applied. Prior to the Acts of Parliament (Commencement) Act 1793, the courts presumed that an Act of Parliament came into force on the first day of the parliamentary session in which it was passed, regardless of the date of Royal Assent, unless it contained a provision to the contrary or specified the date of Assent.[50] Although it was widely accepted that this could cause injustice, it also seems that it served the same purpose as modern practice of backdating of fiscal legislation to prevent forestalling. *Vickars v Attorney-General of Ireland* provides an example: the claimant objected to an additional duty on goods, on the basis that he had imported them before the relevant Act received Royal Assent.[51] However, the duties were still payable, because the Act was deemed to be in force at the start of the parliamentary session, which was well before the goods were imported.[52] The case is interesting because the Attorney-General's argument foreshadowed the modern practice, as he said that there was no injustice because the parliamentary votes occurred before the importation and hence the importers would have known that the higher duties would be payable.[53] This provided a limited safeguard for rule of law in those cases where

see D Natzler and M Hutton, *Erskine May's Treatise on the Law, Privileges, Proceedings and Usage of Parliament*, 25th edn (LexisNexis UK, 2019) para 36.36. For the historical background, see J Jaconelli, 'The "Bowles Act" – Cornerstone of the Fiscal Constitution' (2010) 69 *Cambridge Law Journal* 582.

[48] In the debate on the Finance Bill 1978, John Pardoe, a Liberal MP, said that no retrospection was involved in the practice of backdating tax changes to the budget resolutions: HC Deb 12 July 1978, vol 953, col 1673. His speech is not entirely clear, but he may have been saying that there is no retrospection because budget resolutions are given legal effect by the Provisional Collection of Taxes Act 1968. In any case, he was correct in saying that the backdating is not seen as raising constitutional issues.

[49] The fast track procedure was used for the Jobseekers Bill 2013 and came in for heavy criticism from the Constitution Committee: see House of Lords Constitution Committee, *Jobseekers (Back to Work Schemes) Bill* (HL 2012–13, 155) paras 5–12; on the retrospective aspects, see below text to n 167ff. As discussed above text to n 26, section 75 of the Banking Act 2009 enables the Treasury to issue orders for the retrospective change of the law, which does not allow Parliament advance scrutiny. However, neither one of these were intended to deal with forestalling.

[50] This is now covered by the Interpretation Act 1978, s 4. See M Gobbi, 'When to Begin: A Study of New Zealand Commencement Clauses with Regard to Those Used in the United Kingdom, Australia, and the United States' (2010) 31 *Statute Law Review* 153, 154–59.

[51] *Vickars v Attorney-General of Ireland* (1779) 6 Bro PC 491; 2 ER 1220.

[52] The tax had retrospective effect, but the Court noted that the Act was passed by the Irish Parliament on 21st December and sent to England for Royal Assent; the goods were imported on 28th December; Royal Assent was given on 1st January but the usual rule applied so that the duties took effect from the start of the parliamentary session, which was before the importation.

[53] The argument was that 'And that these several proceedings having been circulated in the printed votes of the House of Commons, the intention of the legislature to continue this ancient additional duty must therefore have been publicly known; consequently, the imposition was made with full notice, and critically at that juncture, to evade, in fraud of the revenue, the payment of the additional duty.' 6 Bro PC 491, 497; 2 ER 1220, 1224.

the ordinary legislative processes made it known that changes were about to come into force. Clearly, the older approach did not always hit the target, as it applied when there was no risk that forestalling would frustrate the legislative aims or cause injustice.[54] Accordingly, the Acts of Parliament (Commencement) Act 1793 acknowledged that injustice could occur, and henceforth the Clerk was required to endorse the date of Assent on the Act.[55]

Constitutional issues may arise where there are questions regarding the risk of forestalling or the breadth of measures. For example, in its evidence to the Treasury Committee on the reduction in Entrepreneur's Relief from £10 million to £1 million under the Finance Bill 2020, the Chartered Institute of Taxation expressed doubts about the breadth of the forestalling measures.[56] In its view, the measures were too broad, as they would have also applied to taxpayers entering transactions for sound business reasons. In Parliament, the point was raised by Bridget Phillipson, Shadow Chief Secretary to the Treasury, to which Jesse Norman, Financial Secretary to the Treasury, responded that there were exceptions in the Bill for those acting for purposes other than avoidance.[57] Neither referred explicitly to constitutional standards specifically relating to forestalling, but their comments do reflect the policies behind the exception.

C. Retrospection and Litigation

Most of the modern examples of retrospection involve legislation that sets aside a judgment. Plainly, reversing a judgment raises serious questions about the rule of law. Not only does it violate fundamental principles regarding the separation of powers, but it undermines the stability that the rule of law should foster. It is therefore quite interesting that governments often justify the reversal of a judgment on the basis that, in the specific circumstances, retrospection would do more to ensure stability than allowing the judgment to stand. That is, governments often say that retrospective action is needed because the judgment was unexpected. It may have been contrary to settled professional opinion,[58] or raise issues that had not been previously identified[59] or been caused by an entirely unintended slip in

[54] Gobbi (n 50) 155–57 discusses *Panter v Attorney-General* (1772) 6 Bro PC 486; 2 ER 1217 (HL), where counsel argued that the courts should not give a retrospective interpretation on the basis of the rule that statutes took effect from the first day of the parliamentary session, but the House of Lords decided to follow precedent.

[55] This still left a degree of retrospection, although only to the start of the day.

[56] Written evidence submitted by the Chartered Institute of Taxation (FB08); Finance Bill 2020 – Submission to the Public Bill Committee, available at publications.parliament.uk/pa/cm5801/cmpublic/Finance/memo/FB08.pdf. See also Brooks Newmark, in relation to changes to the APD, HC Deb 1 May 2007, vol 459, col 1429: there is no need for anti-forestalling provisions if the affected individuals would not be able to change their decisions or behaviour in any event. Newmark argued that retrospection was unnecessary to stop forestalling, because it was highly unlikely that anyone would move their flight dates forward to avoid the increase in the duty. The Government did not respond to his argument.

[57] PBC Deb (Finance Bill) 9 June 2020, col 68 (Bridget Phillipson) and col 71 (Jesse Norman).

[58] eg Charitable Trusts (Validation) Act 1954.

[59] eg Wireless Telegraphy (Validation of Charges) Act 1954.

legislative drafting.[60] It has been pointed out that no judgment could be completely unexpected: why would the litigant have commenced proceedings?[61] Nevertheless, it is not surprising that a government would raise this point. Indeed, it would be more surprising to find that a government had anticipated an unfavourable judgment in an important matter and yet it had not bothered to amend the law before causes of action could vest. In effect, it would admit that it had been governing on the basis of an interpretation of the law that it had not believed to be correct. Nevertheless, it leaves an odd impression of the rule of law as a tool for ensuring stability. That is, Parliament has often enacted retrospective legislation because the strict observance of the rule of law would be more destabilising than reversing it. It is reasonably clear from the practice, however, that the unexpected nature of a judgment is not sufficient justification for its reversal. As noted in the Introduction, in the debates on the War Damage Bill 1965, the Attorney-General, Elwyn Jones, put forward broad propositions on retrospective legislation: it is 'in general wrong and contrary to the rule of law', but there may be 'exceptional circumstances which make it just and equitable to depart from that rule'.[62] In his view, these propositions were not controversial: they were accepted by the Government and 'broadly accepted by the House', although there could be disagreement on their application to a specific case.[63]

The War Damage Bill provoked some of the most protracted and controversial debates on retrospection and proceeded through Parliament twice before approval by the House of Lords. It arose when Burmah Oil and eight other British companies sought compensation for the destruction of their oil refineries and other property in Burma by British forces in World War II. This was a case of 'denial damage', where the property is destroyed to stop it falling into the hands of the enemy. After the War, the British Government made *ex gratia* payments to the companies of about one-quarter to one-third of the value of their losses.[64] However, the companies wanted full compensation. They made claims in the Burmese courts but, when those courts rejected them, they brought proceedings in the UK. In *Burmah Oil v Lord Advocate*, the House of Lords held that the destruction was a lawful exercise of the Crown's prerogative right and duty to protect the realm and subjects in war and peril.[65] However, it was subject to a duty to compensate for the damage. The quantification of damages was left for further proceedings, but the Government introduced the Bill before proceedings could resume.[66]

[60] eg Finance Act 1926, s 22, which took effect as of the commencement of Part III of the Finance Act (No 2) 1915.

[61] P Ridd, 'Hole and Plug' in P Harris and D de Cogan (eds), *Studies in the History of Tax Law* (Hart Publishing, 2021) vol 10, n 179.

[62] HC Deb 12 May 1965, vol 712, col 600; see also HC Deb 25 June 2007, vol 462, cols 48–49, 57, 59.

[63] HC Deb 12 May 1965, vol 712, col 600.

[64] See HC Deb 3 February 1965, vol 705, cols 1091–99 on the background.

[65] *Burmah Oil v Lord Advocate* [1965] AC 75.

[66] In the House, Niall MacDermott stated that the claims totalled about £80 million: HC Deb 12 May 1965, vol 712, cols 544–45. As Lord Reid noted in his opinion, the property was destroyed when it was almost certain that it would fall into the hands of the Japanese, so arguably it had little or no value at that point: *Burmah Oil v Lord Advocate*, ibid 113.

Niall MacDermott, Financial Secretary to the Treasury, opened the Commons debate on Second Reading. He offered a more precise version of the Attorney-General's second proposition, as he stated that 'retrospective legislation is justified when it is necessary to obtain justice or equity between one citizen or class of citizens and another, to ensure that people in like circumstances receive the same treatment and enjoy the same rights'.[67] This raised further questions: what were 'like circumstances'? In this case, governments during and after the War gave support to individuals and companies to 'rehabilitate'. This was intended to be enough to allow them to resume work or re-open businesses, but not to provide the financial equivalent of all their wartime losses or to restore them to their pre-War state. This represented fair and just treatment, and it had already been provided to the companies in the form of the *ex gratia* payments. Hence, the Government argued that it would be contrary to fairness and justice if the law gave them more than others who had suffered injuries and loss during the War. Rehabilitation, in its view, should have been enough.

MacDermott also framed his argument in terms of legitimate expectations. In the debates on the Iron and Steel Bill 1949, Sir David Maxwell-Fyfe focused on the necessity for an advance warning, as he said that 'the justification for retrospective legislation is that a reasonable and definite warning has been given to people likely to practice the matter to be struck at, and they have been given the opportunity to avoid that course'.[68] The Government pressed this point, as Ministers of different governments had refused compensation demands from the companies, starting with Stafford Cripps in 1949, RA Butler in 1951, Harold Macmillan in 1956, Selwyn Lloyd in 1957 and Reginald Maudling in 1961.[69] MacDermott also cited a Commons statement given by the Chancellor in 1943, stating that colonial and British governments would support the replacement or repair of damaged and destroyed property and goods, but only as far as resources permitted.[70] Against the consistency of this position, the claimants could not have had any realistic expectation of recovery or that retrospection would not be used if needed.

In terms of the comparators in the assessment of fairness, the opposing MPs claimed that fairness was on their side, as some wartime victims did receive full compensation.[71] However, this only applied to victims within the UK, as the legislation only secured compensation for damage to property in the UK. Hence, the claimants had no effective remedy, except through the common law action.

[67] HC Deb 12 May 1965, vol 712, cols 530–31.

[68] HC Deb 28 April 1949, vol 464, cols 499–500; E Fletcher, 'Retrospective Fiscal Legislation' (1959) 1959 *British Tax Review* 412, 425.

[69] HC Deb 3 February 1965, vol 705, cols 1097–98. Indeed, the War Damage Bill was drafted by the previous Conservative Government, but the general election intervened before it had time to be introduced to Parliament.

[70] HC Deb 3 February 1965, vol 705, cols 1095–96, quoting Sir Kingsley Wood, Chancellor of the Exchequer, at HC Deb 18 February 1943, vol 386, col 1942.

[71] In particular, full compensation was payable for property located in the UK under the Compensation (Defence) Act 1939 and the War Damage Act 1941.

The opposing MPs dismissed the relevance of the warnings, on the basis that the companies were entitled to access to the courts for a final judicial determination of their rights. Indeed, as discussed below, the issue of warnings was a key element in anti-avoidance tax legislation, going back to the pre-World War II period. In several debates, MPs argued that a warning had no constitutional status: citizens were entitled to follow the law until it was changed, and it could only be changed by Parliament. In effect, warnings were being used as a form of unconstitutional executive lawmaking. However, by 1965, the argument had been raised and dismissed on several occasions and there were already numerous precedents where laws had been backdated to a warning of the intention to legislate.[72]

The War Damage Bill provoked lengthy and vigorous debate, but ultimately it neither created new precedents nor extended the existing ones. It cannot be said, for example, that MPs reached any kind of consensus on principles beyond those identified by Niall MacDermott, and they did not represent a departure from existing precedent in any case. However, it did show that precedent was important, as the Ministers and Law Officers structured their arguments around precedent and provided specific examples when challenged by the opposition. The next section therefore considers the precedents in more detail, by dividing them into two categories. The first includes the situations where the judgment resolves a private dispute. In such cases, the Government has no direct interest in the outcome and hence, arguably, the constitutional concerns with the abuse of power should not be as great. The second covers the reversal of a judgment against a government department or agency. The two categories raise similar issues concerning the rule of law, but the precedents show that the justifications for retrospection can be different.

i. The State is Neutral

Governments rarely seek to reverse judgments in which the state has no direct interest. When governments do seek retrospective legislation, they often argue that the judgment has caused such disruption that it would be contrary to the public interest to allow it to stand. A clear example is the Churches (Scotland) Act 1905. The case arose when the trustees of the Free Church of Scotland voted to merge with the United Presbyterian Church and form the United Free Church (UFC). A much smaller group, concentrated in the Highlands, continued under the original name. The two bodies were unable to agree on a division of the assets. Litigation ensued, with the House of Lords ultimately deciding in *General Assembly of Free Church of Scotland v Overtoun* that the remaining Free Church was entitled to the assets.[73] As a charitable body, the UFC churches and institutions were not just

[72] In the debates regarding the Finance Bill 1958, the Chancellor noted the concerns of some Conservative backbenchers in this respect, but did not doubt the legitimacy of backdating to a sufficiently precise warning: see below, text to nn 111–13.

[73] *General Assembly of Free Church of Scotland v Overtoun* [1904] AC 515.

providing religious services but also schools, other educational institutions and overseas missions. The judgment threatened these services and the security of the ministers and staff, many of whom faced eviction from homes attached to their positions.

In practical terms, it seemed obvious to outsiders that the two parties should have agreed on a division of assets that would have allowed each to continue to provide services for their own communities. However, even after the judgment, no agreement could be reached. The disruption was such that a Royal Commission was appointed to investigate the matter.[74] The Commission stated that a reversal of the judgment should be avoided if at all possible. As its report put it, 'The Legislature cannot reverse or nullify the final decision of the Law Courts without a violation of constitutional principle, much more mischievous than any consequence, however harsh, which may follow from the legal decision in a particular case.'[75] Despite this, the Commission concluded that the judgment did not present an 'insuperable obstacle to an equitable adjustment'.[76] This was put in place by the Churches (Scotland) Act 1905, which provided for the appointment of a second commission to divide the assets between the parties, 'in such manner as appears to the Commission fair and equitable, having regard to all the circumstances of the case'.[77]

The Churches (Scotland) Act 1905 was not controversial in Parliament, despite having the same effect as an uncompensated expropriation. However, the reversal of a later Scottish case was much more so. In *Kerr v Bryde*, the House of Lords held that landlords had not followed the procedure for increasing rents that was required by the Increase of Rent and Mortgage Interest (Restrictions) Act 1920.[78] As a result, they were obliged to reimburse their tenants who had paid increased rents for their overpayments. On 1 December 1922, a few days after the judgment, the Prime Minister stated in the House of Commons that the Government would introduce a bill to excuse landlords from returning the overpayments.[79] The Rent Restriction (Notices of Increase) Bill 1923 followed, and it provoked strong criticism on constitutional grounds from both the opposition parties and from the Conservative backbenches. Ramsay MacDonald, for example, described

[74] The Warrant gave some indication of the eventual solution to the problem, as it stated that the Commission was called in part because 'it is doubtful how far the Free Church are or may be in a position to carry out the Trusts as declared by the House of Lords': Royal Commission on Churches (Scotland) *Report of the Royal Commission on Churches (Scotland)*, vol 1 (Cd 2494, 1905) 1.

[75] ibid 17.

[76] ibid 20.

[77] Churches (Scotland) Act 1905, s 1(1). Strictly speaking, the Act was not retrospective. There was no change to the law of trusts (prospective or retrospective) and the judgment was not overturned. Nevertheless, the Free Church was clearly denied the benefit of the judgment and assets were taken from it without compensation.

[78] *Kerr v Bryde* [1922] AC 16. For a detailed review of the case and legislation, see PQ Watchman, 'Retrospective Legislation: A Gift from the Gods?' in EPH Keane and P Robson (eds), *The Ian Willock Collection on Law and Justice in the Twenty-First Century* (Fairleigh Dickinson University Press; Rowman & Littlefield, 2023).

[79] HC Deb 30 Nov 1922, vol 159, col 901.

it as a 'specially objectionable example of retrospective legislation'.[80] The Attorney-General, Sir Douglas Hogg, defended the Bill on the basis that requiring landlords to return the rent increase would cause 'a very great crisis', because many landlords had not retained the overpayments.[81] The Act passed in any event, but it has not been cited in subsequent debates, perhaps because the retrospective reversal of a judgment in a private matter is so rare. Nevertheless, as Paul Watchman points out, there have been echoes of the Law Officers' defence of constitutionality.[82] The Attorney-General argued that the judgment was based on an unintended technical defect or gap in the law, which Parliament had not been aware of when the Bill was before it.[83] As the defect was unintended, the Act would not have a serious impact on individuals, as it merely restored the position that most landlords and tenants had assumed to be true. This is now regularly employed by governments in their justification of retrospection in cases where the state does have an interest, as shown below.

The approach taken by the Commission and Parliament in 1905 therefore suggests a hierarchy of constitutional principle. That is, the compulsory redistribution of property between private parties was less serious, and more easily justified, than the retrospective reversal of a judgment regarding the same set of assets. Both override the consent of private parties, but a reversal of judgment also interferes with the judicial process. Arguably, this was the view of the opposition to the War Damage Bill, except that specific assets were not in dispute and hence expropriation and redistribution were not in issue. This was not, however, the policy behind the Charitable Trusts (Validation) Act 1954, which reversed judgments that had invalidated a number of charitable trusts (but with savings for individuals who had become entitled to property under the judgments).[84] The judgments turned on model purpose clauses that were widely used by legal professionals when setting up charitable trusts. In a series of cases brought by the Inland Revenue Commission, the courts found that the clauses did not set up charitable trusts, as intended. The consequences went beyond taxation, as distributions under the putative trusts were invalid and subject to tracing. Furthermore, as with the Scottish churches case, the judgment had wide implications, as property that had been devoted to charitable purposes would now be held for private purposes. Moreover, many of

[80] HC Deb 8 May 1923, vol 163, col 2199.

[81] HC Deb 22 February 1923, vol 160, col 1305; see also the Solicitor-General, Sir Thomas Inskip, at ibid col 1401.

[82] Watchman (n 78) 257: 'With the benefit of hindsight, the Rent Restriction (Notices of Increase) Act 1923 may be a watershed, marking the beginning of the modern use of retrospective legislation by Government as a blunt legal tool to protect the public purse, the State or the establishment.'

[83] HC Deb 22 February 1923, vol 160, cols 1253–1313 *passim*; and HC Deb 1923, vol 163, col 2305–2306 (Attorney-General).

[84] *Ellis v Inland Revenue Commissioners* (1949) 31 TC 178 and *Oxford Group v Inland Revenue Commissioners* [1949] 2 All ER 537 and the earlier case *Chichester Diocesan Fund v Simpson* [1944] AC 341; see G Gleason Bogert, 'Nathan Report and the Supervision and Enforcement of Charitable Trusts' (1954) 29 *New York University Law Review*; DW Logan, 'Report of the Committee on the Law and Practice Relating to Charitable Trusts [Cmd. 8710]' (1953) 16 *MLR* 343; PS Atiyah, 'Charitable Trusts (Validation) Act, 1954' (1955) 18 *MLR* 152.

the putative trusts had not been identified, so the impact on the public was uncertain. In this case, given the number of trusts that would be affected, empowering a commission to redistribute assets was not practical. Instead, the Government and Parliament opted for the retrospective reversal of the judgments. Accordingly, the Charitable Trusts (Validation) Act 1954 retrospectively validated the trusts, but with savings for individuals who had become entitled to trust property on their invalidation.

The Charitable Trusts (Validation) Act 1954 suggests that the Royal Commission on the Scottish churches had overstated the constitutional principle when it suggested that the reversal of any judgment would be unconstitutional. This seems to have been the view of MPs, as the 1954 Act passed through Parliament without trouble. The constitutional issues were raised but were not regarded as a serious obstacle by the Government or most MPs. Indeed, the Act was unusual, in that the litigation was pursued by a government department, in the public interest, on the basis of an understanding of the law that it had held for some time.

Hence, the outcome of the cases could hardly be described as unexpected.[85] The justification was simply that implementing the judgments would be disruptive. This followed the recommendations of the Nathan Committee, which reported that

> Retrospective legislation should be avoided whenever possible and the rights of those entitled on the failure of a trust must not be lightly set aside. … In our opinion, however, a legal situation has been created which is somewhat absurd and which appears to us to call for a commonsense solution, saving as much as possible for charity, and to justify, in these highly unusual circumstances, derogation from these rules.[86]

Indeed, there was no change to the law of charities, except for the validation of prior instruments. The easy passage through Parliament was at least partly due to the savings made for private parties, but there were also practical considerations. In 1905, the Commission and Parliament would have been aware that a simple reversal of the judgment would not have resulted in an equitable distribution of assets between the parties. The parties demonstrated no desire to settle their dispute amicably and probably would have returned to the courts, perhaps on multiple occasions. Without a change in the general principles of trust law, the desired solution of a division that allowed both churches to continue to serve their congregations would not have been achieved. By contrast, in 1954, retrospective validation did achieve the desired end. Not only did the charities continue in operation, but there was no need to identify all the trusts that had been affected. The pragmatic concerns were different, but the common concern with the disruption to public services was central to both. As stated above, strict adherence to the rule of law would have undermined social stability.

[85] This was raised in the Commons by Sir Lynn Ungoed-Thomas, especially since some trust instruments were drafted with model clauses after the initial judgments: HC Deb 27 July 1954, vol 531, cols 448–49 and HC Deb 10 March 1954, vol 524, 2301–2304.

[86] *Report of the Committee on the Law and Practice Relating to Charitable Trusts* (Cmd 8710, 1952) paras 497–98.

ii. The State is not Neutral

The Introduction quotes Willes J in *Philips v Eyre*, which concerned a colonial Act of Indemnity that retrospectively gave legal authority for the acts of public officials who suppressed the Morant Bay rebellion in Jamaica. As Willes J observed, there was nothing novel about retrospective legislation. Indemnity and amnesty laws are now rare, as the practice is to prospectively confer special powers on specific classes of public officials in relation to defined duties. The modern focus falls on the retrospective correction of gaps in tax or regulatory laws that only emerge after enactment of the initial legislation. This arises most frequently in relation to tax avoidance schemes, where the repeated use of retrospection has led to attempts to codify the constitutional standards.

In these cases, there are usually financial reasons to reverse a judgment: either an expected source of tax revenue has been lost or an unexpected liability has been created. However, the immediate loss is not usually put forward as the primary or sole reason for retrospection. Instead, governments often focus on the effectiveness of a wider administrative system. It may be the case, for example, that the Government wants to avoid the risk that multiple claims will divert resources and attention from the system's wider aims.[87] Or, the practical cost of dealing with claims may be excessive when set against their amount.[88] In most cases, however, the Government's main concern is with the wider impact of unchecked avoidance. The burdens and benefits of regulation should, in theory, fall according to principles of general application. This, in turn, should help to reduce costs by securing voluntary compliance. If the system is seen as replete with loopholes and exceptions, even if lawful, there is a risk that those who do comply voluntarily will become less likely to do so.[89] Accordingly, governments may argue that retrospective laws are needed to restore faith in the system. Paradoxically, restoring faith in the law may require a departure from the rule of law.

In these situations, the moral condemnation of avoidance often features in the justification of retrospection. It is not just that the judgment confers an undeserved and unintended advantage on some people, but that they deliberately sought to exploit a loophole so as to obtain it. An early example is the War Charges Act 1925, which reversed a judgment that exposed a gap in an administrative scheme for controlling profiteering in World War I. The scheme operated by setting milk prices by region, so that dairies in different regions would make similar profits on sales. Dairies could sell surplus milk outside their region, but they required a special licence to do so. There was a charge for a licence, which was intended to ensure that their profits would be no greater than if they had sold in their own region.

[87] As in the case of the Loan Charge, below text to n 147ff.

[88] As in the case of the Wireless Telegraphy (Validity of Charges) Act 1954.

[89] Conversely, there is a risk that anti-avoidance measures may be seen as heavy-handed and may therefore undermine confidence in the system and raise the cost of securing compliance: see M Blackwell, 'The April 2019 Loan Charge' (2019) 2019 *British Tax Review* 240.

In *Attorney-General v Wilts United Dairies*, a dairy obtained a judgment to say that the charge was not lawful.[90] The Act therefore validated the charges, retrospectively. In Parliament, MPs described the judgment holders as profiteers, because they had taken positive steps to obtain an advantage that they were never intended to have.[91] Similarly, with many retrospective tax avoidance laws, the taxpayers entered highly contrived schemes solely for the purpose of avoiding tax.

The first searching debates on constitutional standards relating to anti-avoidance laws occurred during the debates on the Finance Bills of 1936 and 1937. The concern was with the avoidance of tax on income by transferring it abroad.[92] In 1936, the Chancellor, Neville Chamberlain, addressed the most fundamental point, as he said that retrospection was a necessary tool in the battle against tax avoidance. This was aimed at Conservative backbenchers who argued that retrospective taxation should never be accepted.[93] Chamberlain acknowledged that retrospection should be used sparingly but argued that there were several aspects of the avoidance schemes that justified it. First, they were highly artificial, in that they served no purpose other than tax avoidance. Secondly, it would be unfair to those who paid their taxes if the schemes were allowed to stand. Finally, the schemes provided no wider social or economic value. These points do not appear to have satisfied the backbenchers, and so the Chancellor ultimately decided not to seek retrospective legislation to re-open closed assessments. However, he did not wish to give an 'invitation to devise further and still more ingenious methods' of avoiding tax. Accordingly, he issued a warning:

> I would wish to make it quite clear that I do not consider that, in the future, people will be entitled, if they find new methods of avoiding taxation of a similar character to these which are dealt with here in this Bill, to say that they are protected by anything I do now from retrospective legislation. I give them fair warning, and after that fair warning I think that they will have no reason to complain if retrospective legislation should be found necessary in this particular class of case.[94]

In the 1937 Budget speech, he announced that he would introduce measures to follow from the warning given in the previous year.[95] However, he became Prime Minister before the introduction of the Finance Bill. The new Chancellor, Sir John Simon, was clearly closer to the doves than the hawks. He stated that, as a 'general proposition', that 'if we find that there is a hole in the tax law which is open for people to use, and we have failed to stop the hole, we shall not go back and treat

[90] *Attorney-General v Wilts United Dairies* (1922) 38 TLR 781. Note that the claimant was exempted from the Act.

[91] HL Deb 19 July 1922, vol 51, cols 587–88 (Lord Buckmaster) and HL Deb 3 March 1925, vol 60, col 348 (Marquess of Salisbury).

[92] See Fletcher (n 68) for a detailed analysis of retrospective tax laws in this period.

[93] Daniel Somerville, for example, said that 'retrospective legislation is a dangerous thing and not in accordance with the practice of the House': HC Deb 9 June 1937, vol 322, col 1917.

[94] HC Deb 1 July 1936, vol 314, cols 442–43.

[95] HC Deb 20 April 1937, vol 322, cols 1610–12.

the tax retrospectively'.[96] However, in this case, the warning given by the Chancellor justified action. The schemes, although 'perfectly within the law', were 'of the same general nature as those which my predecessor set out to stop in the Finance Bill last year'.[97] Accordingly, the provisions to counter them would be retrospective to the warning: this was 'a very special case', justified by the 'ample notice' that had been given.[98]

This leads to a further point. Chamberlain and Simon made it clear that the target for retrospection should be specific. They were not claiming a general authority to take retrospective action against avoidance schemes, even where the schemes were highly artificial, unfair to other taxpayers, and served no wider public interest. Some form of advance warning was necessary. Moreover, a vague warning against avoidance in general would not be sufficient: it should identify the type of scheme to which retrospection might apply. Accordingly, in 1936, Chamberlain referred to schemes 'of a similar character' to the income transfer schemes to which the surtax would attach. This still went too far for some Conservative backbenchers, but there were also strong views against the need for any warning, especially from Labour MPs. They argued that tax avoidance was wrong, even if strictly legal, and so there should be no need to provide any warning. Or, if a warning were required, it could be expressed in general terms.[99] Indeed, as discussed below, the Labour Paymaster-General, Dawn Primarolo, did just this in 2004.

It is worth noting that the 1937 Finance Bill was seen as unprecedented, despite the War Charges Act 1925.[100] The analysis therefore proceeded from the general principles rather than precedents. Two general points emerged from the debate. The first relates to the rule of law as embodying fundamental ideas of fairness and equality. Usually, the focus falls on procedural aspects, but it was clear substantive fairness and equality were important to MPs. The MPs who were opposed to retrospection argued that avoidance did not represent a breach of any moral duty or communal obligation. Sir Irving Albery, a Conservative, said that

> the taxpayer is entitled to pay as little tax as he is compelled to pay by law. He has the right to study the law and to arrange his business or his liability for taxation in such a manner that he will be liable for as little taxation as possible.[101]

Hence, when considering fairness and equality, the tax avoider should be compared to someone who was never within the expected scope of the tax provisions, rather than someone who did pay the tax that was avoided. Accordingly, it

[96] HC Deb 9 June 1937, vol 324, col 1909. A similar statement was made by David Mellor, Chief Secretary to the Treasury, in 1991: above text to n 29.

[97] HC Deb 9 June 1937, vol 324, col 1916.

[98] ibid.

[99] HC Deb 1 July 1936, vol 314, col 443 (Hastings Lees-Smith).

[100] eg Sir Alfred Beit (Conservative) HC Deb 9 June 1937, vol 324, col 1919 protested against 'the innovation of retrospective legislation'; see also HC Deb 9 June 1937, vol 322, col 1917 (Annesley Somerville).

[101] HC Deb 16 June 1936, vol 313, col 684.

would be unfair to target tax avoiders with retrospective legislation merely because they avoided tax. This argument was squarely rejected by other MPs. For example, Hastings Lees-Smith argued that Albery confused legal duties with moral duties. It did not follow that someone who lawfully avoided tax had not breached a moral duty to the community.[102] These issues of fairness and the competing claims of the users of schemes and the general body of taxpayers has resurfaced in most subsequent debates on tax avoidance.

The second aspect concerned the role of rule of law in enabling individuals to plan their affairs. Retrospection undermines certainty; without certainty, individuals will become reluctant to enter contracts. Not only does this compromise their autonomy as individuals, but it may lead to wider social and economic harm.[103] This explains the requirement of warnings. As noted above, in the debates on the Finance Bill 1936, the Chancellor stated that retrospection should not be used in the absence of a warning.[104] This established a practice that was followed during World War II and thereafter: first, the Chancellor (or a Treasury Minister) would issue a warning in Parliament that certain types of avoidance schemes could be subject to retrospective legislation in future. Then, when introducing the Budget, the Chancellor would say that the Bill would include retrospective measures and refer to the warning when justifying them. In principle, warnings should be given in relation to any bill where they would allow individuals to choose a course of action. This makes choice and personal autonomy the driving concern behind the requirement for a warning. If retrospection seems harsh, it is only because the targeted individuals did not heed the warnings.

Through this period, Labour accepted that retrospection required justification, but did not explicitly accept that specific notice was necessary. Nevertheless, in the debates on retrospective provisions of the Finance Bill 1950, the Financial Secretary to the Treasury, Douglas Jay, said that 'though I agree it would be undesirable to propose a retrospective measure even of this kind without due warning, the situation is entirely different when due warning has been given'.[105] He also said that 'It has been a well established practice in the past, followed by Conservative as well as other Governments, to act retrospectively in taxation matters when due warning has been given.'[106] He gave specific precedents, listing the Finance Acts of 1936, 1937, 1938, 1939 and 1940 as examples specifically concerned with the

[102] HC Deb 1 July 1936, vol 314, col 443.

[103] See, eg, T Bingham, *The Rule of Law* (Penguin, 2010) 38: 'No one would choose to do business, perhaps involving large sums of money, in a country where the parties' rights and obligations were vague or undecided.'

[104] Above text to n 94. Interestingly, he also said that the threat of retrospection was valuable: without it, the incentive to search for new avoidance schemes would remain strong. If this were the case, however, it would apply to retrospection prior to a warning. By committing only to retrospection from the date of a warning, he left untouched the incentive to engage in avoidance prior to its detection by the tax authorities and the subsequent warning: see HC Deb 1 July 1936, vol 314, col 442.

[105] HC Deb 16 May 1950, vol 475, col 1025.

[106] ibid col 1026.

surtax. This falls short of saying that a warning is strictly necessary, but it does indicate that Labour Ministers also felt that warnings would normally be required.

Questions concerning warnings surfaced again in relation to retrospective provisions of the Finance Bill 1958. During the progress of the Finance Bill 1955, Henry Brooke, Financial Secretary to the Treasury, expressed concern regarding dividend stripping schemes. He warned that, if dividend stripping continued, legislation would be introduced to take effect retrospectively from the date of the warning.[107] The practice did continue, and in his Budget Day speech in 1958, the new Chancellor, Derick Heathcoat-Amory, said the Finance Bill would include retrospective measures consistent with the 1955 warning.[108] However, at Second Reading, he announced that the measures would only be retrospective to Budget Day. It appears that he came under considerable pressure from his own MPs to remove the retrospective element, as the Labour opposition remained in favour. The point of interest concerns Heathcoat-Amory's explanation for the change, as it cast doubt on the use of retrospection in any form. On the one hand, he said that retrospection could be used legitimately, but only after a suitable warning, because 'those concerned should have every reason to be aware of the taxation consequences of their specific actions and, therefore, have a chance of avoiding it if they wish'.[109] Thus far, his position is consistent with the precedents established since the Finance Bill 1936. However, in this case, he stated that the warnings were not sufficiently precise to be acted upon, because 'there were some doubts as to whether the terms of the warnings were wide enough to cover all the new forms of dividend stripping which have arisen since then'.[110] Labour MPs argued that Heathcoat-Amory was, in effect, requiring a warning to be as detailed as a statutory provision.[111] As warnings were used because governments needed time to draft a bill with the adequate level of precision, Heathcoat-Amory was making it virtually impossible for the Treasury to backdate provisions to the warning. Tax avoidance would continue, at least until the introduction of the next Finance bill, despite the Treasury's knowledge that it was occurring.

The Chancellor also expressed doubts that a Ministerial warning in the Commons was sufficiently public to put tax avoiders on notice. He did not say where or how warnings should be given, but only that he did not feel certain that a Ministerial statement should be sufficient to justify retrospection. Indeed, he was careful to say as little as possible:

> In this case, the warning took the form of a statement by Ministers in the House and recorded in Hansard. Different views are held about whether such a warning constitutes

[107] HC Deb 13 December 1955, vol 547, col 1022 (Brooke said that the warning was delivered 'with the authority' of the Chancellor).
[108] HC Deb 15 April 1958, vol 586, cols 61–62.
[109] HC Deb 18 June 1958, vol 589, col 1132.
[110] ibid cols 1136–37 (GR Mitchison and Harold Wilson).
[111] See, eg, ibid cols 1137ff (John Diamond).

> a valid warning which can be assumed to be available to, and in the mind of, anyone contemplating this kind of action at any time in the future.[112]

Later in the debate, he explained that:

> That was one of the factors on which I have still some doubt, namely, whether it is reasonable to expect everyone concerned in future decisions on commercial matters like this to be conscious – by itself and without anything else – about what a Minister said in the House of Commons on a particular day.[113]

He did not, however, commit himself to a clear position, saying only that there were points of doubt. As shown below, neither the Labour Government nor the Opposition critics took such a narrow view in the debates on the Finance Bill 1978 or thereafter. However, critics of the Loan Charge (imposed by the Finance Act (No 2) 2017 raised similar points, although without referring to Heathcoat-Amory's comments. As discussed below, they put forward an amendment that would have limited retrospection to cases where the individual knew that disguised remuneration in the form of loans should have been declared as income.[114] To be sure, the situation was different, as the Treasury insisted that the loan schemes had never been effective to avoid tax, whereas the dividend stripping schemes did lawfully avoid tax. Nevertheless, in both cases, the real objective seems to be that the requirement for a warning should be so specific that retrospection legislation would become largely irrelevant in countering avoidance schemes.[115]

iii. The Rees Rules

Questions concerning the nature and timing of warnings became prominent in the latter years of the Callaghan Government. In November 1977, the Chief Secretary to the Treasury, Joel Barnett, stated that he was aware of new avoidance schemes involving the artificial creation of tax losses through the use of commodity straddles. He told the Commons that the Chancellor 'will be considering from what date legislation against a claim to loss relief contrived in this kind of way should be effective'.[116] In the Budget speech of April 1978, the Chancellor, Denis Healey, announced that retrospective measures would be introduced. However, the measures would not take effect from Barnett's warning, but from April 1976, when it was believed that the schemes were first used.[117]

The Labour Government took the view that retrospection prior to the warning was justified because the schemes served no purpose other than the avoidance of tax and they had cost the Treasury a significant amount in lost revenue

[112] ibid col 1132.
[113] ibid col 1137.
[114] See below text to n 163.
[115] The Chancellor raised these schemes again with the Finance Bill 1960; for a thorough discussion, in Parliament and then the courts, see Ridd (n 61).
[116] HC Deb 25 November 1977, vol 939, cols 965–66W.
[117] HC Deb 11 April 1978, vol 947, cols 1202–1203.

over a short period.[118] Barnett also argued that the key moral point was equality: there was no justification for allowing a small group to shift the tax burden to others, where there was no other purpose to the transaction than the avoidance of tax. Moreover, the unfairness would be minimal because the tax avoiders would pay no more tax than anyone who had not engaged in the scheme.[119] His points were not novel; in substance, they were the same as Neville Chamberlain had made when introducing retrospective measures in Finance Bill 1936. However, the Conservatives focused on backdating prior to a warning. Peter Rees, who later served as Chief Secretary to the Treasury, identified core principles for retrospective provisions aimed at tax avoidance.[120] As summarised by Sir Geoffrey Howe, the Shadow Chancellor, they provide that:

> First, warning must have been given to the taxpayer of the intention to legislate in this way and the warning must have been precise in form. Second, the problem at which the warning has been directed should immediately be referred to what is known as the tax reform committee for consideration – that is the committee that meets between the professions and the Inland Revenue. Third, if the committee can devise an appropriate legislative provision the draft clauses should be published immediately so as to give a second clear intimation to those who are likely to be affected. Finally, such a clause must without fail be introduced in the following Finance Bill.[121]

In the Standing Committee, Rees explained that these rules were a compromise. He rejected the purist line that retrospection should never be permitted, on the basis that it would not go far enough to control tax avoidance. However, his proposal would ensure that taxpayers had the information they needed to plan their affairs; anything else would be unconstitutional.[122] The Liberals took an even more restrictive line: John Pardoe, the Spokesperson for the Treasury, recognised that retrospective legislation had been used before, but said that the Liberals stood for the proposition that 'retrospective legislation, when it is against the interests of the individual, is always wrong'.[123]

A separate issue arose in relation to provisions aimed at schemes based on artificial transactions in land. The opposition argued that, although the Government had issued a specific warning regarding these schemes in December 1976, it had not acted quickly enough in seeking legislation from Parliament. As put by Geoffrey Howe, the Shadow Chancellor, draft clauses should always be prepared and published as soon as possible after the warning is issued, 'so as to give a second clear intimation to those who are likely to be affected'.[124] Once this is done, the

[118] The loss was estimated at £200 million; John Pardoe, the Liberal Spokesperson, described the figure as 'the utmost piece of poppycock': HC Deb 12 July 1978, vol 953, col 1647.
[119] ibid cols 1643–44 and cols 1683–84.
[120] SC Deb (A) 6 June 1978, cols 718–19.
[121] HC Deb 12 July 1978, vol 953, col 1641.
[122] SC Deb (A) 6 June 1978, col 720.
[123] ibid cols 735–36 and HC Deb 12 July 1978, vol 953, col 1648.
[124] HC Deb 12 July 1978, vol 953, col 1648.

clause must 'without fail be introduced in the following Finance Bill'.[125] This addresses a concern raised by Conservative backbenchers in the debates on the Finance Bill 1958 over the impact of warnings: instead of assisting taxpayers, a warning puts them in the impossible situation where the Government, without parliamentary authority, makes it hazardous to act within the law. For Howe, this concern was addressed by minimising the time from the warnings to enactment. Accordingly, the Conservatives proposed amendments to limit retrospection to the Budget Day announcement.

Barnett accepted that allowing retrospection prior to the date of the announcement would be 'somewhat novel'.[126] He also described the 'Rees Rules' as 'interesting' and accepted them in general terms.[127] However, he did not accept that precedent or principle strictly limited retrospection to the date of a warning. Barnett focused on the practical consequences of a rigidity: in most cases, avoidance schemes are in operation before they come to the attention of the tax authorities, which means that at least some tax avoidance remains untouched. This, he argued, would not be right: instead, it was legitimate to use retrospection whenever necessary for 'not allowing tax relief that was never intended to be allowed', especially as the impact was slight.[128] On the impact, he noted that there was no criminal penalty involved and the taxpayer would pay no more tax than they would have been required to pay without the avoidance scheme. From this, a precise warning should be given as soon as the Government becomes aware of a scheme and decides to act, but retrospection can pre-date the warning in these cases. In this case, April 1976 was appropriate, as that was the date that the schemes were first used.

The debates raised important points, but where did they leave the Rees Rules?[129] As noted in chapter two, Peter Rees stated that the constitution 'depends on precedent and convention'.[130] He continued: 'If we enact these two clauses in their present form, we shall embody in our constitution a practice and a precedent which we shall regret in years to come.'[131] The amendments were defeated and the clauses passed into law, despite the objections. By Rees's reasoning, not only were the amendments rejected but his principles were also rejected. From this, it seems that the constitutional requirement for a specific warning is not as strict as Rees and Geoffrey Howe had argued. Nevertheless, Conservative MPs in opposition during the Blair and Brown governments repeated the Rees Rules as though they expressed the constitutional standards, without any reference to their

[125] ibid col 1641.
[126] ibid col 1647.
[127] ibid col 1646.
[128] ibid col 1647.
[129] Note that neither Rees nor Howe questioned the use of parliamentary announcements as warnings, which Heathcoat-Amory had done as Chancellor in 1958.
[130] HC Deb 12 July 1978, vol 953, col 1682.
[131] ibid.

earlier rejection.[132] Indeed, Labour also seems to have accepted the Rees Rules: in the debates on the APD, John Healey, the Financial Secretary to the Treasury, acknowledged that 'the main constitutional conventions on retrospective tax law are known as the Rees rules', and that 'Over the past 10 years, the Government have used and followed those rules, just as previous Governments did on many occasions.'[133] At the very least, the Rees Rules now provide points of reference for constitutional scrutiny of retrospective tax bills. As such, they confirm the existence of a culture of justification relating to constitutional rights. They do not resolve all issues, as there are still important political differences between the leading political parties. The Conservatives would not allow legislation to address tax avoidance prior to the warning, on that basis that the interference with the rule of law and the rights of taxpayers is too great. By contrast, Labour puts more weight on the morality of tax avoidance. They see the tax savings as an unearned benefit; in other cases, such as compensation for land, unearned values are less deserving of protection. The context is important: it is not enough to say that the individual holds property but also to understand how they came to own it.

iv. The Primarolo Statement

The desire to address avoidance schemes led to the 'Primarolo Statement' of 2004.[134] The Paymaster-General, Dawn Primarolo, announced plans to deal with specific schemes by which bonus payments were used to disguise income, thereby avoiding employment tax and National Insurance contributions. However, she also announced that the Government would introduce further retrospective bills to deal with any avoidance schemes that it was not currently aware of, or that might be developed in future. Her statement included the following:

> I am therefore giving notice of our intention to deal with any arrangements that emerge in future designed to frustrate our intention that employers and employees should pay the proper amount of tax and NICs on the rewards of employment. Where we become aware of arrangements which attempt to frustrate this intention we will introduce legislation to close them down, where necessary from today.[135]

This became known as the 'Primarolo Statement'. It was controversial because it did not limit retrospection to a specific scheme or class of scheme. Indeed, it was intended to apply to schemes that had not yet been designed or put into effect. At one level, it was consistent with the Rees Rules, as it indicated that warnings should be provided in advance of retrospective legislation. However, Primarolo

[132] PBC Deb (Finance Bill) 8 May 2008, cols 329, 330–31 (Mark Hoban); PBC Deb (Finance Bill) 22 May 2008, col 369 (David Gauke).

[133] HC Deb 25 Jun 2007, vol 462, col 59.

[134] On the general background from the Rees Rules through to the Primarolo Statement, see A Seely, 'Retrospective Taxation: Earlier Debates' (2012) House of Commons Library Standard Note SN04369.

[135] HC Deb 2 December 2004, vol 428, col 46WS.

did not make any comment on the Rees Rules, and as the Statement did not refer to specific schemes, it is doubtful that Peter Rees or Geoffrey Howe would have accepted that the Statement was sufficiently precise to constitute the kind of warning that they would have required.

In January 2005, the Treasury Select Committee considered the Statement. Several tax practitioners told the Committee that the profession saw it as a radical change and possibly contrary to human rights.[136] The Chancellor, Gordon Brown, gave evidence saying that the Statement was broad enough, on its own, to justify retrospective legislation that might be introduced in future. This was, however, in response to the suggestions that reliance on the Statement would not satisfy human rights standards. There was no separate discussion of UK constitutional standards and precedents.[137] The Committee's report stated that

> It would be helpful if, at this stage, and without jeopardising their position, the Inland Revenue were to publish a paper setting out their thinking on the principles which will guide future decisions as to whether a scheme is reckoned to be within or outside the terms of the announcement.[138]

It was noted in subsequent debates that no such paper has been published.[139]

Indeed, there may be strong tax policy reasons for declining to issue further clarification or narrowing of the Statement. The Primarolo Statement was released as part of a shift in tax policy regarding anti-avoidance measures. In 1997, the Chancellor, Gordon Brown, indicated that the Government would introduce a general anti-avoidance measure, but after consultation it decided not to proceed.[140] Nevertheless, there was still a deep dissatisfaction with the piecemeal approach to avoidance, under which the Treasury could only act when it identified a specific type of scheme. Instead of a general anti-avoidance rule, the Finance Act 2004 introduced new rules on the disclosure of avoidance schemes. It was hoped that, in combination with the Primarolo Statement, they would deter the more aggressive avoidance schemes. There is some evidence that they have had this effect. The estimate in the Pre-Budget Report 2004 was that the anti-avoidance announcement would raise an additional £200 million for 2004/05 and then £500 million annually for the rest of the forecast period. In 2009, HMRC released an analysis showing that there was 'robust evidence' to show that the announcement secured an additional £110 million in 2004/5, and £210 million in the following year.[141]

[136] Treasury Committee, *The 2004 Pre-Budget Report* (HC 2004–05, 138) Ev 13, Ev 88 (see especially John Whiting) and Ev 77 (Anne Redstone).

[137] ibid Ev 50.

[138] ibid 42.

[139] See, eg, Colin Breed, calling for the report: PBC Deb (Finance Bill) 22 May 2008, cols 366–67.

[140] A Seely, 'Tax Avoidance: A General Anti-Avoidance Rule – Background History (1997–2010)' (2020) House of Commons Library Briefing Paper Number 2956; J Freedman, 'Defining Taxpayer Responsibility: In Support of a General Anti-Avoidance Principle' (2004) *British Tax Review* 331.

[141] HMRC KAI: Personal Tax, 'Evaluation of the Government's December 2004 Announcement Warning That Anti-Avoidance Legislation in Respect of Remuneration-Based Avoidance Schemes Could Be Back-Dated' (2009) Working Paper 6, 2.

Whilst the amounts fell below the projections, they were still significant. Chris Tailby, the former Director of the Anti-Avoidance Group of HM Customs & Excise, commented in 2011 that the Primarolo Statement was particularly useful because the threat of retrospective legislation against avoidance schemes 'is the best weapon of all against tax avoidance'.[142] Not only did it make schemes less attractive to taxpayers, and less marketable by tax professionals, but from the Treasury's side, there would be 'a huge saving in litigation resource as it will no longer have to challenge the scheme through the courts'.[143]

Subsequently, the Government relied on the Primarolo Statement in justifying retrospective provisions of the Finance Bill (No 2) 2006. The target was tax avoidance schemes that sought to disguise income through the issue of options. They were backdated to the date of the Primarolo Statement (2 December 2004). Mark Hoban, Shadow Treasury spokesman, proposed an amendment to move the date of the budget announcement (22 March 2006).[144] In response, Dawn Primarolo argued that it was legitimate to backdate the measures to the Statement, as delaying the budget date 'would undermine not only the clear warning that I gave on 2 December 2004, but future Government action to tackle avoidance'.[145] Hoban withdrew the amendment. He said that not everyone had understood how broad the Government had intended the Statement to be, but accepted that there could be no doubt henceforth.[146] This undermines the need for precise warnings, at least as an inflexible requirement. However, there has been little elaboration since then, and no government has sought to rely upon it when justifying retrospective legislation.

v. *The Loan Charge*

The Loan Charge saga is the most recent case to provoke lengthy debate in Parliament on retrospection.[147] The HMRC has consistently taken the view that offshore schemes were not effective to avoid tax on the loan amount. Moreover, it took the view that this had been the law since 1999. In 2017, the Government introduced the Finance Act (No 2) 2017 to capture the lost revenue from these schemes, by requiring scheme users to include the balance of loans made from 5 April 1999

[142] C Tailby, 'Some Reflections on Tax Avoidance' (2011) *Private Client Business* 43, 46.

[143] ibid.

[144] Finance (No 2) Bill Deb 6 June 2006, col 436. Hoban did not argue strenuously for the amendment, as he said that he tabled it 'to push them [the government] on issues of the breadth and variety of schemes to which it will apply': Finance (No 2) Bill Deb 6 June 2006, col 438.

[145] Finance (No 2) Bill Deb 6 June 2006, col 442.

[146] ibid cols 443–44.

[147] For comprehensive summaries of parliamentary activity on the Loan Charge, see A Seely, 'The 2019 Loan Charge' House of Commons Library Research Briefing no 8811, 9 February 2023; A Seely, 'Introduction of the 2019 Loan Charge' House of Commons Library Debate Pack, Number CDP-2019/0078, 4 April 2019; for a critical review, see Blackwell (n 89).

that were still outstanding by 5 April 2019 as income in that year's assessment.[148] Further provisions were introduced in the Finance Act 2018, although they did not alter the basic scheme.

One might have thought that constitutional questions would have been prominent when the Bill was introduced, given that the Loan Charge depended on transactions that could have occurred as much as 20 years previously. However, as noted above, Ministers did not regard the Loan Charge as retrospective. It upset expectations that the offshore schemes would be effective, but the HMRC did not share the view that the schemes were effective and, in any case, the Loan Charge measures did not reverse the law with retrospective effect.[149] Nevertheless, given the controversy that later arose, it is surprising that the measures initially raised little concern in Parliament. At the Committee stage of the Finance Act (No 2) 2017, Annelise Dodds, Shadow Financial Secretary to the Treasury, briefly asked about hardship but did not suggest that the provisions were incompatible with constitutional or human rights standards.[150] Neither were constitutional or human rights issues raised when the Finance Bill 2018 was debated. Indeed, at that point, Dodds suggested that the provisions should have incorporated enhanced penalties.[151] However, on 8 May 2018, well after the two Acts had come into force, Stephen Lloyd MP (Liberal Democrat) tabled an Early Day Motion stating that 'retrospectively taxing something that was technically allowed at the time, is unfair' and proposing that 'the [Loan] Charge to apply only to disguised remuneration loans entered into after the Finance Act (No 2) 2017 received Royal Assent'.[152] From that point, Members in both Houses regularly raised questions about the Loan Charge[153] and an All-Party Parliamentary Group was created to review it.[154] The Government eventually agreed to an independent review, which was carried out by Sir Aymas Morse, the Auditor General. He published his review in December 2019.[155] He agreed with the policy behind the Loan Charge but made 20 recommendations for change, including a recommendation that the Loan Charge should not apply to loans received prior to 9 December 2010, on the basis that there may have been some doubt about the legal situation before the Finance Act 2011. However, from that point, there could have been no doubt that tax was payable on loans.[156]

[148] Alternatively, the taxpayer could settle the tax balance with HMRC before the loan charge came into effect.

[149] See above nn 18, 19.

[150] PBC Deb (Finance Bill) 19 October 2017, cols 101.

[151] PBC Deb (Finance Bill (No 2) 9 January 2018, col 30.

[152] 132 EDM 1239 of 2017/19, 8 May 2018 (the Act received Royal Assent on 16 November 2017).

[153] Economic Affairs Committee, *The Powers of HMRC: Treating Taxpayers Fairly* (HL 2017–2019, 242) paras 53–84.

[154] Information about the group is available at www.loanchargeappg.co.uk.

[155] Sir Aymas Morse, 'Independent Loan Charge Review: Report on the Policy and its Implementation' (2019), available at assets.publishing.service.gov.uk/government/uploads/system/uploads/attachment_data/file/854387/Independent_Loan_Charge_Review_-_final_report.pdf.

[156] The Finance Act 2011 inserted new provisions (Part 7A) into the Income Tax (Earnings and Pensions) Act 2003. Under these provisions, income tax and National Insurance Contributions are chargeable on the full value of a loan made to an employee from a third party.

The Government accepted all but one of Morse's recommendations.[157] Jesse Norman, Financial Secretary to the Treasury, introduced the changes as amendments to the Finance Bill 2020 but did not discuss the constitutional considerations, although he did acknowledge that the amendments implemented the recommendations.[158] This was the pattern of all the debates on the Loan Charge: parliamentarians gave very little consideration to its constitutional aspects. Members did not explicitly raise, for example, the Rees Rules or the Primarolo Statement in the debates. Morse briefly referred to the Primarolo Statement in his report but the Government did not do so in its response.[159]

This is not to say that the debate was not principled, but the focus fell on the principles of tax policy rather than the constitutional precedents or principles on retrospection. The apparent lack of interest in the constitutional standards makes it unclear whether any sort of constitutional precedent was set (or challenged). MPs raised several concerns that might have raised debate on the constitutional standards. The first relates to the nature of retrospection and hence the scope of the constitutional standards, as discussed above.[160] The remaining concerns over the relevance of legal certainty, the provision of warnings and individual hardship are considered below.

a. Relevance of Certainty

As noted above, Sir Aymas Morse recommended that the law should only apply from the Finance Act 2011, when it put the legal position beyond doubt. In any case, even if the law had been clear before then, the 'HMRC did not consistently articulate this to taxpayers before the 2011 legislation' and did not open an investigation into the pre-2011 tax years in about 40 per cent of cases. He concluded that 'For the twenty year look-back period of the Loan Charge to be proportionate and justified, taxpayers would need to have acted in a way that was perverse in light of a clear legal position.'[161] That was not the case, and hence he recommended that the Loan Charge should not apply to loans made before 9 December 2010, 'being the point at which the law became clear'.[162] The Government accepted this recommendation.

[157] HM Treasury, 'Independent Loan Charge Review: Government Response to the Review' (2019), available at assets.publishing.service.gov.uk/government/uploads/system/uploads/attachment_data/file/854490/20191219_Government_response.pdf. The Government rejected the recommendation that any unpaid tax liability of lower income individuals should be written off after 10 years.

[158] He made no explicit reference to principles, but only that Morse had concluded that law was not entirely clear prior to that: see PBC Deb (Finance Bill) 4 June 2020, col 32. Labour and SNP members commented on the Bill but did not explicitly raise constitutional issues. It was not raised by Mel Stride when he introduced the Bills in the Commons in 2017, or by Annelise Dodds when she responded on behalf of Labour.

[159] Morse (n 155) 17 refers to the Primarolo Statement but says 'It did not specifically mention loan schemes.'

[160] See above text to n 5ff.

[161] Morse (n 155) 4.

[162] ibid.

Did Morse's reasoning reflect the constitutional standard? Ministers and MPs had not previously said that tax avoidance must be 'perverse' to be targeted by retrospective legislation. Previous constitutional debates suggest that retrospection can be justified where Parliament did not intend to allow the tax advantage and the scheme had no purpose other than to save tax, and it would be inequitable to allow it to stand. In many cases, it would strain the language to describe a scheme user's actions as perverse. Indeed, it might be entirely rational to enter an avoidance scheme, even in the knowledge that there is a high risk that the courts would find it ineffective or that Parliament would reverse the law with retrospective effect. From the perspective of the scheme user, it is merely a question of costs and benefits, assessed in the light of all risks, including the legal risks.

It may be unfair to read the Morse report as suggesting that a scheme user must have acted perversely for retrospection to be justified. Perhaps he meant only that, given the uncertainty prior to 2011, an appropriate warning should have been issued. By the Rees Rules, once a government forms the intention to legislative retrospectively, it should warn taxpayers so that they can plan accordingly. Nevertheless, as explained above, it is questionable whether this applies in every case. Labour accepts that warnings are important but it has indicated that there may be circumstances where retrospection may take effect prior to the warning. The Conservatives have argued that warnings should always be issued and retrospection should never reach back prior to the warning (although in this case, it seems that they were adopting Labour's position that a warning was not necessary). The Liberal Democrats and previously the Liberals have taken the view that retrospection is never permitted, except to prevent forestalling. Accordingly, the Loan Charge provided an opportunity to consider the Rees Rules on this point. However, they were not considered. Neither, as noted above, was there any discussion of the Primarolo Statement.

b. Requirement for Actual Notice

As noted above, Sir Aymas Morse said that looking back prior to 2011 could not be justified, in part because the HMRC had not 'consistently articulated' its view on the law to taxpayers before then. This recalls Heathcoat Amory's statement in 1958, where he expressed doubts that a Ministerial warning in Parliament would be sufficient to put taxpayers on notice. Since then, the practice has confirmed that parliamentary warnings are sufficient. Indeed, neither Rees nor Howe questioned their efficacy in 1978. There is still a lack of clarity on the breadth of a warning: in particular, it is not clear whether the Primarolo Statement would provide adequate warning for all or only some disguised remuneration schemes. Nevertheless, this raises the question: does the Government's acceptance of Morse's recommendation suggest that there is now an additional aspect of actual notice? On this point, it is worth noting that David Davis tabled an amendment restricting the loan charge to cases where taxpayers 'knew that the loan or quasi loan should have been accounted for as income in the relevant year'.[163] This would, of course, put a heavy burden on the HMRC to notify taxpayers and to establish the absence of actual knowledge. If so, it would suggest that the Government (through the HMRC) cannot act in future against new schemes unless it has ensured that tax avoiders were actually aware that their schemes were suspect. The amendment was defeated, but without clarity on the nature of warnings that are constitutionally required. Indeed, David Davis and the other supporters of the amendment did not seek to justify the clause in terms of constitutional standards.

c. Relevance of Individual Hardship

The Joint Committee on Human Rights considered the issue of hardship in relation to the Finance Bill 2008, although only in relation to Article 1 of the First Protocol. In a Westminster Hall debate, Loan Charge critics raised hardship as the key factor that should have led to a revision of the law.[164] They pointed out that HMRC data and anecdotal evidence showed that many users had been lower-income employees of public sector bodies whose work was outsourced. The former employees then worked for agencies that sought to avoid PAYE and NIC contributions by paying their workers through the offshore loan schemes. Clearly, the workers benefited by avoiding tax, but it was said that their reason for entering the scheme was simply to continue working rather than avoid tax. Indeed, many of them were under the impression that they had no choice but to be employed through the offshore scheme. In other cases, outsourced former employees set themselves up as independent contractors, and were mis-sold schemes by tax advisors. In addition, many individual scheme users felt misled by the HMRC, as they had declared on their tax return that they had used a tax avoidance scheme and were given a DOTAS (disclosure of tax avoidance schemes) number for it. However, they reported that the HMRC often failed to take action, which gave them the impression that it had decided that they had no tax to pay. The Loan Charge therefore caught many unsuspecting individuals by surprise and put them into serious financial difficulty.

The Government was not unaware that the Loan Charge would have a serious impact on some scheme users. Its impact assessment, published on 22 November 2017, stated that

> Some of these individuals [the scheme users] will be unable to repay the loans, agree a settlement with HMRC before 5 April 2019, or pay the loan charge arising on

[163] HC Deb 1 July 2020, vol 678, col 434. In terms of proving actual knowledge, Davis argued that there was precedent for the 20-year period, from the Finance Act 2008: see HC Deb 1 July 2020, vol 678, col 452. It is not clear from his speech, but he may have been referring to section 118(2), by which the Act inserted provisions into section 77(4) (4A) and (4B) of the Value Added Tax Act 1994 that allow the HMRC to look back 20 years and assess whether the taxpayer participated in a transaction knowing that it was part of an arrangement attempting to bring about loss of tax (an arrangement that creates 'a loss that arises as a result of a deliberate inaccuracy'); if so, the concern is with tax evasion rather than avoidance, and would be of limited relevance as a precedent in this case.

[164] HC Deb 20 November 2018, vol 649, cols 270WH-96WH.

> 5 April 2019. The government anticipates that some of these individuals will become insolvent as a result.[165]

There was an awareness of the potential impact, but no discussion of ameliorating measures. Whilst not explicitly referring to human rights standards, Sir Aymas Morse made a number of recommendations regarding hardship in his report. The Government accepted all of them, except a recommendation that any unpaid tax liability of lower income individuals should be written off after 10 years.[166] Again, there was no debate on the constitutional precedents, which was unfortunate because the question of hardship has arisen on several occasions without any real analysis or resolution.

The Loan Charge saga raises fundamental questions about the purpose of the constitutional standards relating to retrospection. Are they primarily concerned with reliance, expectation and the individual's capacity to plan their affairs? Or is the real question whether retrospection produces hardship and, if so, how it should be approached within a bill? And, either way, does the focus on warnings adequately capture these concerns? More generally, are the standards still relevant: as with the Finance Act 2008, it seems that parliamentarians find the European Convention on Human Rights to be a more useful and appropriate focus for scrutiny relating to the protection of the rights of the individual.

vi. The Jobseekers Allowance

In some cases, the Government's enthusiasm to condemn the behaviour of the targets of retrospection seems calculated to override constitutional concerns. This was the case with the Jobseekers (Back to Work Schemes) Act 2013, where the Government not only legislated retrospectively, but used the fast-track procedure to push the legislation through Parliament as quickly as possible. This was in the face of constitutional concerns, including those of the Constitution Committee.[167] The Bill was a response to *R (Reilly and Wilson) v The Secretary of State for Work and Pensions*, which concerned sanctions imposed by the Department of Work and Pensions under the Jobseekers Act 1995.[168] Under the 1995 Act, recipients of the Jobseekers Allowance could have benefits withdrawn if they declined to participate in employment programmes as instructed by their Jobcentre.

[165] HMRC, 'Disguised Remuneration: Further Update' (22 November 2017), available at www.gov.uk/government/publications/disguised-remuneration-further-update/disguised-remuneration-further-update.

[166] Morse (n 155) 55. The Government rejected it on the basis that it 'would reduce taxpayers' incentive to pay off the debt and would have unwelcome wider impacts that change how HMRC and those in debt interact' HM Treasury (n 157) 9.

[167] House of Lords Constitution Committee, *Jobseekers (Back to Work Schemes) Bill* (HL 2012–13, 155).

[168] *R (Reilly and Wilson) v The Secretary of State for Work and Pensions* [2013] EWCA Civ 66; upheld on appeal (*R (Reilly and Another) v The Secretary of State for Work and Pensions* [2013] UKSC 68, although not until after the Jobseekers (Back to Work Schemes) Act 2013 came into effect.

The instructions were purportedly issued under 2011 Regulations, but the Supreme Court held that the Regulations were *ultra vires*, as they fell outside the scope of the Jobseekers Act. *Reilly and Wilson* was a test case, and it left the Department owing about £130 million for similar claims. The 2013 Act retrospectively validated the instructions and therefore the sanctions as well.

No advance warning of the intention to legislate retrospectively was given. This is not unusual in social welfare cases.[169] Clearly, it runs contrary to the principles in tax law, especially as the consequences are more severe: not only are benefits recovered, but sanctions are imposed. In Parliament, Mark Hoban, the Secretary of State for Work and Pensions, stated that no specific warning was required because 'the people taking part in the schemes knew at the start that, if they did not take part, they would be sanctioned. They knew there was a penalty for not taking part in the schemes'.[170] Hoban described the failure to give adequate information to the claimants as a purely technical matter.[171] By contrast, the Supreme Court in *Reilly and Wilson* pointed out that individuals had not been given enough information to know what they needed to do to avoid sanctions. Hoban referred to claimants taking 'all reasonable steps', but the Supreme Court said that the individual must be able to ascertain those steps before penalties can be imposed: 'Fairness therefore requires that a claimant should have access to such information about the scheme as he or she may need in order to make informed and meaningful representations to the decision-maker before a decision is made.'[172] Instead of providing greater clarity, the 2013 Act simply validated the instructions.[173] Moreover, parliamentary scrutiny was limited by the fast-track procedure, and hence there was very little discussion of constitutional implications. This was partly due to the indifference of the Labour opposition, as it supported the Bill, for two reasons: first, it regarded the general principle of imposing sanctions for social welfare as sound and certainly not novel (it had been introduced in 1911); and the Bill retained provisions that allowed for exceptions to be made in cases of hardship.[174] Nevertheless, some Labour members were very critical, especially as the provisions would target the vulnerable and the regulations and instructions were often too vague or complex to understand.[175]

The strongest criticism on constitutional grounds came from the Constitution Committee. Its report included a recommendation that the House 'consider

[169] See C Harlow and R Rawlings, '"Striking Back" and "Clamping down": An Alternative Perspective on Judicial Review' in J Bell, M Elliott, J Varahus and P Murray (eds), *Public Law Adjudication in Common Law Systems: Process and Substance* (Hart Publishing, 2016) 23–26; M Adler, *Cruel, Inhuman or Degrading Treatment?: Benefit Sanctions in the UK* (Springer International Publishing, 2018).

[170] HC Deb 19 March 2013, vol 560, col 843; *cf* ibid cols 843–45 (Ian Lavery).

[171] See the exchange between Derek Twigg and Hoban, HC Deb 19 March 2013, vol 560, col 830.

[172] *R (Reilly and Another)* (n 168) para 65 (Lord Nueberger and Lord Toulson).

[173] Jobseekers (Back to Work Schemes) Act 2013, s 1.

[174] HC Deb 19 March 2013, vol 560, col 832 (Liam Byrne and Mark Hoban).

[175] See, eg, ibid col 842 (Ian Lavery), col 846 (Russell Brown), cols 853–56 (John McDonnell) and col 864 (Graham Morris). The Liberal Democrats did not voice their usual opposition to retrospection of any type, perhaps because they were part of the Coalition Government that promoted the Bill.

whether retrospectively confirming penalties on individuals who, according to judicial decision, have not transgressed any lawful rule is constitutionally appropriate in terms of the rule of law.'[176] The Committee did not raise the point, but the 2013 Act was much more draconian than any of the examples concerned with retrospective legislation aimed at tax avoidance schemes, as there were no advance warnings and penalties were imposed. Mark Hoban justified retrospection on the basis that

> It is vital that scarce public resources are targeted at those who need and deserve them most. It would be unacceptable for claimants who have failed to take all reasonable steps to increase their chances of finding work to receive an undeserved windfall payment.[177]

Does this identify a different constitutional standard for social welfare as opposed to tax avoidance? Hoban argued that retrospection was appropriate because the individuals were taking from 'those who need and deserve [public resources] most'. However, as the funds for any department come from the Treasury, the burden did not fall solely on other recipients of the jobseeker benefits. Rather, it fell on taxpayers in general, as it does with tax avoidance. Moreover, in financial terms, the 'undeserved windfall payment' is equivalent to the undeserved windfall savings from tax avoidance. Arguably, there is a distinction between retrospection that imposes a liability that did not previously exist, as in the case of anti-avoidance measures, and retrospection that takes away a benefit that was freely conferred by the state. However, Parliament has not made these distinctions for all benefits: when planning permission is withdrawn, compensation may be paid to offset wasted expenditures.[178] The difference seems to lie in the perceived need to condemn and punish those who appear to avoid the requirements for obtaining social welfare benefits. With social welfare, the need was so great that warnings were not necessary and penalties could be imposed.[179] Indeed, in one sense, tax avoidance is more deserving of condemnation, as the investment in avoidance schemes does not produce anything of value. By contrast, the successful claimants in *Reilly and Wilson* took voluntary internships to gain experience and not solely to avoid workfare or to obtain the Jobseekers Allowance. With pure avoidance, the individual gains nothing from entering the scheme other than the avoidance of the burden and there is no wider public benefit from their actions. Nevertheless, moral condemnation of tax avoidance sits uneasily with many MPs. Moreover, there are political differences in taxation that are not seen in social welfare: the Conservative and Liberal Democrats are more inclined than Labour to restrict retrospection in tax, but they have all taken a similarly harsh line with social welfare. Hence,

[176] House of Lords Constitution Committee, *Jobseekers (Back to Work Schemes) Bill* (HL 2012–13, 155) para 15.
[177] HC Deb Tuesday 19 March 2013, vol 560, col 833.
[178] See B Denyer-Green, *Compulsory Purchase and Compensation*, 11th edn (Routledge, 2018) 362–75.
[179] The Constitution Committee also raised the use of the fast-track legislative procedure.

for many MPs, questions of fairness of retrospection in tax focus on the treatment of the avoider; however, with social welfare, it is on other beneficiaries and the wider public. In effect, the constitutional standard allows moral condemnation as a valid justification for harsher treatment but allows scope for political differences on the types of conduct that require condemnation.

IV. Conclusion

It is worth making several points that, although they may seem obvious, are still important. First, is that the evidence shows that the practice on retrospection is consistent with the Attorney-General's statement in the War Damage Bill debates, as quoted in the Introduction. That is, governments and MPs agree that retrospective legislation should be treated as exceptional and that it should require specific justification from the Government.[180] There are exceptions, but only where restrictions that address constitutional concerns have developed through long practice. For example, provisions that are curative, or address forestalling, do not raise serious concerns, but Parliament would still want to satisfy itself that the provisions are indeed curative or are necessary to address forestalling.

The second point is that MPs and governments take the constitutional arguments on retrospection seriously. In general, Ministers do not ignore constitutional points of opposing MPs. They may dispute them, but they do not usually ignore them. Indeed, even where governments argue that measures are not in fact retrospective, they seek to justify them as though they were retrospective. Moreover, MPs and Ministers approach constitutional questions as matters of principle that transcend the policy concerns of the immediate case. To be sure, there have been some exceptions. It is difficult to believe, for example, that the Government or the opposition front bench had any real concern over constitutional propriety of the Jobseekers Act 2013. The desire to condemn those who, in the view of MPs, had sought to obtain an unfair social welfare advantage outweighed the constitutional considerations. However, in other cases, constitutional rhetoric seems to carry such authority that it is employed even where it is of questionable relevance. For example, with VED, the core argument against the increase was that it would hit those who lacked financial resources much harder than the better-off.[181] The real concern was not that the increase would undermine decisions that had already been made, but that it was a form of regressive tax. The clearer approach would have been to say that any regressive tax should be subject to closer scrutiny by Parliament, perhaps through the Treasury Committee.

[180] In the case of criminal retrospection, no exceptions have been identified.

[181] This is also one of the arguments behind the Loan Charge campaign, although it is a case of avoidance; that is, it was not that the tax itself was regressive, but that the means of collecting it (through the Loan Charge) had a regressive impact.

Finally, it also seems clear that constitutional scrutiny is declining in importance, despite its growing influence since the reforms of the late twentieth century. The concluding chapter draws on evidence across the different areas examined by this work. However, in relation to retrospection, it is worth noting that the most contentious debates since the Human Rights Act 1998 have either ignored UK constitution or focused on the European Convention on Human Rights as the source of standards.

Conclusions

In the political constitution, a right to property should enhance the parliamentary scrutiny of measures that affect rights of private property. Indeed, many MPs and Ministers have used it in this way. However, it is no longer as central as it once was: none of the bills over the last two or three decades that have affected private property have produced debates as contentious or as protracted as those concerning the People's Budget, the Attlee and Callaghan nationalisation programmes, tenancy reforms, or the Thatcher government's poll tax legislation. In addition, the delegation of private bill business to administrative bodies has meant that parliamentarians do not regularly consider specific issues relating to property. Their scrutiny is at a general level, and even then, it rarely leads to the invocation of a constitutional right to property. This chapter, as a conclusion to the book, reviews some of the common themes of the previous chapters and asks how important a right to property is, in today's constitution.

I. Identifying Standards

In its search for evidence of a constitutional right to property, this book follows the description of parliamentary constitutional standards given by Jack Simson Caird and Dawn Oliver and discussed in chapter one.[1] Accordingly, beginning with the first of their four criteria, it has focused on norms that have been articulated by parliamentary actors in parliamentary fora. Hence statutes, parliamentary debates, resolutions, conventions, Standing Orders, committee reports and the rulings of Speakers, Examiners and Referees provide the primary sources for consideration. Each helps identify standards, although in different ways. Statutes exhibit what Parliament believes the unwritten constitution allows it to do, but not the negative: they do not show what Parliament considers unconstitutional. Moreover, they do not show the reasoning behind judgements on constitutionality. The other sources – especially debates – can fill the gaps. However, in practice, this book shows that they often fail to do so. MPs often make assertions regarding constitutionality, but careful arguments that move from the statutory precedents to the contested measures of the bill are not seen as frequently. Nevertheless, there are sufficient examples to show that there is the accepted method of constitutional

[1] J Simson Caird and D Oliver, 'Parliament's Constitutional Standards' in A Horne and A Le Seuer (eds), *Parliament: Legislation and Accountability* (Hart Publishing, 2016).

interpretation: statutory precedents are the primary source, and debates and the other parliamentary materials can shed light on the reasoning behind Parliament's choices.

Simson Caird and Oliver's second criterion concentrates on the constitutional nature of standards. Standards deal with issues that transcend the immediate policy issues of the specific bill; constitutional standards, for this work, focus on the relationship between the state and the individual, specifically in relation to rights of private property. The book has therefore sought to distinguish constitutional standards from other types of standards, with the Treasury Committee's *Principles of Tax Policy* as a prominent example of a non-constitutional set of principles intended to guide Parliament and governments.[2] The book has also sought to distinguish practices that are pragmatic; if concerned solely with ensuring that the legislative policies are implemented, or to achieve a bargain in Parliament, rather than the issues between state and individual that transcend the immediate concerns, they would not qualify as constitutional standards. One example arose in chapter five, concerning compensation for the destruction of diseased animals. The debates show that MPs and Ministers did not regard compensation as a constitutional right, but as a means for securing compliance with the law. It was clearly important to the success of the statutory programme, but it did not proceed from constitutional principles.

Simson Caird and Oliver also state that constitutional standards are not partisan. This is the case with property: it is clear that a substantial majority of MPs, from all parties, share a commitment to the protection of rights of private property. They often differ on precisely what this requires in a specific context, but the general commitment is still present. For example, chapters three and four show that there has been agreement that compensation should be paid on an expropriation or nationalisation and that it should counter-balance the owner's loss. However, MPs do not always agree on the choice of the valuation standard to be applied under specific bills. If there are alternative ways of measuring loss, the Conservatives generally argue that legislation should apply the most generous method, so as to minimise the risk that the holder would suffer an uncompensated loss. Similarly, with the retrospective tax avoidance measures discussed in chapter six, the Conservatives have argued that Parliament should take a very narrow view of what is legitimate. Labour, in general, gives rights of property less weight in the balance than the Conservatives have done. Perhaps the clearest and most recent example is in Labour's 2019 Manifesto, which included nationalisation plans based on compensation principles that seemed to be aimed at minimising compensation. Nevertheless, despite the differences with the Conservative policies, Labour did not suggest that owners would not have been compensated for their loss. On that fundamental point, there was agreement.

[2] House of Commons Treasury Committee, *Principles of Tax Policy* (HC 2010–11, 753).

Finally, Simson Caird and Oliver emphasise the parliamentary nature of the standards. The courts have no role in their interpretation and application of the standards in the legislative processes. Moreover, parliamentarians do not consider judicial precedents as a source of parliamentary standards. As with other standards, Parliament does not operate in isolation: bills are drafted and debated against expectations regarding their interpretation by the courts and their implementation by the executive. As shown in chapter five, when Parliament granted administrative bodies the authority to grant powers of compulsory purchase, care was taken to ensure that they did not have unlimited discretionary power; as Paul Craig pointed out, there was an expectation that the courts would allow judicial review against the requirements of these provisions.[3] Similarly, tax legislation and the system of assessment carefully incorporates administrative discretion in order to ensure that taxpayers are treated fairly.[4] The question that arises under different issues, and addressed in the final section of this chapter, is whether the legal version of a right to property – from the European Convention on Human Rights – is overtaking the political version of the unwritten constitution.[5] At various points in history, parliamentarians would have had a strong preference for a political rather than a legal version of a right to property (or, indeed, a version under a constitution with executive supremacy). However, as discussed below, the political version seems to be yielding to the legal version found in the European Convention.

II. Specific Standards

The preceding chapters uncover good evidence for parliamentary constitutional standards for some aspects of a right to property. The general principle that all legislation should be justified by the promoter has specific application for property: historically, all subjects held the right to petition for a private bill overriding the property rights of others; conversely, anyone whose rights would be overridden had the right to appear before the parliamentary committee to object to the bill. There were no specific criteria for justification, but the processes ensured that the burden of proof lay on the promoter and that the specific case for the bill would be tested. The process is now handled by administrative bodies, but the fundamental principles developed in parliamentary proceedings are reflected in statute. With the Town and Country Planning Act 1947 and the Transport and Works

[3] P Craig, 'Proportionality and Judicial Review: A UK Historical Perspective' in S Vogenauer and S Weatherill (eds), *General Principles of Law: European and Comparative Perspectives* (Hart Publishing, 2017).

[4] C Stebbings, 'The Equity of the Executive: Fairness in Tax Law in Nineteenth-Century England' in PG Turner (ed), *Equity and Administration*, 1st edn (Cambridge University Press, 2016).

[5] Convention for the Protection of Human Rights and Fundamental Freedoms (Rome, 4 November 1950); Protocol to the Convention for the Protection of Human Rights and Fundamental Freedoms (Paris, 20 March 1952).

Act 1992, the process is now almost entirely handled by administrative bodies, but the fundamental principles developed in parliamentary proceedings are reflected in statute.

Chapters three and four discuss the principle that compensation for loss must be provided on an expropriation or nationalisation, with an independent assessment and rights of appeal. Compensation is not so generous so as to allow the owner to claim a share of surplus that the acquiring body hopes to gain from the use of the property; conversely, it is not so generous to promoters so as to enable them to profit simply by acquiring the property at an undervalue. There is flexibility with these standards: for example, from the late nineteenth century, legislation allowed for a reduction in compensation where part of the value was attributable to the owner's moral or legal defaults. Nevertheless, the core principle was robust: chapter four shows that some Labour MPs resisted compensation for the Coal Act 1938, but Labour Ministers have consistently sought to provide fair compensation on nationalisation.[6] To be sure, where there are alternative reasonable valuations, they have not committed governments to the most generous one; however, they have not seen compensation as a confiscation or penalty. Standards have also emerged in relation to retrospective laws that interfere with rights of property. These cases usually arise in response to unexpected judgments that are highly disruptive to private parties. Or, in the case of avoidance, activity comes to light that causes loss to Treasury or significant demoralisation to others, or both; if so, Parliament would consider whether the avoider should have been aware that Ministers would seek retrospective legislation.

With other types of interference with property, there is general agreement that legislation should be fair. This includes regulatory laws that interfere with property without a transfer of title (including the complete extinction or destruction of property), as well as laws imposing rates, taxes and other contributions. In these cases, however, there are several difficulties in the way of concluding that fairness is a constitutional standard. The first is that, even if there is evidence of standards and practices, they are not constitutional in nature. For example, the Treasury Committee's *Principles of Tax Policy* cite fairness as a core principle of taxation. In practice, however, the primary aim of fairness in taxation is voluntary compliance, as it recognises that most people are more likely to pay taxes that they perceive to be fair. Avoidance and evasion are reduced, without a heavy cost of enforcement. In many other cases, Parliament may support a bill that authorises payments to relieve hardship where due to unexpected disruptions beyond the owner's control, such as war damage, or the loss of employment due to nationalisation or emergency regulations for outbreaks of disease (animal or human). Most of these concern isolated events, but legislation may also provide support for particular classes over a longer period: social welfare support and subsidies

[6] See E Shinwell, *Conflict Without Malice* (Odhams Press, 1955) 172–73 and the discussion in chapter four, section II.

for some industries are examples. In most cases, there is no acknowledgement of a constitutional obligation to provide support. Rather, the general view seems to be that these depend heavily on the specific context, rather than some overarching constitutional obligation. As such, payments or other measures of one case do not create precedents for another.

The second difficulty is that, even if there is a constitutional aspect, fairness is often raised in a way that is too vague on its own to enhance parliamentary scrutiny of a bill. That does not mean that principles cannot emerge from more general values, such as fairness. Indeed, this is the experience with right to property under the European Convention on Human Rights. Article 1 of the First Protocol provides that

> Every natural or legal person is entitled to the peaceful enjoyment of his possessions. No one shall be deprived of his possessions except in the public interest and subject to the conditions provided for by law and by the general principles of international law. The preceding provisions shall not, however, in any way impair the right of a State to enforce such laws as it deems necessary to control the use of property in accordance with the general interest or to secure the payment of taxes or other contributions or penalties.[7]

It does not include an explicit right to compensation on expropriation; nor does it include the 'justifiable in a democratic society' wording of the qualified rights of the Convention. Nevertheless, through repeated re-examination, the European Court of Human Rights has produced a structure for reviewing state action against reasonably clear criteria: there is both the general structure of the proportionality test and principles for its application to specific categories of issues.[8] A similar evolution happened with some aspects of constitutional standards. As in the courts, the clearest evidence for standards follows from repeated consideration of specific issues, as in the case of private bills on compulsory purchase, public Acts on nationalisation, and Finance Acts with retrospective anti-avoidance provisions. However, this evolution is not evident with regulatory laws. This raises questions regarding the conceptions of fairness that seem to underpin constitutional discussions of rights of property. That is, a bare assertion that a bill is unfair may not be enough to enhance scrutiny of bills, but there have also been debates in which clearer conceptions of fairness are evident. The question is whether they provide a basis for constitutional scrutiny of bills, in those cases where the precedents are not clear.

There is some evidence that this is the case, as two conceptions of fairness emerge from the debates. The first concentrates on the impact of an interference on the property holder. It is very similar to the human rights principle of

[7] Protocol to the Convention for the Protection of Human Rights and Fundamental Freedoms (Paris, 20 March 1952).

[8] European Court of Human Rights, *Guide on Article 1 of Protocol No. 1 – Protection of Property* (Council of Europe/European Court of Human Rights, 2022).

proportionality, as applied under Article 1 of the First Protocol to the European Convention on Human Rights. At its most general, this view accepts that any law may have an adverse impact on some aspects of the lives of some people, but Parliament should be very cautious about enacting a law that would have a highly disruptive impact on anyone. To take an extreme case, confiscatory laws that would put some people into poverty would be seen as an unconstitutional excess of power by most MPs, at least in the absence of a very compelling justification. In some cases, such as expropriation of land or nationalisation of enterprises, Parliament has regularly required compensation as a means of moderating the impact on property holders. In some cases, the question of impact depends on moral considerations relating to the conduct of the rights holder: for example, with retrospective anti-avoidance laws, Ministers often say that the targeted individuals obtained a benefit that should not have been available to them. Ultimately, retrospection only requires them to pay the tax that they should have expected to pay.

The issue of impact therefore partly explains the constitutional position and could provide a guide for scrutiny where specific standards have not emerged. However, although MPs do show a concern with the fairness of the impact of measures, they also seem to overlook some of its implications. If it is a matter of impact, one would expect that similar principles would apply to non-proprietorial interests – such as employment, social welfare support and occupancy interests short of tenancy – where legislation could be highly disruptive for affected parties. This also applies to the comparatively well-off: for example, most business enterprises prefer reasonably stable and predictable fiscal policies, and yet they have no constitutional right to the continuation specific rules of taxation. In addition, the right to property does not cover all losses to property, but only to the direct interference with the legal rights of the holder that the constitutional right applies. For example, as shown in chapter two, there is no right of standing before parliamentary committees for anyone whose rights of property would not be directly and specially affected by a bill. The committee has a discretion to allow them to appear, but there is no right to appear. Similarly, the taking of the right to develop under the Town and Country Planning Act 1947 was not compensated, on the basis that there was no constitutional right to compensation for regulatory losses. The issue of impact also fails to explain the differences in treatment for different types of deprivations of property rights. As discussed in chapter five, there is no general right to compensation for regulatory losses, even where the asset is extinguished or destroyed. By contrast, in *R (on the application of Mott) v Environment Agency*, the Supreme Court found that regulatory controls violated Article 1 of the First Protocol to the European Convention on Human Rights, because they deprived a lease of almost all its economic value.[9] The legislative aim was legitimate, as it concerned the protection of the environment, but the Court held that the impact

[9] *R (on the application of Mott) v Environment Agency* [2018] UKSC 10.

was so severe that it should not have gone forward, at least without compensation to the rights holder. This would not have been required under the constitutional right to property, as shown by the animal disease controls: the compulsory destruction of diseased animals could destroy a business, and yet Parliament did not recognise a right to compensation to the owners. It may be provided in some cases: for example, although the Government took the view that there was no constitutional obligation to compensate for the taking of the right to develop under the Town and Country Planning Act 1947, it did provide *ex gratia* payments to those who would have been most seriously affected. There was, however, no concession from the Government that there was a constitutional right to the payments.

A second theme in the debates on fairness has been equity, in the sense of fairness across groups. Equity arises in two ways. The first is illustrated by the London Passenger Transport Act 1933, where the Government decided not to reduce compensation for some of the companies to be nationalised despite a drop in their value, as it could appear unfair when set against the compensation awarded for other targets.[10] Similarly, with the Aircraft and Shipbuilding Industries Act 1977, opposition members argued that the compensation for shareholders of unlisted companies was unfair. In theory, the 'hypothetical share price' model should have achieved equity with the shareholders of listed companies, but the argument was that it did not do so in practice. In these cases, it was suggested that the failure to provide equitable treatment across a group was a breach of constitutional standards. In practice, however, equity usually arises as a justification for an interference with rights of property. It has been central to retrospective laws, where Ministers often claim that the measures are necessary to ensure fairness to those who did not avoid the laws or benefit from an unexpected judgment. Chapter six quotes Niall MacDermot, Financial Secretary to the Treasury, in his defence of the War Damage Bill 1965: 'retrospective legislation is justified when it is necessary to obtain justice or equity between one citizen or class of citizens and another, to ensure that people in like circumstances receive the same treatment and enjoy the same rights'.[11] Equity, in this sense, can justify the redistribution of private rights.

MPs often raise questions regarding the equitable distribution of burdens, but there are aspects of equity that do not seem to raise constitutional issues in the UK. In human rights law, these questions arise when governments seek to support vulnerable groups, but they do so by imposing burdens on other private parties, and hence without a cost to the Treasury. For example, rent controls provide support for tenants, without any direct state subsidy to either tenants or landlords.[12] Similarly, there are statutory schemes requiring all industry participants to contribute to a scheme for the protection of customers or employees, irrespective

[10] See chapter four, section I.
[11] HC Deb 3 February 1965, vol 705, col 1098.
[12] There may be indirect costs: for example, the Treasury is likely to lose tax revenue if the controls reduce the profitability of the property owner.

of any misconduct or profiteering on the part of the contributors.[13] Plainly, this raises questions of fairness and equity: would it be better to spread the cost of support across taxpayers in general? Governments and MPs often focus on pragmatic considerations: in particular, if the burden is significant, investment may shift elsewhere, potentially with longer term adverse implications for the group that the legislation was intended to support. Put this way, the issues are matters of politics and policy and would vary from one situation to another. However, the European Court of Human Rights has also considered this from the perspective of the burdened party. Initially, it allowed states a very wide discretion in this area. In *James v United Kingdom*, it found that the UK could provide below-market compensation under the Leasehold Reform Act 1967 because it was legitimate for it to question whether the landlords had a moral entitlement to the full value.[14] As put by the Court, states have a wide discretion when enacting measures aimed at achieving social justice. Similarly, in *Mellacher v Austria*, it found no violation in respect of rent controls that deprived many landlords of any realistic prospect of earning a profit.[15] However, in later cases, it doubted whether the cost of providing social welfare support should be imposed on other parties where there are no suggestions of unfair enrichment, exploitation or morally questionable conduct on their part. Hence, in cases where rent and tenancy controls over a lengthy and indefinite period cause a significant deprivation of value, the Court is now much more inclined to hold that these burdens should be widely spread.[16] That is, it is entirely legitimate for states to support tenants facing unaffordable rents or insecure tenancies, but where their vulnerability is due to general economic issues rather than exploitation by the landlords, the burden should be spread across taxpayers in general. A government might choose, for example, to provide social housing at low cost or to subsidise rents specifically or to increase general social welfare payments, but leaving the cost entirely on landlords may be questionable under human rights law. This has emerged as an issue in human rights law, but it has not been addressed in Parliament as a matter of the constitutional rights of the landlord. In relation to the specific question of rent controls, the Rent Act 1977 still applies to some tenancies. The Rent Acts (Maximum Fair Rent) Order 1999 allowed landlords to obtain above-inflation increases to rents controlled by the Rent Act 1977, but not necessarily to the level of current market rents for uncontrolled properties. This was, ultimately, adjudged by the House of Lords and the European Court of Human Rights to comply with the Convention.[17] The burden

[13] See, eg, the compulsory contributions required for the Air Travel Trust Fund, under the Civil Aviation Act 1982, s 71A and for the Pension Protection Fund, under the Pensions Act 2004, Part 2.

[14] *James v UK* (1986) Series A No 98.

[15] *Mellacher v Austria* (1990) Series A No 169.

[16] See *Hutten Czapska v Poland* ECHR 2006-VIII 57 paras 224–25; *Lindheim v Norway* App nos 13221/08 and 2139/10 (ECtHR, 12 June 2012) paras 119–36; see also European Court of Human Rights (n 8) paras 295–303.

[17] *Spath Holme Ltd v UK* App no 78031/01 (ECtHR, 14 May 2002); *R v Secretary of State for the Environment, Transport and the Regions, ex parte Spath Holme Ltd* [2001] 2 AC 349.

on landlords was not so onerous that the UK was obligated to consider alternative means of supporting tenants. Nevertheless, the reasoning suggests that the human rights analysis raises questions that do not arise under the constitutional standards.

In conclusion, these two conceptions of fairness in relation to legislation affecting property do not completely explain constitutional principles. However, they suggest that there is a framework that would support constitutional scrutiny of bills that interfere with the right of property. There are gaps and inconsistencies in reasoning from these general values, but it is not the case that MPs have been unable to articulate general values. This suggests that the constitutional right to property could develop and adapt to new issues. This leads to a more general question about the future of the constitutional standards: how relevant are they, in the light of the increasing influence of the Human Rights Act (HRA) 1998? At its most basic, a parliamentary constitutional standard provides a set of reference points for debate and discussion of bills affecting rights of private property. In this respect, however, the right to the peaceful enjoyment of possessions, under Article 1 of the First Protocol, is a competitor. The UK ratified the Protocol in 1952, but the most contentious legislation affecting property since then – the War Damage Act 1965, Leasehold Reform Act 1967 and the Aircraft and Shipbuilding Industries Act 1977 – went through Parliament with no discussion of the UK's Convention obligations. Neither were they considered in any detail one of the few debates where MPs have sought to consolidate constitutional principles: that is, the debate on the Finance Bill 1978, where Peter Rees summarised the effect of the statutory precedents on retrospective anti-avoidance measures[18] or subsequently, in the debates on the measures that retrospectively reversed *Padmore v IRC*[19] or the *Woolwich* cases.[20] With the enactment of the HRA 1998 and the establishment of the Joint Committee on Human Rights (JCHR), the parliamentary scrutiny of retrospective provisions against the Convention standards has been given additional strength and prominence. The relevant Minister must make a statement on a bill's compatibility with Convention rights, and the JCHR provides specialist scrutiny on Convention issues. The Convention therefore provides an alternative to parliamentary constitutional standards as a focus for scrutiny. MPs could, of course, frame arguments in terms of both the constitutional standards and the Convention right. However, as a practical matter, time is a scarce commodity in Parliament and MPs tend to rely on one or the other. Increasingly, it is the Convention rather than parliamentary constitutional standards that they prefer to use. An early post-HRA example arose in March 2002, when Harriet Harman, the

[18] SC Deb (A) 6 June 1978, cols 718–19; see chapter six, section III.C.

[19] *Padmore v IRC* [1989] STC 493 (CA): see HC Deb 15 July 1987, vol 119, cols 1178–87.

[20] *R v Inland Revenue Commissioners ex p Woolwich Equitable Building Society* [1990] 1 WLR 1400 and *Woolwich Building Society v Inland Revenue Commissioners* [1993] AC 70; Peter Bottomley, Conservative, briefly referred to the likelihood of a challenge to the 'European courts' HC Deb 4 April 1991, vol 190, cols 185–99 and HC Deb, 1 June 1992, vol 208, col 776.

Solicitor-General, provided a statement to Parliament on the Government's policy on retrospective legislation. She said that:

> The Government's policy before introducing a legislative provision having retrospective effect is to balance the conflicting public interests and to consider whether the general public interest in the law not being changed retrospectively may be outweighed by any competing public interest. In making this assessment the Government will have regard to relevant international standards including those of the European Convention for the Protection of Human Rights and Fundamental Freedoms which was incorporated into United Kingdom law by the Human Rights Act 1998.[21]

Harman made no reference to constitutional standards, but only to the 'general public interest in law not being changed retrospectively'. It does not seem that she thought that the constitutional standards were a significant concern. Or, Harman may have been saying nothing more than the balancing of public interests is all that the UK constitution requires. Indeed, Harman's statement suggests that the European Convention on Human Rights is the primary basis for considering whether public interest has been correctly balanced against the rights of the individual. This is consistent with the Constitution Committee's list of basic constitutional tenets, as it includes international and European law, including the Convention.[22] However, the Constitution Committee also saw individual rights as an aspect of the rule of law, and this seems to be missing from Harman's statement.

Examples where MPs still rely on constitutional rather than human rights standards are rare but do exist. One occurred in March 2008, when the Chancellor, Alistair Darling, announced that the Finance Bill would include retrospective provisions aimed at avoidance schemes involving offshore trusts and double taxation treaties.[23] David Gauke, the Shadow Treasury Minister, expressed doubt that the Bill complied with the constitutional precedents, primarily because the Government had not acted quickly enough to introduce legislation after discovering the loophole.[24] However, Jane Kennedy, the Financial Secretary to the Treasury, defended the relevant clause in terms of human rights law rather than the constitutional precedents, saying that 'I am satisfied that in these unusual circumstances, retrospective clarification of the law is fair, proportionate and in the public interest. That is the human rights test that we must apply.'[25] It appears that Kennedy,

[21] HC Deb 6 March 2002, vol 381 col 409-10W. The statement was given in response to a request from the Conservative MP, Jonathan Sayeed.

[22] House of Lords Constitution Committee, *Reviewing the Constitution: Terms of Reference and Method of Working* (HL 2001–02, 11) para 51.

[23] See A Seely, 'Retrospective Taxation: Section 58 of the Finance Act 2008', House of Commons Library Standard Note SN6361, 28 Aug 2013.

[24] Gauke argued that 'It is not acceptable that the Government permit something that they consider unacceptable to exist for some years, and then seek to introduce retrospective legislation to address it.' PBC Deb (Finance Bill) 22 May 2008, col 369.

[25] He also expressed doubt that the Primarolo Statement was broad enough to apply in this case: PBC Deb (Finance Bill) 22 May 2008, col 372. The Joint Committee on Human Rights, *Twentieth Report* (2008–2009 HL 133/HC 882) paras 1.18–1.24 considered the measures and suggested that the absence

like Harman, believed that compliance with human rights standards was sufficient to address the constitutional issues: either they superseded the constitutional requirements or there was no difference between them.[26]

Arguably, a shift to a human rights focus would not leave a significant gap so far as the interests of individuals are concerned, as the constitutional and human rights principles on property rights are similar in content. This is not to say that there are no differences. As discussed above, the constitutional principles do not seem as broad as the Convention in respect of regulatory controls that effectively deprive assets of all or virtually all their value, or for controls that put the cost of social programmes on those who are not responsible for creating the conditions that the programmes respond to. This is due to the judicial development of Article 1 of the First Protocol of the Convention as a general right to property, with proportionality as the overarching principle. In constitutional matters, MPs frequently refer to fairness as the underlying value relevant to legislation that may interfere with private rights. However, unlike proportionality, fairness has not provided a clear structure for review in relation to all issues relating to property. This does not, of course, rule out the possibility that Parliament may adopt a more general structure for review in future, based on its conceptions of fairness. Neither does it rule out the possibility that constitutional standards relating to property will become even less important in parliamentary scrutiny, regardless of the future of European human rights law. This is, however, their history: in a system of parliamentary supremacy, standards are possibilities rather than fixed elements.

of a published impact assessment meant that there was 'an arguable breach of Article 1 Protocol 1' (at para 1.22). In *Huitson v HM Revenue and Customs* [2011] EWCA Civ 893, paras 85–92, the Court of Appeal held, inter alia, that the failure to conduct an impact assessment did not make the provisions disproportionate.

[26] See also the debates on the retrospective anti-avoidance measures of the Finance Bill 2009, PBC Deb (Finance Bill) 16 June 2009, cols 422–23: David Gauke questioned compliance with constitutional standards; Stephen Timms, the Financial Secretary to the Treasury, stated that the constitutional (and human rights) standards had been met.

BIBLIOGRAPHY

Adler M, *Cruel, Inhuman or Degrading Treatment?: Benefit Sanctions in the UK* (Springer International Publishing, 2018)

Albert W, *The Turnpike Road System in England, 1663–1840* (Cambridge University Press, 1972)

Allen RC, 'The Price of Freehold Land and the Interest Rate in the Seventeenth and Eighteenth Centuries' (1988) 41 *Economic History Review* 33

Allen T, *The Right to Property in Commonwealth Constitutions* (Cambridge University Press, 2000)

——, 'Liberalism, Social Democracy and the Value of Property under the European Convention on Human Rights' (2010) 59 *International and Comparative Law Quarterly* 1055

——, 'Constitutional Rights in the Irish Home Rule Bill of 1893' (2018) 39 *Journal of Legal History* 187

Anderson, Sir Iain, *Foot and Mouth Disease 2001: Lessons to be Learned Inquiry Report* (HC 2002, 888)

Anderson S, 'Parliament' in W Cornish and others (eds), *The Oxford History of the Laws of England: Volume XI: 1820–1914 English Legal System* (Oxford University Press, 2010)

Anns A, 'The History of the National Telephone Company: Part III' (1911) 6 *National Telephone Journal* 208

Atiyah PS, 'Charitable Trusts (Validation) Act, 1954' (1955) 18 *MLR* 152

Aulakh PS, 'British Empire, Land Tenure and the Search for an Ideal Proprietor: 1868–1875' PhD thesis (York University, 2022)

Bailey M, 'The 1844 Railway Act: A Violation of Laissez-Faire Political Economy?' (2004) 12 *History of Economic Ideas* 7

Baker JH, *The Oxford History of the Laws of England* (Oxford University Press, 2004) vol 6

Baldwin NDJ, 'The House of Lords and the Labour Government 1974–79' (1995) 1 *Journal of Legislative Studies* 218

Bellamy R, 'Political Constitutionalism' in H Kumarasingham and P Cane (eds), *The Cambridge Constitutional History of the United Kingdom: Exploring the Constitution*, (Cambridge University Press, 2023) vol 1

Bennion F, Bailey D and Norbury L, *Bennion, Bailey and Norbury on Statutory Interpretation*, 8th edn (LexisNexis UK, 2022)

Besly N and others, *How Parliament Works*, 8th edn (Routledge, 2019)

Biagini EF, *Liberty, Retrenchment and Reform: Popular Liberalism in the Age of Gladstone, 1860–1880* (Cambridge University Press, 1992)

Bingham T, *The Rule of Law* (Penguin, 2010)

Bitterman R and McCallum M, 'Upholding the Land Legislation of a "Communistic and Socialist Assembly": The Benefits of Confederation for Prince Edward Island' (2006) 87 *Canadian Historical Review* 1

Blackwell M, 'The April 2019 Loan Charge' (2019) 2019 *British Tax Review* 240

Blake L, '"Hybrid Bills" and Human Rights: The Parliament Square Litigation 2002–2007' (2008) 19 *King's Law Journal* 183

Blick A, *The Codes of the Constitution* (Hart Publishing, 2016)

Bobbett CS, 'Retroactive or Retrospective? A Note on Terminology' (2006) 1 *British Tax Review* 15

Bogart D and Richardson G, 'Property Rights and Parliament in Industrializing Britain' (2011) 54 *Journal of Law and Economics* 241

Bogert GG, 'Nathan Report and the Supervision and Enforcement of Charitable Trusts' 29 (1954) *New York University Law Review*

Booth P and Huxley M, '1909 and All That: Reflections on the Housing, Town Planning, Etc. Act 1909' (2012) 27 *Planning Perspectives* 267

Brand P, 'Petitions and Parliament in the Reign of Edward I' (2004) 23 *Parliamentary History* 14
Bridge JW, 'Retrospective Legislation and the Rule of Law in Britain' (1967) 35 *University of Missouri Kansas City Law Review* 132
Broad J, 'Cattle Plague in Eighteenth-Century England' [1983] *Agricultural History Review* 12
Buckingham WS, 'Compensation and Profits in British Nationalized Industries' (1953) 8 *Journal of Finance* 422
Bull P, *Land, Politics & Nationalism: A Study of the Irish Land Question* (Gill & MacMillan, 1996)
Cabinet Office, *Cabinet Manual* (Cabinet Office, 2011)
——, *Guide to Making Legislation* (Cabinet Office, 2022)
Cairns MB, 'Some Legal Aspects of Compensation for Nationalized Assets' (1951) 16 *Law and Contemporary Problems* 594
Calamita N, 'The British Bank Nationalizations: An International Law Perspective' (2009) 58 *International and Comparative Law Quarterly* 119
Cannan E, *The History of Local Rates in England, Five Lectures* (Longmans, 1896)
Chairman of Ways and Means, House of Commons and Senior Deputy Speaker, House of Lords, *Hybrid Bill Review Report* (2022), available at www.parliament.uk/globalassets/about-parliament/how-parliament-works/how-are-laws-made/hbr-final-covered-doc.pdf
Chew HM and Kellaway W, 'Introduction', *London Assize of Nuisance, 1301–1431: A Calendar* (London Record Society, 1973)
Clay C, 'The Price of Freehold Land in the Later Seventeenth and Eighteenth Centuries' (1974) 27 *Economic History Review* 173
Clifford F, *A History of Private Bill Legislation* (Butterworths, 1885) vol 1
——, *A History of Private Bill Legislation* (Butterworths, 1885) vol 2
Committee on the Law and Practice Relating to Charitable Trusts, *Report of the Committee on the Law and Practice Relating to Charitable Trusts* (Cmd 8710, 1952)
Company Law Amendment Committee, *Report* (Cmnd 2657, 1926)
Conservative Party (Great Britain), *Conservative Manifesto, 1979* (Conservative Central Office, 1979)
Corwin ES, 'The "Higher Law" Background of American Constitutional Law' (1929) 42 *Harvard Law Review* 365
Cox A, *Adversary Politics and Land: The Conflict Over Land and Property Policy in Post-War Britain* (Cambridge University Press, 1984)
Craig P, 'Proportionality and Judicial Review: A UK Historical Perspective' in S Vogenauer and S Weatherill (eds), *General Principles of Law: European and Comparative Perspectives* (Hart Publishing, 2017)
Crompton G, 'The Railway Companies and the Nationalisation Issue 1920–50' in R Millward and J Singleton (eds), *The Political Economy of Nationalisation in Britain, 1920–1950*, 1st edn (Cambridge University Press, 1995)
——, '"A Very Poor Bag of Assets": The Railway Compensation Issue 1921–47" (1996) 6 *Accounting, Business and Financial History* 73
Dale I, *Conservative Party General Election Manifestos, 1900–1997* (Psychology Press, 2000)
Darian-Smith E, *Bridging Divides: The Channel Tunnel and English Legal Identity in the New Europe* (University of California Press, 1999)
Davis J, 'Baking for the Common Good: A Reassessment of the Assize of Bread in Medieval England' (2004) 57 *Economic History Review* 465
Davis RW, 'The House of Lords, the Whigs and Catholic Emancipation, 1806–1829' (1999) 18 *Parliamentary History* 23
Denyer-Green B, *Compulsory Purchase and Compensation*, 11th edn (Routledge, 2018)
Department of Industry, *The Regeneration of British Industry* (Cmnd 5710, 1974)
Deringer W, 'Pricing the Future in the Seventeenth Century: Calculating Technologies in Competition' (2017) 58 *Technology and Culture* 506
Dicey AV, *Introduction to the Study of the Law of the Constitution*, 10th edn (MacMillan, 1959)
Dimitruk K, '"I Intend Therefore to Prorogue": The Effects of Political Conflict and the Glorious Revolution in Parliament, 1660–1772' (2017) 22 *European Review of Economic History* 261

Dooley T, 'Land and Politics in Independent Ireland, 1923–48: The Case for Reappraisal' (2004) 34 *Irish Historical Studies* 175
Duxbury N, 'Ex Post Facto Law' (2013) 58 *American Journal of Jurisprudence* 135
Dymond G and Deadman H, 'The Salisbury Doctrine' (2006) House of Lords Library Note Number LLN 2006/006
Economic Affairs Committee, *The Powers of HMRC: Treating Taxpayers Fairly* (HL 2017–2019, 242)
Elliott M and Hughes K, *Common Law Constitutional Rights* (Bloomsbury, 2020)
Ellis CT, *Practical Remarks, and Precedents of Proceedings in Parliament* (B McMillan, 1802)
Erickson AB, 'The Cattle Plague in England, 1865–1867' (1961) 35 *Agricultural History* 94
European Court of Human Rights, *Guide on Article 1 of Protocol No. 1 – Protection of Property* (Council of Europe/European Court of Human Rights, 2022)
Examiners of Petitions for Private Bills, *Holocaust Memorial Bill: Report from the Examiners and Statement of Reasons* (HC 2022–23, 1403)
Expert Committee on Compensation and Betterment, *Final Report* (Cmd 6386, 1942)
FRD, 'British Nationalization of Industry. Compensation to Owners of Expropriated Property' (1949) 97 *University of Pennsylvania Law Review* 520
Fari S, *Victorian Telegraphy Before Nationalization* (Springer, 2015)
Fisher JR, 'British Physicians, Medical Science, and the Cattle Plague, 1865–66' (1993) 67 *Bulletin of the History of Medicine* 651
Fletcher E, 'Retrospective Fiscal Legislation' (1959) 1959 *British Tax Review* 412
Foulkes D, 'The Post Office and Its Services' (1980) 11 *Cambrian Law Review* 11
Freedman J, 'Defining Taxpayer Responsibility: In Support of a General Anti-Avoidance Principle' (2004) *British Tax Review* 331
Fryde EB, 'Edward III's Wool Monopoly of 1337: A Fourteenth Century Royal Trading Venture' (1952) 37 *History* 8
Gadd S, 'The Emergence and Development of Statutory Process for the Compulsory Purchase of Land for Transport Infrastructure in England and Wales, c.1530–1800' (2019) 40 *Journal of Legal History* 1
Gee G, 'The Political Constitutionalism of JAG Griffith' (2008) 28 *Legal Studies* 20
Gee G and Webber GCN, 'What Is a Political Constitution?' (2010) 30 *OJLS* 273
Gibson J, 'The Presentation of the Poll Tax' (1989) 60 *Political Quarterly* 332
Gobbi M, 'When to Begin: A Study of New Zealand Commencement Clauses with Regard to Those Used in the United Kingdom, Australia, and the United States' (2010) 31 *Statute Law Review* 153
Gough JW, *Fundamental Law in English Constitutional History* (Clarendon, 1955)
Grant M, 'Environmental Court Project Final Report: Report to the Department of Environment, Transport and the Regions' (DETR, 2000)
Greenhalgh G, 'The Sizewell Inquiry – Is There a Better Way?' (1984) 12 *Energy Policy* 283
Grey TC, 'Origins of the Unwritten Constitution: Fundamental Law in American Revolutionary Thought' (1977) 30 *Stanford Law Review* 843
Grez Hidalgo P, 'Legislative Scrutiny on Constitutional Grounds in the United Kingdom Parliament' PhD thesis (Edinburgh, 2019)
Grieve D, 'The Role of Human Rights in a Law Officer's Work: Challenges Facing the HRA and the ECHR' (2012) 17 *Judicial Review* 101
Griffith JAG, 'The Place of Parliament in the Legislative Process. Part I' (1951) 14 *MLR* 279
——, 'The Political Constitution' (1979) 42 *MLR* 1
Griffiths GLH, 'The Hundred Years War – The Development of the Movement towards Leasehold Enfranchisement in Wales' (2003) *Conveyancer* 289
Habakkuk HJ, 'The Long-Term Rate of Interest and the Price of Land in the Seventeenth Century' (1952) 5 *Economic History Review* 26
Habakkuk J, 'Presidential Address: The Rise and Fall of English Landed Families, 1600–1800: II' (1980) 30 *Transactions of the Royal Historical Society* 199
Hagman DG, 'Betterment For Worsenment: The English 1909 Act and Its Progeny' (1977) 10 *University of Queensland Law Journal* 29

Hanley JG, *Healthy Boundaries: Property, Law, and Public Health in England and Wales, 1815–1872* (Boydell & Brewer, 2016)
Harlow C and Rawlings R, '"Striking Back" and "Clamping down": An Alternative Perspective on Judicial Review' in J Bell, M Elliott, J Varahus and P Murray (eds), *Public law Adjudication in Common Law Systems: Process and Substance* (Hart Publishing, 2016)
Harris P, *Income Tax in Common Law Jurisdictions: Volume 1, From the Origins to 1820* (Cambridge University Press, 2006)
Hart PE, 'Competition and Control in the British Sugar Industry' (1953) 5 *Oxford Economic Papers* 317
Hayward M, '"Outlandish Superfluities": Luxury and Clothing in Scottish and English Sumptuary Law from the Fourteenth to the Seventeenth Century' in G Riello and U Rublack (eds), *The Right to Dress* (Cambridge University Press, 2019)
Hazlewood A, 'The Origin of the State Telephone Service in Britain' (1953) 5 *Oxford Economic Papers* 13
Heatley MK, 'The Continued Use of Private Acts of Parliament in United Kingdom' (*UK Constitutional Law Association*, 4 October 2021), available at ukconstitutionallaw.org/2021/10/04/mark-k-heatley-the-continued-use-of-private-acts-of-parliament-in-united-kingdom
Henriques URQ, 'The Jewish Emancipation Controversy in Nineteenth-Century Britain' [1968] *Past & Present* 126
Higham RD, 'The British Government and Overseas Airlines, 1918–1939' (1959) 26 *Journal of Air Law and Commerce*
HM Treasury, 'Independent Loan Charge Review: Government response to the Review' (2019), available at assets.publishing.service.gov.uk/government/uploads/system/uploads/attachment_data/file/854490/20191219_Government_response.pdf
——, 'Tampon Tax Abolished from Today' (*GOV.UK*), available at www.gov.uk/government/news/tampon-tax-abolished-from-today
HMRC KAI: Personal Tax, 'Evaluation of the Government's December 2004 Announcement Warning That Anti-Avoidance Legislation in Respect of Remuneration-Based Avoidance Schemes Could Be Back-Dated' (2009) Working Paper 6
Holcombe AN, 'The Telephone in Great Britain' (1906) 21 *Quarterly Journal of Economics* 96
Holliday I, 'The Politics of the Channel Tunnel' (1992) 45 *Parliamentary Affairs* 188
Hoppit J, 'Patterns of Parliamentary Legislation, 1660–1800' (1996) 39 *Historical Journal* 109
——, 'Compulsion, Compensation and Property Rights in Britain, 1688–1833' [2011] *Past & Present* 93
——, 'The Nation, the State, and the First Industrial Revolution' (2011) 50 *Journal of British Studies*
House of Commons Treasury Committee, *Principles of Tax Policy* (HC 2010–11, 753)
House of Lords Constitution Committee, *Reviewing the Constitution: Terms of Reference and Method of Working* (HL 2001–02, 11)
——, *Nationality, Immigration and Asylum Bill Further Report (Seventh Report)* (HL 2001–02, 129)
——, *Prevention of Terrorism Bill (Second Report)* (HL 2004–05, 66)
——, *Tribunals, Courts and Enforcement Bill (First Report)* (HL 2006–07, 13)
——, *Serious Crime Bill (Second Report)* (HL 2006–07, 41)
——, *Child Maintenance and Other Payments Bill (Third Report)* (HL 2007–08, 27)
——, *Banking Act 2009: Supplementary Report on Retrospective Legislation* (HL 2008–09, 11)
——, *Part 1 of the Legal Aid, Sentencing and Punishment of Offenders Bill (Twenty-First Report)* (HL 2010–12, 222)
——, *Jobseekers (Back to Work Schemes) Bill* (HL 2012–13, 155)
House of Lords Select Committee on Town Improvements (Betterment), *Report* (HC 1894, 292)
Hutchison NE and Rowan-Robinson J, 'Utility Wayleaves: A Compensation Lottery?' (2002) 20 *Journal of Property Investment & Finance* 159
Innes J, *Inferior Politics: Social Problems and Social Policies in Eighteenth-Century Britain* (Oxford University Press, 2009)
Jack S and Jack A, 'Nineteenth-Century Lawyers and Railway Capitalism: Historians and the Use of Legal Cases' (2003) 24 *Journal of Legal History* 59

Jaconelli J, 'The "Bowles Act" – Cornerstone of the Fiscal Constitution' (2010) 69 *Cambridge Law Journal* 582

Jaffe LL and Henderson EG, 'Judicial Review and the Rule of Law: Historical Origins' (1956) 72 *LQR* 347

Johnston A, 'Takeover Regulation: Historical and Theoretical Perspectives on the City Code' (2007) 66 *Cambridge Law Journal* 422

Johnston N, 'Referendums' (2016) House of Commons Library Briefing Paper Number 7692

Joint Committee on Private Bill Procedure, *Private Bill Procedure* (1987–88, HL 97, HC 625)

Jones WR, 'Keeping the Peace: English Society, Local Government, and the Commissions of 1341–44' (1974) 18 *American Journal of Legal History* 307

——, 'Purveyance for War and the Community of the Realm in Late Medieval England' (1975) 7 *Albion: A Quarterly Journal Concerned with British Studies* 300

Joy NV, 'Fair Compensation Under the British Labor Government' (1950) 65 *Political Science Quarterly* 538

Kavanagh D, Dale I and Nfa ID, *Labour Party General Election Manifestos 1900–1997* (Taylor & Francis Group, 2000) vol 2

Kelf-Cohen R, *British Nationalisation 1945–1973* (Springer, 1973)

Kellett JR, 'Municipal Socialism, Enterprise and Trading in the Victorian City' (1978) 5 *Urban History* 36

Kelly R, 'Hybrid Bills (Background Paper)' (2018) House of Commons Library Briefing Paper Number 06736

Kieve JL, *The Electric Telegraph: A Social and Economic History* (David and Charles, 1973)

Labour Party, *Housing for the Many: A Labour Party Green Paper* (Labour Party 2018), available at labourhousing.org/wp-content/uploads/2019/05/Labour-Party-Green-Paper-Housing-for-the-Many.pdf

——, *Bringing Energy Home: Labour's Proposal for Publicly Owned Energy Networks* (Labour Party, 2019), available at www.labour.org.uk/wp-content/uploads/2019/03/Bringing-Energy-Home-2019.pdf

——, *Clear Water: Labour's Vision for a Modern and Transparent Publicly-Owned Water System* (2019), available at www.labour.org.uk/wp-content/uploads/2018/09/Conference-2018-Water-pamphlet-FINAL.pdf

——, *It's Time for Real Change: The Labour Party Manifesto 2019* (Labour Party, 2019)

Lambert S, *Bills and Acts: Legislative Procedure in Eighteenth-Century England* (Cambridge University Press, 1971)

Landers T, *Procedure and Practice Relating to Private Bills in Parliament: Shewing the Progress of a Bill from Its Inception to Royal Assent, Together with Numerous Forms and Precedents* (Stevens and Sons, 1919)

Lang JHA, 'The Coal Act, 1938' (1939) 2 *MLR* 301

Langford P, *Public Life and the Propertied Englishman 1689–1798* (Oxford University Press, 1994)

Law Commission, *Towards a Compulsory Purchase Code* (Law Com Nos 286 and 291, 2004)

Le May GHL, *The Victorian Constitution: Conventions, Usages and Contingencies* (Duckworth, 1979)

Lead L, '"They Flow for Country and People": Landowners and Early Canal Development in England' (2014) 38 *Railway & Canal Historical Society* 73

Leasehold Committee, *Final Report* (Cd 7982, 1950)

Lee RG, 'The (Not So) Great Escape: The Legal and Moral Responsibility for the Foot and Mouth Outbreak 2007' in I Kenway, Dr J Gunning and Professor S Holm (eds), *Ethics, Law and Society* (Taylor & Francis Group, 2009) vol IV

Leijten I, 'From Stec to Valkov: Possessions and Margins in the Social Security Case Law of the European Court of Human Rights' (2013) 13 *Human Rights Law Review* 309

——, 'The Right to Minimum Subsistence and Property Protection under the ECHR: Never the Twain Shall Meet?' (2019) 21 *European Journal of Social Security* 307

Lenhoff A, 'Development of the Concept of Eminent Domain' (1942) 42 *Columbia Law Review* 596

Letwin, Sir Oliver, *Independent Review of Build Out: Final Report* (CM 9270, 2018)
Lidbetter A and Randhawa J, 'Developments in Judicial Review of Decisions That Are Wholly or Substantially Commercial' (2016) 21 *Judicial Review* 105
Lienen C, *Shaped by the Nuanced Constitution: A Critique of Common Law Constitutional Rights* (Bloomsbury Publishing, 2023)
Loengard J, 'The Assize of Nuisance: Origins of an Action at Common Law' (1978) 37 *Cambridge Law Journal* 144
Logan DW, 'Report of the Committee on the Law and Practice Relating to Charitable Trusts [Cmd. 8710]' (1953) 16 *MLR* 343
Maitland FW, *The Constitutional History of England*, 1st edn (edited by HAL Fisher) (Cambridge University Press, 1908)
Mann FA, 'Outlines of a History of Expropriation' (1959) 75 *LQR* 188
Manton K, 'The Labour Party and the Land Question, 1919–51' (2006) 79 *Historical Research* 247
Mathews P, 'Forestalling Ahead of Property Tax Changes' [2016] OBR Working Paper no 10
McDonald J, 'Tax Fairness in Eleventh Century England' (2002) 29 *Accounting Historians Journal* 173
McMurtie SN, 'The Constitutionality of the War Crimes Act 1991' (1992) 13 *Statute Law Review* 128
McNulty WD, 'The Power of "Compulsory Purchase" under the Law of England' (1912) 21 *Yale Law Journal* 639
Mendelson M, 'The United Kingdom Nationalization Cases and the European Convention on Human Rights' (1987) 57 *British Yearbook of International Law* 33
Mingay GE, *Parliamentary Enclosure in England: An Introduction to Its Causes, Incidence and Impact 1750–1850* (Longman, 1997)
Minister of Land and Natural Resources, White Paper, *Leasehold Reform in England and Wales* (White Paper, Cmnd 2916, 1966)
Ministry of Reconstruction, *Second Report of the Committee Dealing with the Law and Practice relating to the Acquisition and Valuation of Land for Public Purposes* (Cd 9229, 1918)
Morris RJB, *Private Bill Legislation in the Nineteenth Century: Parliamentary Promotion from 1797 to 1914* (Cambridge Scholars Publishing, 2022)
Morse, Sir Aymas, 'Independent Loan Charge Review: Report on the Policy and its Implementation' (2019), available at assets.publishing.service.gov.uk/government/uploads/system/uploads/attachment_data/file/854387/Independent_Loan_Charge_Review_-_final_report.pdf
Mullett CF, 'The Cattle Distemper in Mid-Eighteenth-Century England' (1946) 20 *Agricultural History* 144
Murray SE, *The Post Office* (GP Putnam's Sons, 1927)
Natzler D and Hutton M, *Erskine May's Treatise on the Law, Privileges, Proceedings and Usage of Parliament*, 25th edn (LexisNexis UK, 2019)
Neale JE, *The Elizabethan House of Commons* (Jonathan Cape, 1949)
Nicol D, *EC Membership and the Judicialization of British Politics* (Oxford University Press, 2001)
Norton P, 'Playing by the Rules: The Constraining Hand of Parliamentary Procedure' (2001) 7 *Journal of Legislative Studies* 13
Offer A, *Property and Politics, 1870–1914: Landownership, Law, Ideology, and Urban Development in England* (Cambridge University Press, 1981)
O'Riordan T, Kemp R and Purdue M, *Sizewell B: An Anatomy of the Inquiry* (Macmillan Press, 1988)
Ormrod WM, '"Common Profit" and "The Profit of the King and Kingdom": Parliament and the Development of Political Language in England, 1250–1450' (2015) 46 *Viator* 219
Owen AEB, 'The Custom of Romney Marsh and the Statute of Sewers of 1427' (1996) 116 *Archaeologia Cantiana* 93
Packer I, *Lloyd George, Liberalism and the Land: The Land Issue and Party Politics in England, 1906–1914* (Royal Historical Society, 2001)
Perceval RW, 'The Origin and Essence of Hybrid Bills' (1949) 2 *Parliamentary Affairs* 139
Pinelli C, 'Constitutional Reasoning and Political Deliberation' (2013) 14 *German Law Journal* 1171
Pozen DE and Samaha AM, 'Anti-Modalities' (2021) 119 *Michigan Law Review* 729

Procedure Committee, *Revisions of Private Business Standing Orders* (HL 2017–19, 34)
Purdue M, Kemp R and O'Riordan T, 'The Context and Conduct of the Sizewell B Inquiry' (1984) 12 *Energy Policy* 276
Quin-Harkin A, 'Imperial Airways, 1924–50' (1954) 1 *Journal of Transport History* 197
Reddaway TF, *The Rebuilding of London After the Great Fire* (Jonathan Cape, 1940)
Reich C, 'The New Property' (1964) 73 *Yale Law Journal* 733
Reynolds S, *Before Eminent Domain: Toward a History of Expropriation of Land for the Common Good* (University of North Carolina Press, 2010)
Richardson HG, 'The Early History of Commissions of Sewers' (1919) 34 *English Historical Review* 385
Ridd P, 'Hole and Plug' in Peter Harris and Dominic de Cogan (eds), *Studies in the History of Tax Law: Volume 10* (Hart Publishing, 2021)
Robins N, *The Corporation That Changed the World*, 2nd edn (Pluto Press, 2012)
Royal Commission on Churches (Scotland), *Report of the Royal Commission on Churches (Scotland)*, vol 1 (Cd 2494, 1905)
Royal Commission on the Housing of the Working Classes, First Report 1885 (C (2nd series) 4402, 1885)
Royal Commission on Water Supply within the Limits of the Metropolitan Water Companies, *Final Report of the Commissioners* (C (2nd series) 25, 1899)
Rowan-Robinson J and Hutchison NE, 'Utility Wayleaves: Time for Reform' (2001) *Journal of Planning and Environmental Law* 1247
Rudden B, *The New River: A Legal History* (Oxford University Press, 1985)
Sandford M and others, 'Coronavirus: Support for Businesses' (2022) House of Commons Library Briefing Paper Number 8847
Scarrow HA, 'Policy Pressures by British Local Government: The Case of Regulation in the "Public Interest"' (1971) 4 *Comparative Politics* 1
Schneiderman D, 'A. V. Dicey, Lord Watson, and the Law of the Canadian Constitution in the Late Nineteenth Century' (1998) 16 *Law and History Review* 495
Scott P, 'Entick v Carrington and the Legal Protection of Property' in A Tomkins and P Scott (eds), *Entick and Carrington: 250 Years of the Rule of Law* (Hart Publishing, 2015)
Seely A, 'Retrospective Taxation: Earlier Debates' (2012) House of Commons Library Standard Note SN04369
——, 'Tax Avoidance: A General Anti-Avoidance Rule – Background History (1997–2010)' (2020) House of Commons Library Briefing Paper Number 2956
Select Committee on the High Speed Rail (London – West Midlands) Bill, *Special Report of Session 2016–17* (HL 2016–17, 83)
Select Committee on the Phase One Bill, *Second Special Report of Session 2015–16* (HC 2015–16, 129)
Select Committee on Town Holdings, *Report* (HL 1889, 190)
Sharman FA, 'River Improvement Law in the Early Seventeenth Century' (1982) 3 *Journal of Legal History* 222
——, 'The History of the Lands Clauses Consolidation Act 1845 – I' (1986) 1986 *Statute Law Review* 13
——, 'The History of the Lands Clauses Consolidation Act 1845 – II' (1986) 1986 *Statute Law Review* 78
——, 'An Introduction to the Enclosure Acts' (1989) 10 *Journal of Legal History* 45
Shinwell E, *Conflict Without Malice* (Odhams Press, 1955)
Simson Caird J, 'Identifying the Value of Parliamentary Constitutional Interpretation' PhD thesis (Queen Mary University of London, 2014)
Simson Caird J, Hazell R and Oliver D, *The Constitutional Standards of the House of Lords Select Committee on the Constitution*, 3rd edn (The Constitution Unit, 2017)
Simson Caird J and Oliver D, 'Parliament's Constitutional Standards' in A Horne and A Le Seuer (eds), *Parliament: Legislation and Accountability* (Hart Publishing, 2016)
Smead EE, 'The Rule against Retroactive Legislation: A Basic Principle of Jurisprudence' (1936) 20 *Minnesota Law Review* 775

Smethurst JM, *A Treatise on the Locus Standi of Petitioners Against Private Bills in Parliament* (Stevens and Haynes, 1867)
Spencer JR, 'Public Nuisance. A Critical Examination' (1989) 48 *Cambridge Law Journal* 55
Stebbings C, 'Consent and Constitutionality in Nineteenth-Century English Taxation' in J Tiley (ed), *Studies in the History of Tax Law* (Bloomsbury, 2009) vol 3
——, 'The Equity of the Executive: Fairness in Tax Law in Nineteenth-Century England' in PG Turner (ed), *Equity and Administration*, 1st edn (Cambridge University Press, 2016)
Steele ED, 'Ireland and the Empire in the 1860s. Imperial Precedents for Gladstone's First Irish Land Act' (1968) 11 *Historical Journal* 64
Stern WM, 'Water Supply in Britain: The Development of a Public Service' (1954) 74 *Journal of the Royal Sanitary Institute* 998
Stoebuck WB, 'A General Theory of Eminent Domain' (1971) 47 *Washington Law Review* 553
Su W, 'What Is Just Compensation?' (2019) 105 *Virginia Law Review* 1485
Tailby C, 'Some Reflections on Tax Avoidance' (2011) *Private Client Business* 43
Taylor J, 'Private Property, Public Interest, and the Role of the State in Nineteenth-Century Britain: The Case of the Lighthouses' (2001) 44 *Historical Journal* 749
Tennent KD and others, 'Blending Public and Private: British Municipal Trading c. 1889–1975' (2020) 2020 *Academy of Management Proceedings* 20352
Tennyson R, 'From Unanimity to Proportionality: Assent Standards and the Parliamentary Enclosure Movement' (2013) 31 *Law and History Review* 199
Tichelar M, *The Failure of Land Reform in Twentieth-Century England: The Triumph of Private Property* (Routledge, 2018)
Tomkins A, 'What's Left of the Political Constitution?' (2013) 14 *German Law Journal* 2275
Trentmann F and Taylor V, 'From Users to Consumers: Water Politics in Nineteenth Century London' in F Trentmann (ed), *The Making of the Consumer: Knowledge, Power and Identity in the Modern World* (Berg, 2006)
Turner M, *English Parliamentary Enclosure: Its Historical Geography and Economic History* (Dawson, 1980)
——, *Enclosures in Britain 1750–1830* (Macmillan Press, 1984)
Waldron J, 'The Dignity of Legislation' (1995) 54 *Maryland Law Review* 633
——, *The Dignity of Legislation* (Cambridge University Press, 1999)
——, 'The Core of the Case Against Judicial Review' (2006) 115 *Yale Law Journal* 1346
Walsh R and Fox O'Mahony L, 'Land Law, Property Ideologies and the British–Irish Relationship' (2018) 47 *Common Law World Review* 7
Watchman PQ, 'Retrospective Legislation: A Gift from the Gods?' in EPH Keane and P Robson (eds), *The Ian Willock Collection on Law and Justice in the Twenty-First Century* (Fairleigh Dickinson University Press; Rowman & Littlefield, 2023)
Watts DCH, 'On the Causes of British Railway Nationalisation: A Re-Examination of the Causes, 1866–1921' (2002) 16 *Contemporary British History* 1
Watts J, '"Common Weal" and "Commonwealth": England's Monarchical Republic in the Making' in A Gamberini, J-P Genet and A Zorzi (eds), *The Languages of Political Society: Western Europe, 14th-17th Centuries* (Viella, 2011)
Webb S and Webb BP, *English Local Government: Statutory Authorities for Special Purposes* (Longmans, Green, 1922)
Wilde ML, 'All the Queen's Horses: Statutory Authority and HS2' (2017) 37 *Legal Studies* 765
Williams O, *The Historical Development of Private Bill Procedure and Standing Orders in the House of Commons*, vol 1 (HMSO, 1948)
Woods A, 'The Construction of an Animal Plague: Foot and Mouth Disease in Nineteenth-Century Britain' (2004) 17 *Social History of Medicine* 23
Yelling JA, *Slums and Slum Clearance in Victorian London* (Routledge, 1986)

INDEX

www.ingramcontent.com/pod-product-compliance
Ingram Content Group UK Ltd.
Pitfield, Milton Keynes, MK11 3LW, UK
UKHW020819290926
15470UKWH00003B/1255